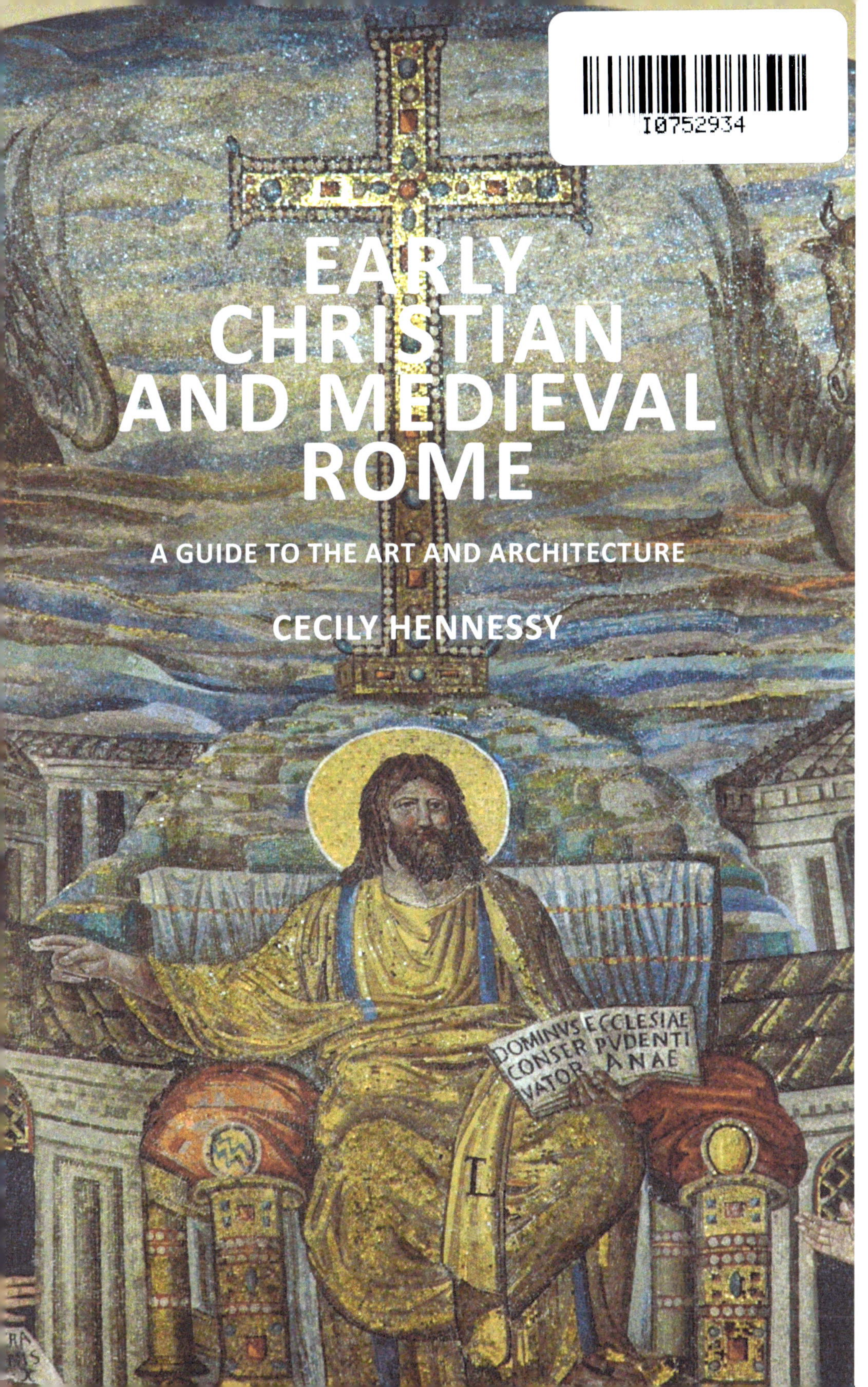

EARLY CHRISTIAN AND MEDIEVAL ROME

A GUIDE TO THE ART AND ARCHITECTURE

CECILY HENNESSY

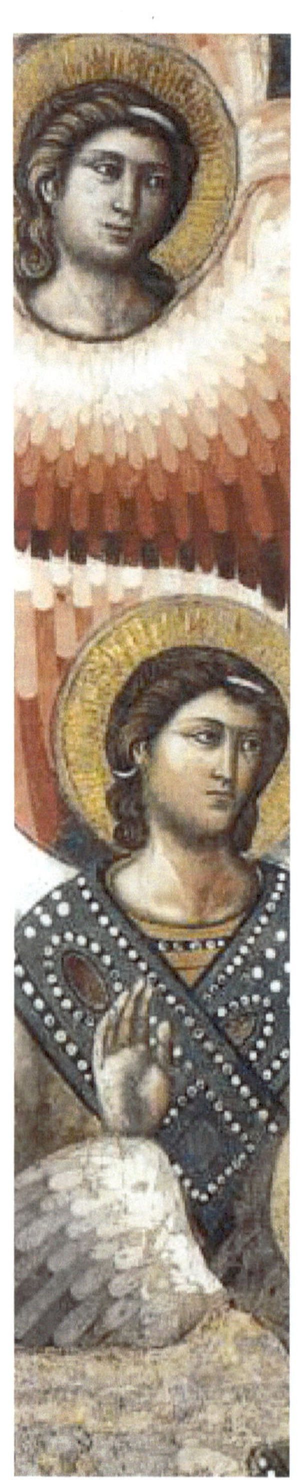

Published by Cecily Hennessy Publications

Design by Simon Firullo

ISBN 978-0-9576628-1-0

Front cover: Angel, *Last Judgement*, S. Cecilia; Cosmati floor, S. Maria Aracoeli; Angelic host, apse, S. Maria Domnica; Floral motif, S. Sylvester Chapel, S. Quattro Coronati; Icon Virgin Mary, S. Maria Nova; Apse mosaic, S. Clemente; Adam and Eve, *Sarcophagus of Junius Bassus*, St. Peter's Treasury; Catacomb painting, Vigna Randanini; Christ, *Last Judgement,* S. Cecilia; back cover: Male figure (Christ?) domus Porta Marina, Ostia; Three Hebrews in furnace, catacomb of Priscilla; Virgin and Child, apse, S. Maria Domnica; front matter page: Angel, *Last Judgement,* S. Cecilia; contents page: *Adoration of Magi*, detail, S. Maria Maggiore; title page: Christ, S. Pudenziana
Photographs: principally by Cecily Hennessy

I would like to give sincere thanks to Anna Kartsonis for first inspiring me with her teaching in Rome, to Robin Cormack for his wisdom and guidance, and to Michael Michael, Richard Plant, Antony Eastmond, Derek Nichols, Ted Sandling, Sabra Raven and Isobel Raven for advice and suggestions. Any errors or omissions remain my own.

EARLY CHRISTIAN AND MEDIEVAL ROME

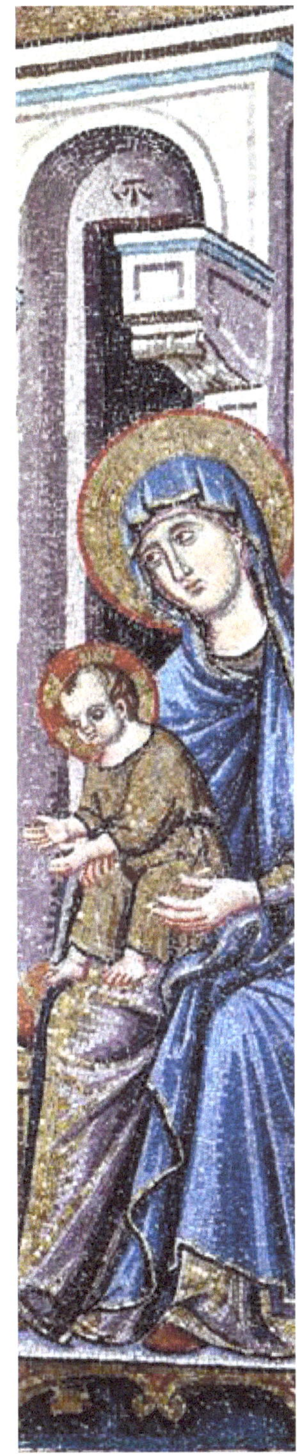

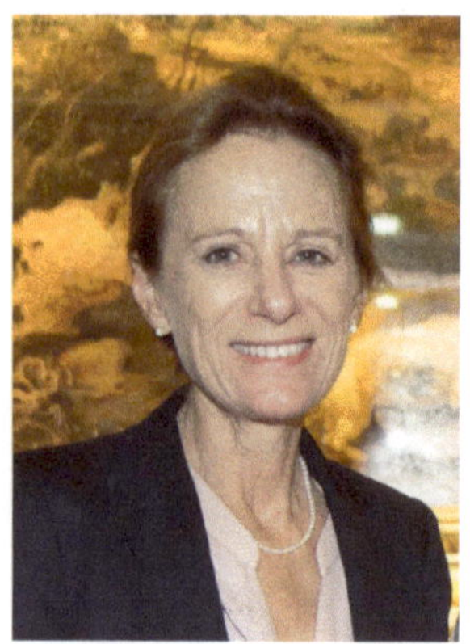

Cecily Hennessy

Content

Early Christian and Medieval Rome looks at the fascinating art and architecture in Rome dating from between about 300 and 1300. In the fourth and fifth centuries, Rome was the most important city in the west for the early development of buildings for Christian use and of imagery employed by both the Church authorities and by the practising Christians. Many Christians still had links with traditional Roman religions and with Judaism. It remained the most prestigious centre in the west in the following centuries, despite political upheavals. With the papacy established at its heart, patronage and artistic production prospered, with high points in the ninth and again in the twelfth and thirteenth centuries.

Material

This book explores churches, baptisteries, houses and catacombs with extraordinary mosaic and painted decoration. It also includes sculpture, reliquaries, icons, ivories and metalwork, which were used throughout the period.

Audience

It is designed to appeal to the casual visitor to the city as well as those seeking an art-historical understanding of the material. It particularly points out the cultural exchange between Christianity in the west and in the east (the Byzantine empire).

How to use

It is organised geographically as a travel guide with sites close to each other grouped together suggesting itineraries. It gives both historical and art-historical information, encouraging exploration. It also aims to suggest how to understand the subject matter, meaning and style in imagery and to look closely at works of art. It is not intended to be comprehensive, but to highlight significant material and to introduce the reader to the remarkable sites and experiences of early Christian and medieval Rome.

A note about names:

In general Italian names of sites and buildings are used with the exception of ones in common English usage such as the Vatican and Saint Peter's. Names of people, including saints, are given for the most part in Italian except, again, when in common usage in English, such as the apostles. A few, where it seems appropriate, are referred to in Italian in terms of labelling their depictions but in English when discussed as people. The Virgin Mary is referred to, for the most part, as the Virgin and Jesus Christ as Christ.

CHAPTER ONE:

INTRODUCTION

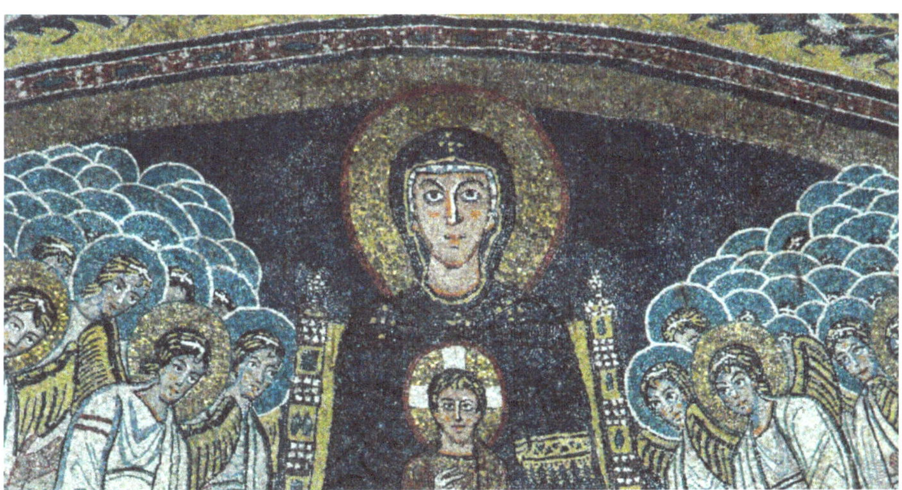

Virgin and Child and Host of Angels, S. Maria in Domnica, apse, 817-24

Rome was the capital of the Roman empire and naturally became a focus for the centre of Christianity in the west. Christ lived and worked in Palestine, but by tradition many of the first and second generations of his followers, principally Peter, his foremost disciple, and Paul, who turned his energies to converting gentiles (non-Jews), went to Rome, to spread the new cult. Tradition suggests that they were both killed in the city of Rome. Those who met together and established communities sharing belief in Christ and his teaching, gathered at sites which became known as *tituli* (see box, p. 70). Many of these were later reconstructed as the early Christian churches in Rome, and they persist to this day, such as Santa Cecilia in Trastevere (see p. 52).

In the first three centuries after Christ's death, his followers were at times persecuted, but not perhaps as consistently as has often been suggested. However, at certain times men, women and children chose to die rather than disavow their beliefs and were put to death, often by the civic authorities. In 311 the emperor Galerius (305-311) introduced an edict which tolerated the practice of Christianity and in 313 this was furthered by the emperor Constantine I (the Great) (306-37) and his co-emperor Licinius (308-324) with a regulation known as the Edict of Milan, which gave people of all religions the right to follow them, an edict probably introduced in order to gain popular support. Constantine's life was recorded by a bishop and

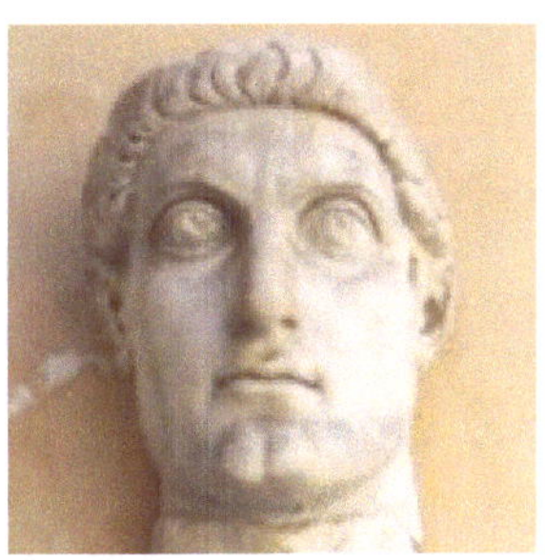

Head of Constantine the Great, Capitoline Museums, ca. 313-24

Constantine I (306-37) was responsible for building several large **basilical churches** in Rome for Christian worship. This colossal head was originally in a secular basilica he built on the **forum**, which was used as a meeting place and court of law, known as the **Basilica of Maxentius and Constantine**. The new churches used a similar form, creating large spaces for people to gather.

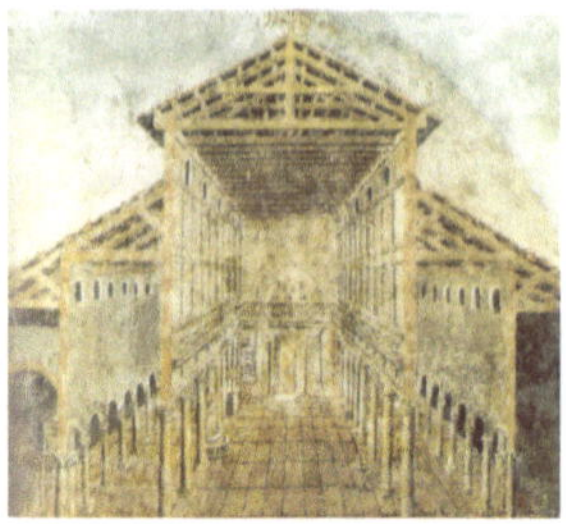

Old St. Peter's, watercolour, Giovanni Battista Ricci da Novara, seventeenth century

St. Peter's was built on the supposed site of Peter's burial. Some believers thought that he was martyred in the nearby Circus of Nero. The church became a major pilgrimage site (see pp. 68-9)

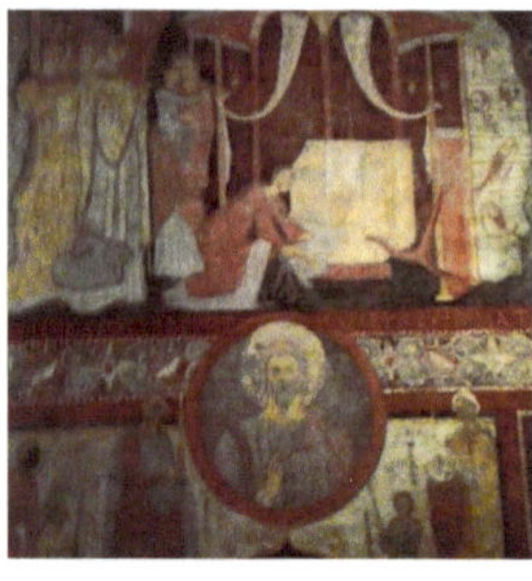

Fresco, narthex, lower church, San Clemente, ca. 1080

This wall painting, shows a miracle about **St. Clement,** whose tomb was in the Black Sea and marvellously revealed each year. According to legend, a child was found there after being lost for an entire year. It was painted shortly before the sack of Rome in 1084. The church was then abandoned and a new one built above.

historian, Eusebius of Caesarea (263-339), who recalled events from a Christian point of view (see box p. 70).

Constantine built several important sites for the use of Christians in Rome, most notably large basilicas for them to gather in and to pray. These had a rectangular plan with a semicircular apse and were derived from secular spaces used as courts of justice and for public assemblies. Christian buildings were often connected with funerary sites, which then became a focus of pilgrimage. After Constantine, the emperors were supporters of Christianity (except for a short period in the fourth century), and Christianity became the state religion by 393 under the emperor Theodosius I (379-95).

Constantine established a new capital to the east in Constantinople, but for the next 150 years there was usually a Roman emperor ruling in the west as well. Rome was sacked in 410 by Alaric the Visigoth, and Germanic kings ruled from 476, though this did not stop the building of churches. In 536, Rome was reclaimed by Belisarius, a talented general, in the name of the Roman (Byzantine) emperor in the east, Justinian I (527-65). It remained to some extent ruled from Constantinople until 751 when the Lombards took control. The popes were then granted power in the city by the Frankish king, Pepin the Short (751-68), and so Rome became the capital of the papal states.

Charlemagne (king of Franks 768, of Lombards 774, Roman emperor 800-814) was crowned in Rome on Christmas Day 800 by Pope Leo III (795-816), and the title Roman emperor was maintained and re-vivified by Otto I (962-73) in 962, who introduced a new dynasty, the Ottonians. However, these rulers did not use Rome as their capital. There was frequent conflict for power with the popes. The city was sacked in 1084 by the Normans, under Robert Guiscard, who came to aid the pope against the emperor Henry IV (1084-1105), who had besieged the city.

In terms of artistic production, a period in the ninth century, sometimes known as the Carolingian renaissance, mainly under a pope named Paschal (817-824) (see box p. 82), is notable for renewed building and a fresh interest in the Early Christian history of the city and its martyrs. The twelfth century was also a period of artistic proliferation and, in the second half of the thirteenth century, many of the artists who were to influence the painters of the early Italian renaissance worked in Rome, using mosaic and fresco to create innovative compositions with a sense of realism and pathos.

The classical tradition

In the Early Christian period, much of the sculpture and painting reflected the techniques and styles used in Ancient Greece and Rome. There is considerable continuity of iconography and style from the pagan to the Christian world and many features of the Christian representational vocabulary were adopted from the past and altered to suit the new narratives and ideologies.

CHAPTER TWO:

THE VIMINAL HILL AND NEARBY

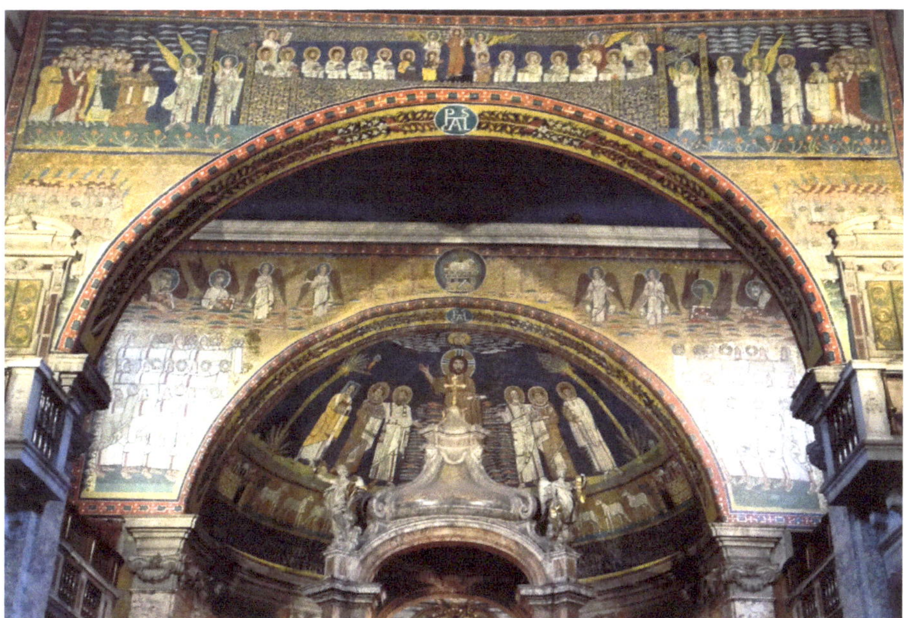

Apse and triumphal arches, S. Prassede, ca. 822

Santa Pudenziana, Santa Maria Maggiore, Santa Prassede, Santa Susanna

Introduction

The first three sites in this chapter form a good introduction to the early churches of Rome, situated near to each other and each with a distinctive history and decoration. Santa Pudenziana and Santa Prassede were by tradition the daughters of a senator named San Pudens who welcomed Saint Peter to his house (ca. 50 C.E.). Both sites had early *tituli* churches (see box p. 70). Santa Maria Maggiore, on the other hand, is one of the five major papal basilicas in Rome (see box p. 79) and was first built by Pope Liberius (352-66) on the site of a miracle. Santa Pudenziana is dated to 390, Santa Maria Maggiore was rebuilt in 432-7 and Santa Prassede dates to 810, so together spanning over 400 years. With different functions and pictorial programmes, these churches introduce key themes. Santa Susanna can be visited afterwards, as it is not far away, or when visiting the Museo nazionale Romano, Palazzo Massimo alle Terme.

The **apses** in Rome's churches often contain key imagery concerning the patrons and dedications of the buildings. They are usually decorated with mosaics, which became the most popular medium for wall decoration. **Mosaics** had been used often in the Roman period, but usually for floors. The mosaics are made from glass tesserae (small pieces) combined with terracotta and stone, and often use gold tesserae in which gold leaf is sandwiched between two pieces of glass.

They were created on site, directly onto the walls and ceilings, unlike modern mosaics which are normally put together on a flat surface and then placed on the wall. The wet plaster was prepared beforehand and the design sometimes sketched out before the tesserae were placed.

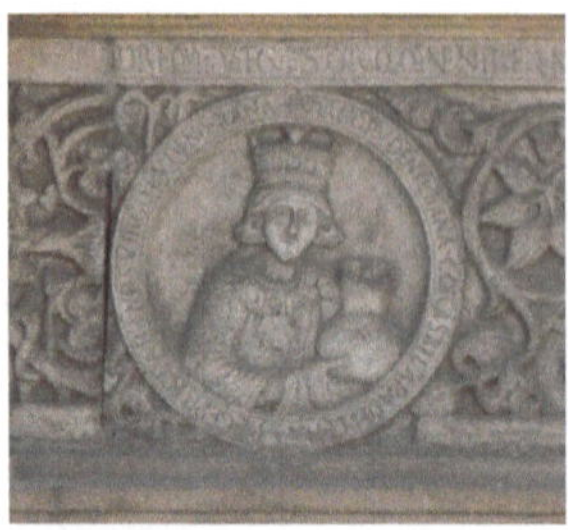

Relief sculpture of S. Pudenziana, lintel over the west door, S. Pudenziana, eleventh century (?)

According to legend this church was built by Pope Pius I (140-54) in 145. The ***domus ecclesiae*** (a house used by early Christians to gather together) was known as the *Titulus Pudentis*, and then became dedicated to **Pudenziana**, whose life is not verifiable.

Over the **entryway** is a distinctive carved lintel with five *clipei*, or roundels, depicting, from left to right, Pastore (who is said to have inherited the site from Pudens' family), Pudenziana, the lamb of God, Prassede and Pudens. The date of the lintel is not known, but it could well be eleventh century.

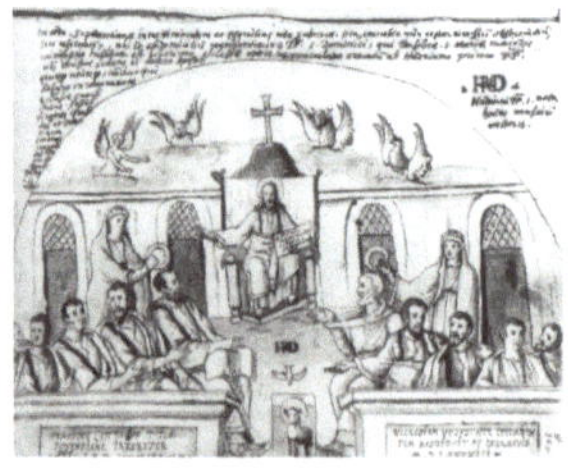

Drawing showing the apse in 1595, Alphonsus Ciacconius

This drawing was made after the 1588 **restoration** when two of the apostles were cut out, leaving only ten. The drawing does not very closely resemble the style of the mosaic.

Santa Pudenziana

This church is one of the earliest in Rome and has a unique mosaic apse decoration. The ground around it has risen over the centuries, so now the courtyard is reached by descending steps. On entering, notice the sculpture on the door lintel.

History

Excavations here have revealed a two-storied house datable by brick stamps to 129 C.E. Later in the second century the site was reconstructed with a terrace and baths with an apsed room *(thermae basilica)*. This was adapted for use as the church, built (mostly) in about 390. The archaeological site below the church can be visited by arrangement. Its entrance is through the Caetani chapel (thought to be the original entry room to the baths) on the north side of the nave.

The apse

When the church was restored in 1588, the apse was cut down and some of the mosaics removed. The scene shows Christ seated in the centre holding a scroll, with the words in Latin, 'The Lord protector of Pudenziana's church'. The mound behind is the Hill of Golgotha and the bejewelled golden cross, representing Christ's crucifixion but also his resurrection and victory over death, may copy one, which was possibly put up on the site by Theodosius I (379-95). Behind is a splendid cityscape, the Heavenly Jerusalem, resembling perhaps Jerusalem as it was in the late fourth century. The domed building to the left of Christ may be the Rotunda built by Constantine the Great (306-37) to mark the site of Christ's tomb.

The apostles sit in the foreground, with Paul to the left of Christ and Peter to the right. Each is being crowned with a victory wreath, perhaps representing their martyrdom. The crowns are placed by female figures who are sometimes said to be the sisters Pudenziana and Prassede, but more likely they represent the two early Christian communities, the churches of the Jews and the Gentiles, known as *Ecclesia* and *Synagoga* (Peter is seen as the apostle to the Jews and Paul to the Gentiles).

Above in the sky are four creatures, known as the *tetramorph* (four shapes/elements). They come to represent the four apostles, the angel for Matthew, the lion for Mark, the ox for Luke and the eagle for John. They derive from the Books of Ezekiel (1.10) and Revelation (4.7), where they appear in relation to Christ's Second Coming.

This is a remarkable mosaic. There is very little similar work that has survived, and it is a vivid example of imagery that was explorative, experimental and not picked up in mainstream iconography. In this period, church authorities, patrons and artisans endeavoured to devise ways of imaging both Christ's nature (as both man and God) and his teachings.

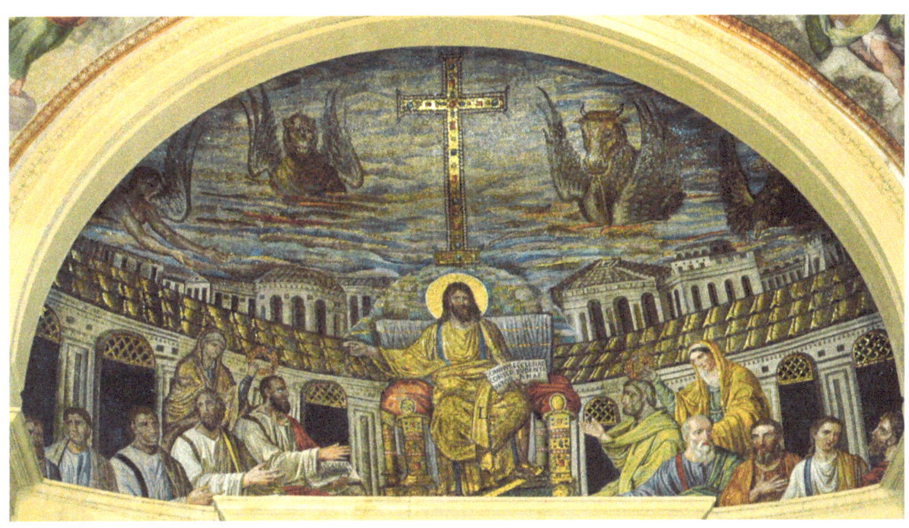

Christ seated before Golgotha, flanked by apostles, apse, S. Pudenziana, ca. 390
Part of the mosaic was restored in the nineteenth century, such as the heads of the apostles on the right.

The portrayal of Christ

In the Early Christian period, Christ is depicted in various ways. In the mosaic at Santa Pudenziana (shown above), he has long dark hair and beard and a strong, sturdy body. In many ways this evokes Zeus or Jupiter the most important god of the Greeks and Romans. He also wears a golden toga, suggesting wealth and resplendence, and is seated on a throne studded with gems behind which is a silken hanging. It is often said that he is depicted as an emperor, but at this time emperors tended to have short hair and were beardless. They did wear togas at times, but often were shown in military dress. The imagery does not replicate an imperial court, but something more celestial and unworldly.

In other representations, often on sarcophagi, Christ is shown as young and beardless, perhaps drawing on images of the beautiful youthful god Apollo.

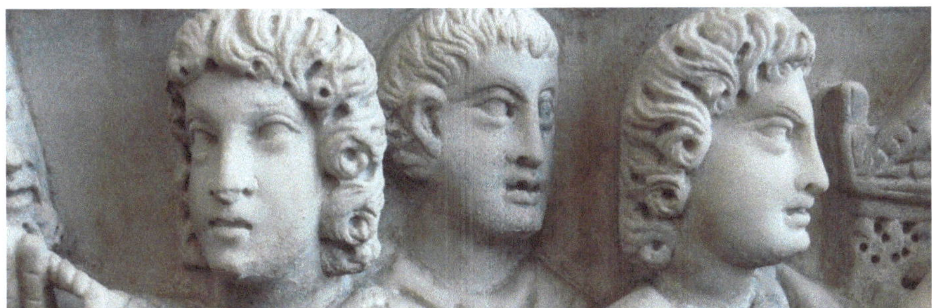

Miracles of Christ, Sarcophagus of Claudianus, Museo nazionale Romano, Massimo alle Terme, ca. 330-40
In this detail, Christ is shown twice, left and right. He appears in several scenes on the sarcophagus.

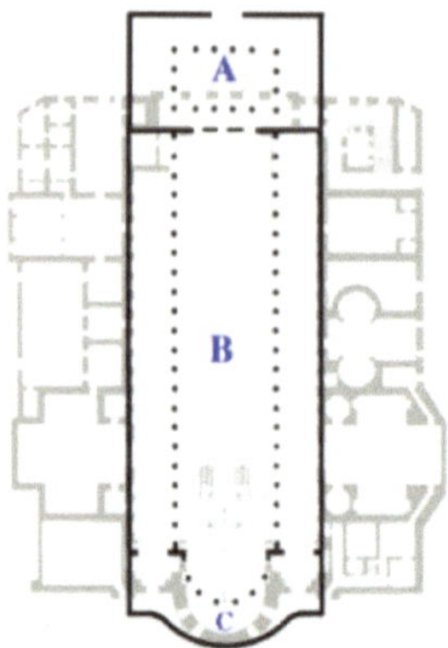

Original plan of S. Maria Maggiore, ca. 432, superimposed over current plan

A=hypothetical atrium
B=nave; C=ambulatory

The church holds several important **relics** including the **crib** of the Christ Child, now in the crypt. A very fine ***presepio*** (nativity scene) was carved by **Arnolfo di Cambio** and is now in the **Museum**, which is accessed from the right aisle.

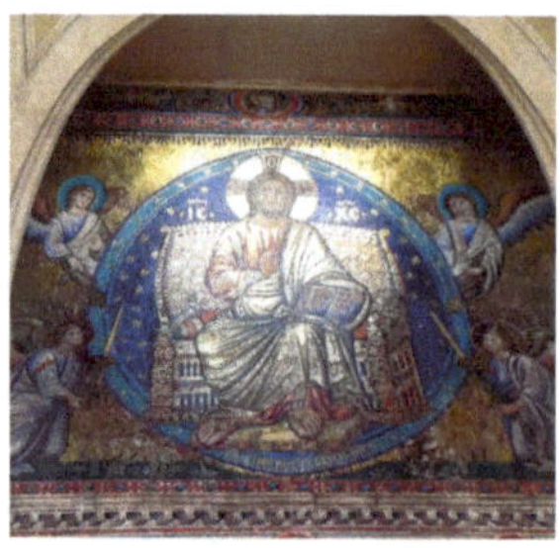

Christ in Majesty, Facade of S. Maria Maggiore, ca. 1288-97

The facade mosaics show **Christ enthroned** with a Gospel open to the words, 'I am the light of the world' and surrounded by angels. It is signed beneath Christ's feet by **Filippo Rusuti**. The Virgin stands to the left with a Greek inscription naming her as the Mother of God. Below are elaborate mosaics detailing the story of the church's **foundation** by Pope Liberius (possibly by Rusuti's workshop).

Santa Maria Maggiore

Just a short walk from Santa Pudenziana, this is one of the most important churches in Rome. Highlights from the early period are the mosaics in the nave and on the triumphal arch (ca. 432, just after the Visigothic sack of Rome), the historically important icon of the Virgin and Child (ca. sixth century, in the Borghese chapel) (see p. 17), the mosaics on the facade above the portico by Filippo Rusuti (ca. 1288-97), the apse mosaics by Jacopo Torriti (ca. 1291-6), and the Chapel of the *Presepio* (nativity), with sculpture by Arnolfo di Cambio (ca. 1291, now in the museum).

History

This church was first built in the fourth century by the pope Liberius (352-60), and rebuilt by Sixtus III (432-40). It is one of five patriarchal basilicas in Rome and has great importance in the city. It is known as Saint Mary of the Snows because of a legend in which the Virgin appeared in a vision to Liberius. The outline of a church miraculously appeared in snow (in August), whereupon Liberius built a church according to this heaven-sent plan, which is unusually oriented with the apse facing northwest. It has been restored and added to at various times (see plan to left).

Facade

Before entering the church at the main southeast doors, look up above the facade to spot the thirteenth-century mosaics which can be visited with a ticket. They were made by Filippo Rusuti (ca. 1255–ca. 1325) and are well worth seeing. There is also an interesting display of ecclesiastical garments and ancient manuscripts.

Mosaics

Inside the church, which is vast and often only partially lit, pick out the mosaics running down the walls of the nave beneath the clerestory windows, and the mosaic on the arch in front of the apse. These are rare examples from the early fifth century.

Nave mosaics

The mosaics in the nave narrate stories from the Old Testament (see pp. 12-13). On the wall to the left as you enter, are scenes, starting from the far end with events in the life of Abraham and ending with Moses, while on the side to the right are scenes from Moses to Joshua (see pp. 8). The Old Testament scenes in the nave prefigure or prepare the worshipper for the triumph of Christ enacted on the altar under the apse during the Eucharist.

Triumphal Arch

The wall in front of the apse at the east end of the church is known as the triumphal arch (see pp 14-15). This term is derived from the arches put up to honour the victories of Roman emperors, sometimes decorated, as is this, with registers depicting important events. The apse is the most important part of the church.

The scenes are connected with Christ's incarnation. The narrative starts in the top left register with an unusual representation of the Annunciation. Rather than dressed in blue or purple with her head covered, the Virgin Mary wears gold, with a coronet on her head. In later images, the archangel Gabriel alone brings her the good news that she is to have a child, but here one angel is in the sky with the dove of the Holy Spirit and a further five angels are present. Two address Joseph, standing on the right.

The story then moves to the right side with a scene which may be the Presentation in the Temple. The woman may, on the other hand, be the midwife (or her companion Salome), who came to witness the birth of Christ in an apocryphal account of the nativity.

Moving back to the left side, the Virgin appears again (in the same dress) in the Adoration of the Magi, seated to the left of a wide purple throne, on which is the Christ Child, sitting up and dressed in white, with a halo of light. He is not a baby as in the iconography that became customary, but rather a small boy or toddler. The woman to the right, who looks as we have come to expect the Virgin to look in a dark veiled robe, may again be the apocryphal midwife or her companion. Alternatively, she may be *Ecclesia*, a personification of the Church or a sibyl. The magi are dressed in Persian costume with leggings and pointed Phrygian caps as wise men from the east. Joseph is to the very far left.

The scene to the right is not now understood. It would chronologically fit with the time the family spent in Egypt. Returning to the left side, the scene shows the soldiers approaching mothers holding their babies in the Massacre of the Innocents which took place while Joseph and family were in Egypt.

On the right, however, is the scene of the Three Magi before Herod, an event that took place before the Adoration. Below are representations of Bethlehem and Jerusalem.

Apse Mosaic

The apse mosaic by Jacopo Torriti (1291-6), combines traditional Early Christian motifs, such as acanthus scrolls, with a relatively new image which became popular in the thirteenth century, the Coronation of the Virgin by Christ. They sit together on a magnificent throne in heaven. St Francis is at the bottom right, who was included because the patron, Pope Nicholas IV (1288-92), was himself a Franciscan and the first Franciscan pope.

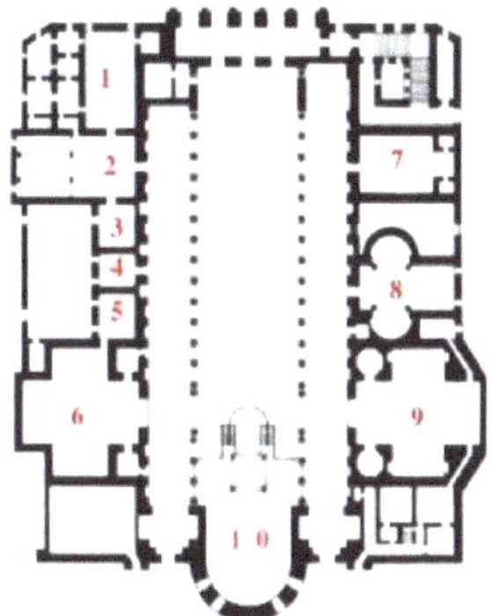

Current plan of S. Maria Maggiore

1=Sacristy; 2=Baptistery; 3=Chapel of SS. Michele e Pietro in Vincoli; 4=Chapel of the Relics; 5=Sacristy; 6=Sistine Chapel, or Chapel of the Holy Sacrament; 7=Cesi Chapel; 8=Sforza Chapel; 9=Borghese Chapel, or Pauline Chapel; 10=apse of Nicholas IV (1288-1294).

The Borghese Chapel (9) houses the early icon known as the *Salus Populi Romani*.

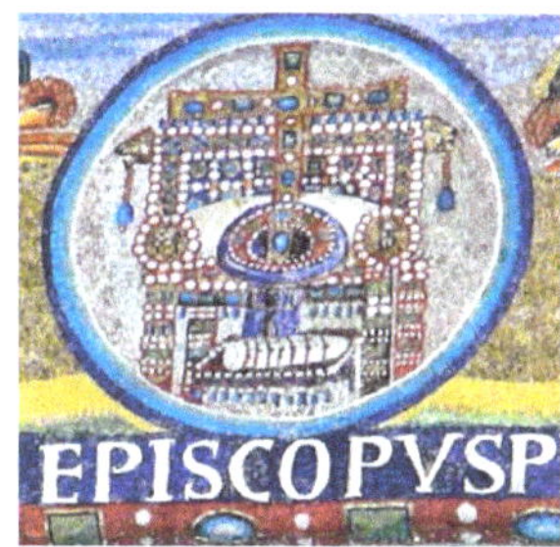

The prepared throne, triumphal arch, Santa Maria Maggiore, ca. 432

In the centre at the top is a **throne** prepared for the return of Christ, shown with a bejewelled cross and crown and below the words in Latin, 'Bishop **Sixtus** to the people of God'. This refers to Sixtus III who rebuilt the church. To the left and right are Peter, Paul and the ***tetramorph***, the symbols of the evangelists.

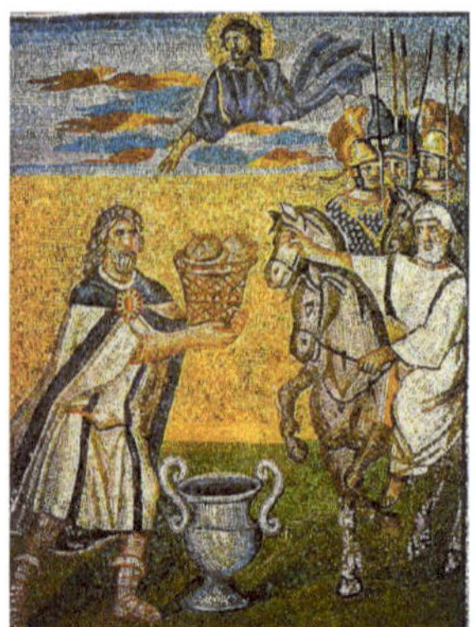

Melchizedek, a high priest from the Old Testament, offers bread and wine to the patriarch Abraham on horseback, nave, S. Maria Maggiore, ca. 432

This scene is interpreted as prefiguring the **Eucharist** of the New Testament, as the priest offers the sacraments to Abraham. This foreshadowing of events in the New Testament with ones in the Old is known as **typology** and was very important in early Christian thinking. The image of Abraham on horseback is perhaps modelled on that of a Roman emperor entering a city in triumph and raising his hand as if addressing the people or his troops.

Scenes in the nave

Left wall as you enter, starting by the altar

1. Melchizedek, King of Salem, blesses Abraham (Genesis 4.17-20)
2. Abraham at the Oak of Mamre (Trinity) (Genesis 18.1-15)
3. Abraham departs from his brother Lot (Genesis 13.5-9)

Three panels are then missing where the arch is.

4. Isaac blesses Jacob; Rebecca is to the right (Genesis 27:1-42)
5. Later painting in fresco, Jacob's Dream (Genesis 28.10-16)
6. Laban, Leah and Rachel welcome Jacob (Genesis 29.1-14)
7. After working for seven years, Jacob is offered Leah (Genesis 29.1-14)
8. After working for seven more years, Jacob is given Rachel and they wed (Genesis 30.25-43)
9. Laban and Jacob divide their flocks (Genesis 29.22-30)
10. God orders Jacob to return to Canaan with his wives and children (Genesis 31.1-21)
11. Later painting in fresco, Joseph's brothers show his coat to Jacob (Genesis 37.12-36)
12. Jacob meets Esau (Genesis 33.1-15)
13. Later painting in fresco (out of place), Sacrifice of Abraham (Genesis 22.1-15)
14. Jacob buys a field and his sons tell him of the rape of Dinah, their sister (Genesis 33.17-20)
15. Jacob and his sons discuss Dinah's marriage with Shechem (Genesis 34.5-19)
16. Later painting in fresco, Elisha strikes the Jordan with Elijah's cloak and makes a spring healthy (II Kings 2.21)
17. Later painting in fresco, Daniel in the Lions' Den (Daniel 6.17-23)
18. Later painting in fresco, Massacre of Jews, women praying, King of Jews taken prisoner (II Kings 25.1-7)
19. Later painting in fresco, Jacob wrestling with an angel (Genesis 32.23-30)

Choice of Iconography

The mosaics at Santa Maria Maggiore are not easy to see from the floor, and it is not clear why they were depicted in this way, with detailed, complex images that are hard to decipher. It is possible that they were modelled on illustrations from manuscripts and the patron (the pope) or the artisans (whoever decided on the iconography) had not realised that they would be so hard to see. On the other hand, it may have been thought sufficient that these great events from the Old Testament were present in the church, reminding the clergy and the lay people of their importance. It is often said that images in the early church were used to teach illiterate people about the biblical texts. It is perhaps not necessary to be able to see the details of the story, but to be shown them with verbal explanations of the narrative.

Scenes in the nave

Right wall as you enter, starting by the altar

1. Later painting in fresco, out of place, Angel and Virgin
2. Moses is adopted by Pharaoh's daughter; he talks with the Egyptian wise men (Exodus 2.9-10)
3. Moses marries Reuel's daughter Zipporah; Moses and the burning bush (Exodus 2.21, 3.1-3)

Three panels are then missing where the arch is.

4. Moses crosses the Red Sea (Exodus 14.19-31)
5. Manna from Heaven and a flock of quail (Exodus 16.4-18)
6. Moses sweetens the waters of Marah; the Amalekites fight the Israelites (Exodus 15.22-5; 17.8)
7. Moses, Aaron and Hur hold up their hands for victory (Exodus 17.10-13)
8. The spies sent to Canaan report to Moses; stoning of Moses, Aaron and Joshua (Exodus 13.26-33; Numbers 14.1-12)
9. Moses hands over the tablets of the Law and dies on Mount Nebo; the ark is carried (Deuteronomy 31.24-9; Joshua 3.6)
10. The ark is carried over the Jordan, the spies arrive at Jericho (Joshua 3.14-17, 2.1-6)
11. The angel of the Lord appears to Joshua; Joshua's spies flee from Jericho (Joshua 5.13-16, 2.13-24)
12. The victory at Jericho, the ark arrives (Joshua 6.12-19)
13. The Amorites besiege Gibeon, God appears to Joshua (Joshua 10.5-9)
14. Joshua defeats the Amorites (Joshua 10.10-11)
15. Joshua halts the sun and moon (Joshua 10.12-14)
16. Joshua punishes the Amorite kings (Joshua 10.22-3)
17. Later painting in fresco, David brings the ark to Jerusalem (II Samuel 6.1-3)
18. Later painting in fresco, David in the Temple (II Samuel 7.1-29)
19. Later painting in fresco, Rehoboam, King of Israel takes advice (1 Kings 12.6-11)

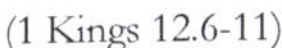

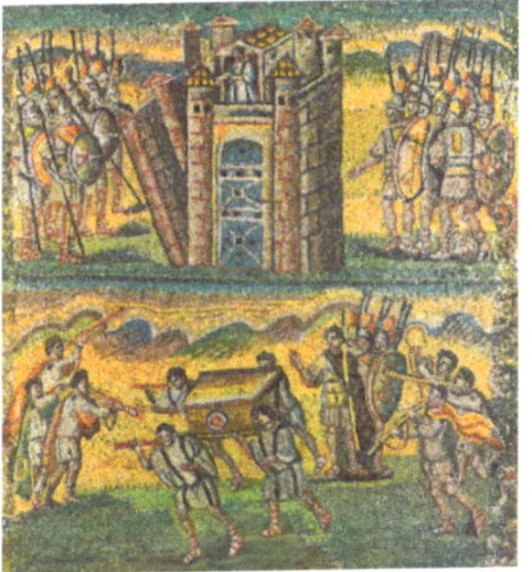

The victory at Jericho, the ark arrives, nave, S. Maria Maggiore, ca. 432

The city of Jericho was besieged by **Joshua** and the Hebrews. This is the moment of triumph.

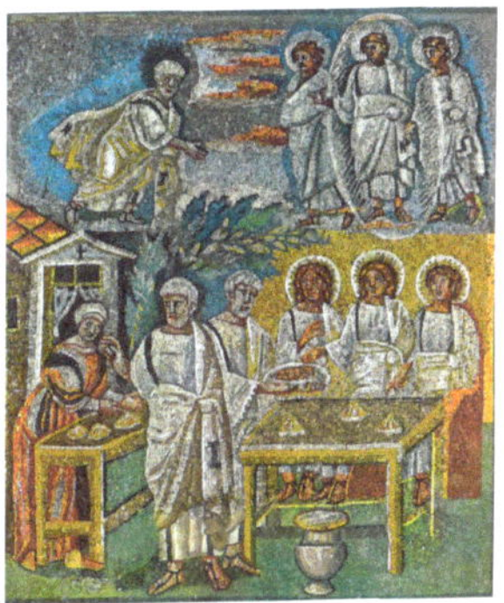

Abraham receiving three visitors, the Trinity, nave, S. Maria Maggiore, ca. 432

Abraham and his wife **Sarah** serve food to their guests who tell them Sarah will have a child.

The Council of Ephesus

In 431 a council of the church hierarchy was called by the emperor Theodosius II and held in Ephesus, now in western Turkey. There were many such councils in the early period, seven of which occurred before 787. In these, the central doctrine of the church was debated and decided. Those who disagreed with the authorities' decision would often leave the main church and start a separate sect and some were persecuted. The discussion in 431 focused on a topic that featured often, the nature of Christ and in what ways he was either or both human and divine. The Nestorians argued that Christ's mother should be called the *Christotokos*, the bearer of Christ, but it was decided she should be the *Theotokos*, the bearer of God. This became the accepted orthodox view and led to a dominant role of the Virgin in Christian doctrine.

Over the main altar in the Borghese Chapel is a painting of the **Virgin and Child**, one of the most famous icons in Rome, known since the nineteenth century as the *Salus Populi Romani*, the Safety of the Roman people. The painting may originally date to the **sixth century** and has been added to at various times, probably in the eighth and twelfth centuries. The Greek letters at the top are abbreviations for the words **Mother of God**, Μήτηρ (του) Θεοῦ as she is known in the east. She is also referred to as the *Theotokos* or bearer of God. There are several important early icons of the Virgin in Rome (see box pp. 16-17).

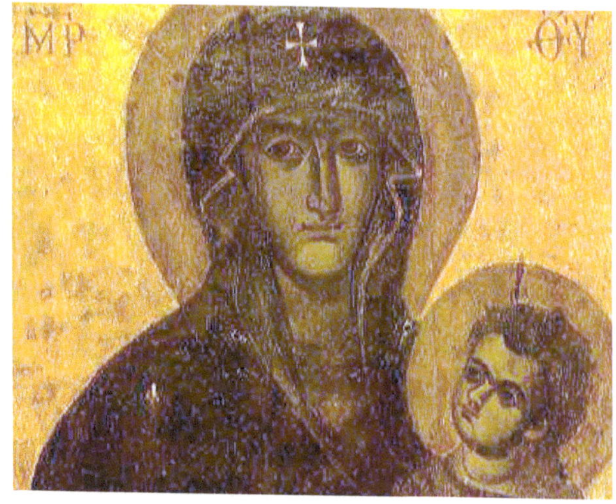

Icon of the Virgin and Child, S. Maria Maggiore, possibly sixth century

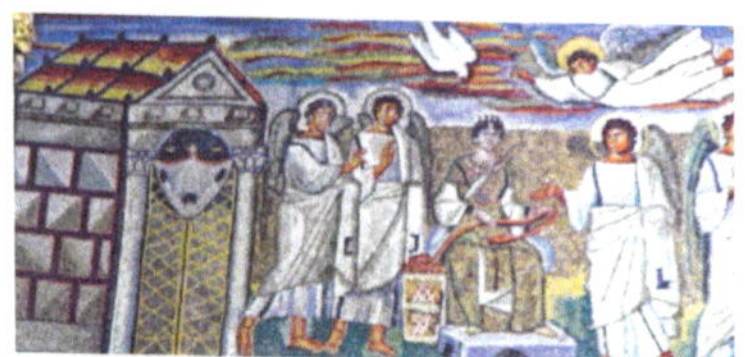

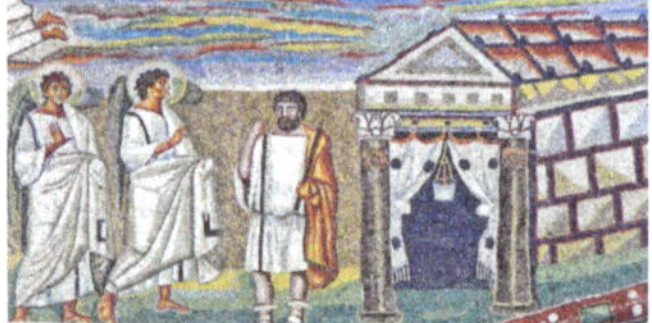

Annunciation to the Virgin Mary
Annunciation to Joseph

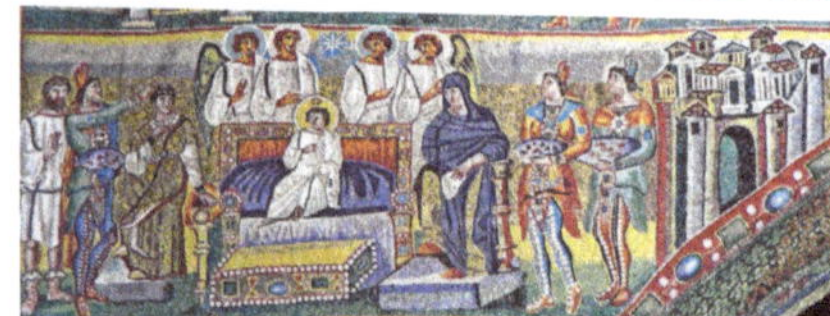

Adoration of the Magi

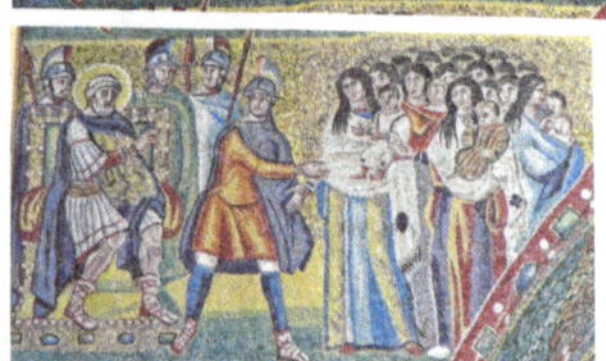

Beginning of Massacre of Innocents

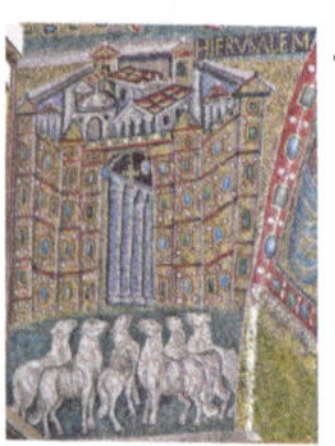

Jerusalem

Guide to the mosaics on the triumphal arch, left side, S. Maria Maggiore, ca. 432

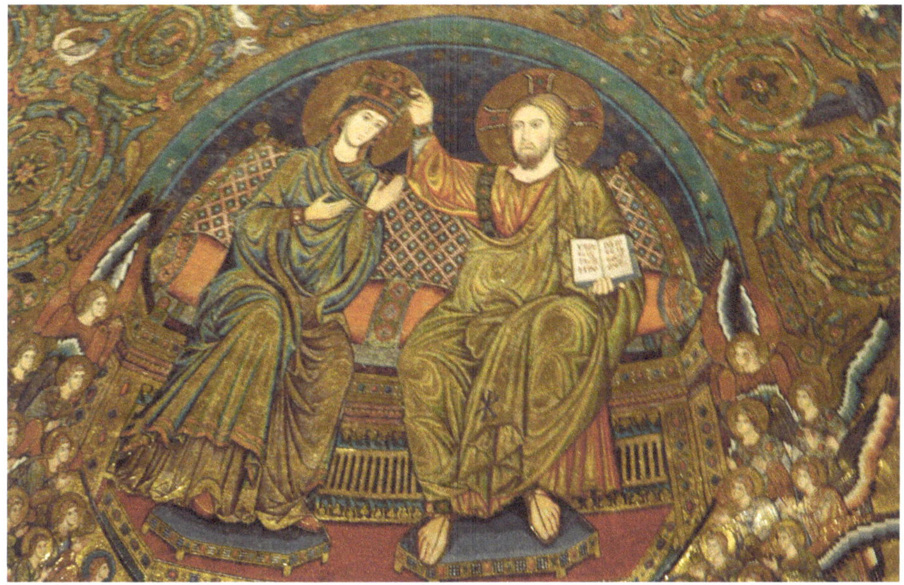

Jacopo Torriti, The Crowning of the Virgin, S. Maria Maggiore, ca. 1291-6

Presentation in the Temple (?) Warning to Joseph

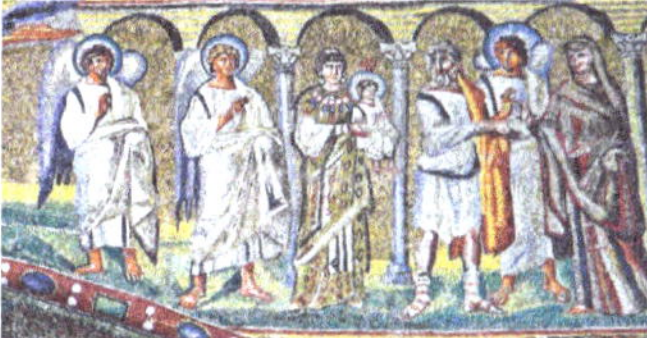

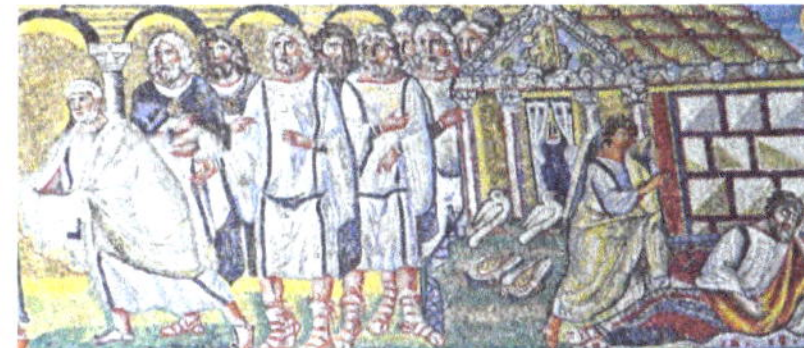

Not known, perhaps scenes in Egypt

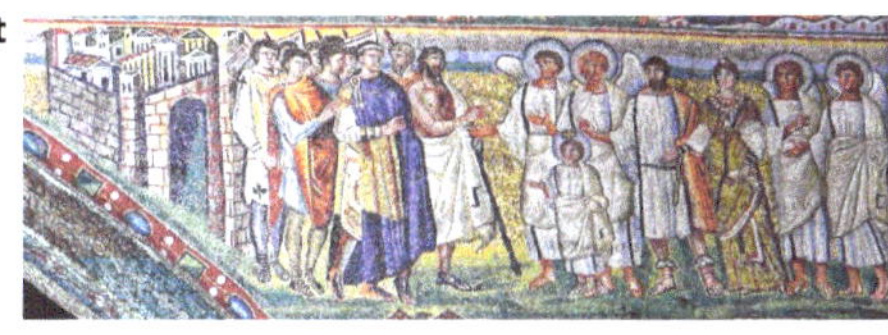

Herod and the Three Magi

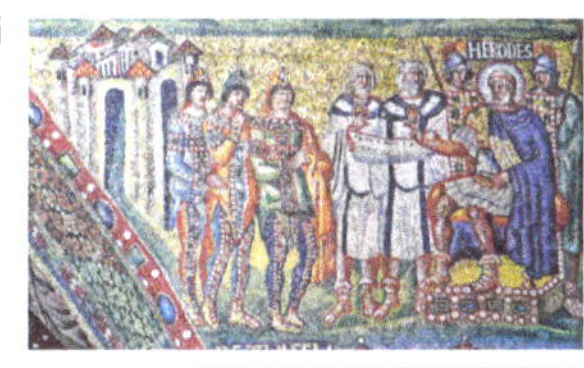

Bethlehem

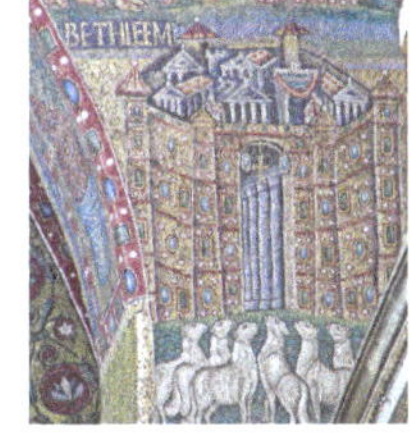

Guide to the mosaics on the triumphal arch, right side, S. Maria Maggiore, ca. 432

Rome's early icons of Christ and of the Virgin

Rome's churches still possess five early icons of the Virgin. The oldest probably dates from the sixth century. They are painted in encaustic, a wax substance, often used on early icons, on either panel or canvas. They were seen as sources of protection and strongly tied to religious worship but also to political and social events. In Rome, as in Constantinople, images seem to have taken on the same role as relics and were actively involved in people's lives, responsible for miracles and for punishing wrong doers.

There are two main types of icons, those that are not painted or made by human hand (*acheiropoieta* in Greek), but rather made miraculously, and those which are painted. The *acheiropoieta* could be miraculously copied. The *Kamouliani* icon of Christ appeared miraculously to a woman in Cappadocia and was taken to Constantinople in the sixth century where it was used as protection in battles. Of the painted images, the most famous was the image of the Virgin and Child said to be painted by Saint Luke and known as the *Hodegetria*. This was housed in Constantinople, but probably only from the tenth century.

From about the sixth century an image of Christ was in Rome and is now in the Sancta Sanctorum by the *Scala Sancta* in the Lateran Palace. It has been very much altered over time. In the tenth century, it was re-covered in silk and the head repainted. It is entirely enclosed in a silver revetment or casing, except for the face. The story of its origin relates that the painting was started by Saint Luke but then miraculously finished by God. It was carried in processions, including one to the forum, where doors at the bottom were opened to wash Christ's feet. On the eve of the Feast of the Assumption of the Virgin, celebrated from 600 on August 15th, it was carried in a procession led by the pope along the Sacra Via in the Roman forum to Santa Maria Maggiore. The icon of Christ 'met' there an icon of the Virgin and Child, which by a later tradition was painted by Saint Luke. At times, other images of the Virgin were visited and joined the procession. This practice continued until 1566.

The pagan temple of the Pantheon was made a church by Pope Boniface IV (608-615) in 609 and dedicated to the Virgin and all the saints. At this time an icon which still survives (a copy is displayed over the altar) was probably made.

A very early and striking icon of the Virgin and Child, perhaps from the sixth century, is held at Santa Maria Nova, also called Santa Francesca Romana, adjacent to the forum. It came from Santa Maria Antiqua, in the forum, in the ninth century and is occasionally displayed there. In Santa Maria Nova, it is not on open display, but it is possible to ask to see it.

In Santa Maria in Trastevere, in the north eastern chapel is a large icon of the Virgin and Child, known as the Madonna della Clemenza. She is pictured as an empress, wearing a crown with hanging pearls, and is flanked by angels who are mentioned in the inscription as the 'awestruck princes of the angels'. A donor (not easy to see) who worships at her feet may be Pope John VII (705-7).

A further image of the Virgin from San Sisto was also said by the beginning of the twelfth century to be painted by Saint Luke and also took part in the August 15th procession. It is now held at Santa Maria in Rosario and is displayed with golden hands studded with pearls and a cross. Precious or semi-precious metals and ornaments are sometimes added to icons to enrich them.

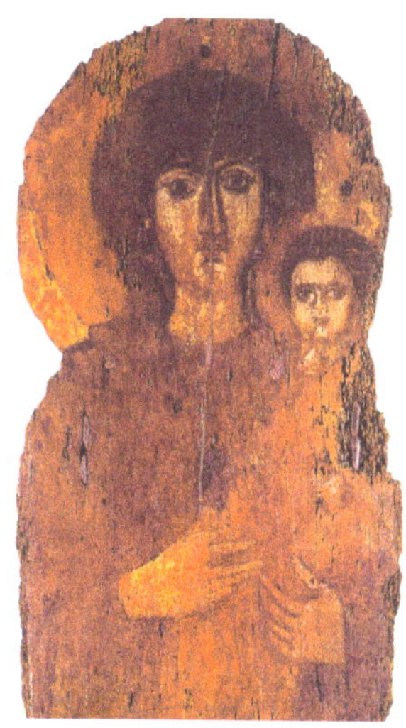

Icon of the Virgin, Pantheon, ca. 609

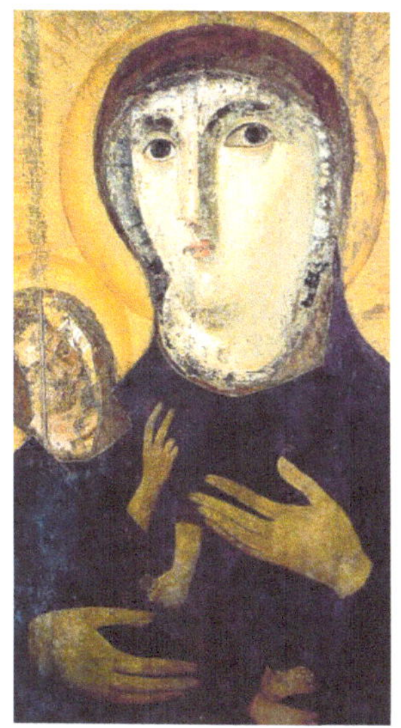

Virgin of S. Maria Antiqua, Santa Maria Nova, ca. sixth century

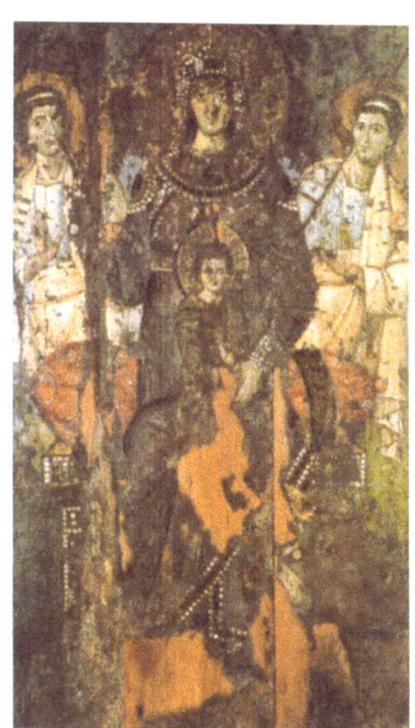

Madonna della Clemenza, S. Maria in Trastevere, early eighth century (?)

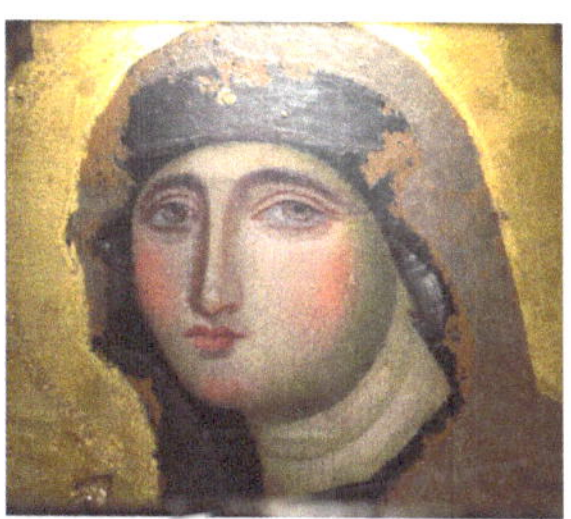

Virgin of San Sisto, S. Maria in Rosario, ca. sixth century

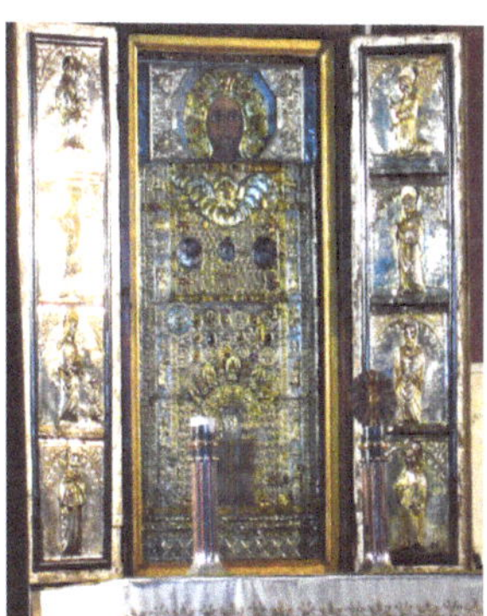

Icon of Christ, Sancta Sanctorum, Lateran, restored

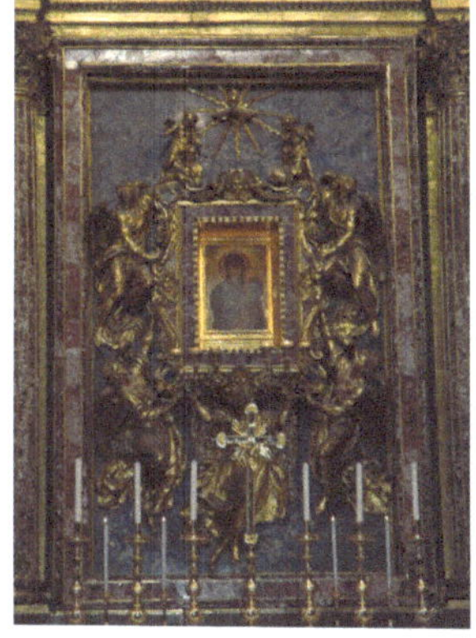

Icon of the Virgin, Borghese Chapel, S. Maria Maggiore, ca. sixth century

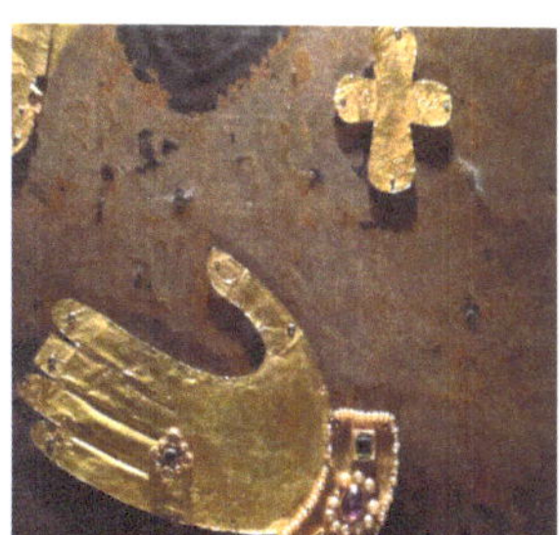

Gold hand and cross, Virgin of San Sisto, S. Maria in Rosario, ca. sixth century

It is clear that some of the **icons** have been heavily restored and over-painted, but they still retain their potency for many and bear witness to the past.

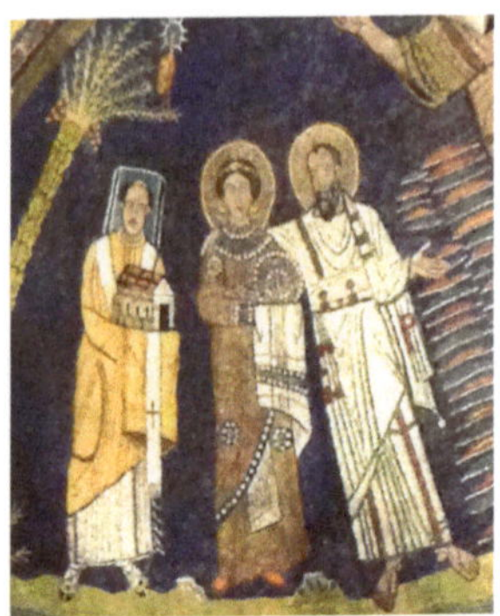

Pope Paschal I presenting a model of the church, S. Prassede, apse, ca. 817

Pope **Paschal I**, on the left, with a **square halo** (which indicates he is living), proffers a model of the church to Christ. He stands with St. Paul and S. Prassede. Above Paschal is a **phoenix**, a symbol of the rising and setting of the sun and so of resurrection.

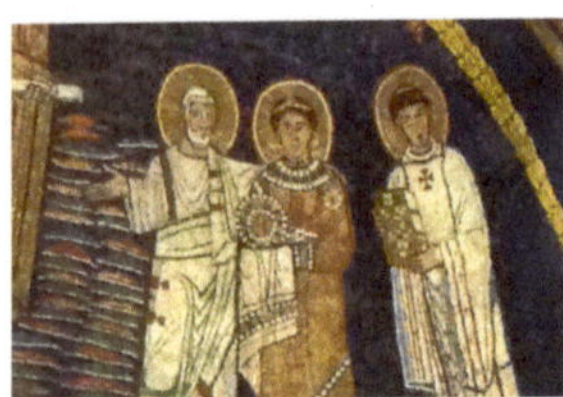

St. Peter, S. Pudenziana and a deacon, S. Prassede, apse, ca. 817

Pudenziana is dressed in a bejewelled gown like a Byzantine empress. The Latin **inscription** running at the bottom of the apse reads, 'Decorated with varied enamels the hall glitters in honour of the devout Prassede, pleasing to the Lord above, through the zeal of Paschal, Supreme Pontiff, member of the Apostolic Seat, who laid in all quarters the myriad bodies of saints beneath these walls, that through them he may deserve to approach the entrance of Heaven'.

Santa Prassede

Again just a short walk, this time from Santa Maria Maggiore, is this important church from the ninth century.

History

Dedicated to Santa Prassede, this church was built by Pope Paschal I in 817 on the site of a house that was mentioned as early as 491. It had been used as a church and was one of the early *tituli* (see box p. 70). Prassede was by tradition the sister of Pudenziana and the daughter of Senator Pudens mentioned by Saint Paul (2 Timothy 4.21). In the ninth century there was a monastery here for Greek monks. Pope Paschal was very active in building churches and reinstating the remains of martyrs (see box p. 82). The design of the church is based on that of Old Saint Peter's. Both the plan and the decoration look back to old traditions.

Apse and Triumphal Arch

The theme of the mosaic at the east end is the Second Coming of Christ. Christ is in the centre of the apse, shown with the nail wounds from the crucifixion in his palms.

On the arch at the east end framing the apse, the imagery comes from the Book of Revelation. In the centre is a lamb representing Christ on a throne over a book with seven seals, to be opened by him. On either side are seven candlesticks, standing for the seven early churches, four angels, the four 'living beings' (who represent the evangelists) and twenty-four elders, dressed in white and adoring the lamb.

On the second arch (further from the apse) is another complex series of images again relating to Christ's Second Coming. At the top is Christ flanked by two angels and below, on the left, the Virgin and John the Baptist and, on the right, Santa Prassede, with apostles on either side and at the ends Moses and Elijah. Beyond are the gates to Heavenly Jerusalem guarded by angels and the 144,000 elect waiting to enter with martyrs on the left and others led by Peter and Paul on the right. Below are further martyrs wearing white and holding palm fronds and martyrs' crowns (Revelation 7).

The lambs below, representing the twelve apostles, come from the cities of Bethlehem and Jerusalem towards Christ, in the form of a lamb, and the four rivers of paradise, referring to the evangelists.

Crypt

The crypt follows the form of the one added to Old Saint Peter's by Pope Gregory I (the Great) (590-604). It holds Roman sarcophagi said to contain the remains of the sisters Prassede and Pudenziana. The sarcophagi are called 'strigilated' because of the curvy pattern on them. Above the altar, the painting from the 1700s copies an earlier one.

San Zeno Chapel

A doorway in the south aisle has a carved Roman lintel and ninth-century capitals imitating ancient Roman examples. It leads to a small colourful chapel dedicated to an unknown saint named Zeno. It was made by Paschal for his mother, Theodora. It is entirely decorated in mosaics, with a design based on the late-fifth-century chapel of Sant'Andrea in Ravenna. Like the main part of the church, the decoration is looking back to Early Christian models. Having entered, look up to the vault to see angels, standing like caryatids, supporting an image of Christ. The background is gold, with tesserae (the small squares forming the mosaic) made of gold leaf placed within two layers of glass.

Above the entrance, through which you just came, is the *Hetoimasia*, an empty throne awaiting the Second Coming of Christ, with Peter on the left and Paul on the right. On the wall to the right are Theodora, shown with a square halo, and three saints, Agnes (wearing a crown), Pudenziana and Prassede. Above is the Lamb of God with the four rivers of paradise. In the tympanum below Theodora are the two sisters, Pudenziana and Prassede, again flanking the Virgin. Within the arch is an apocryphal scene knows as the Harrowing of Hell or *Anastasis*, when Christ goes to Hades to bring back to life Adam and Eve and other blessed people from the Old Testament. On the wall facing the entrance, above the altar, are the Virgin and John the Baptist with a scene representing the Transfiguration. This shows Christ flanked by three apostles, Peter, James and John and two prophets, Moses and Elijah. In the small apse above the altar is a thirteenth-century mosaic showing the Virgin and Child with the two sisters. This is different in style from the earlier mosaics.

The space beyond (to the right as you enter) contains the column to which Christ was said to be tied when he was beaten before his crucifixion. In the medieval period, this was a highly significant relic and made this an important church.

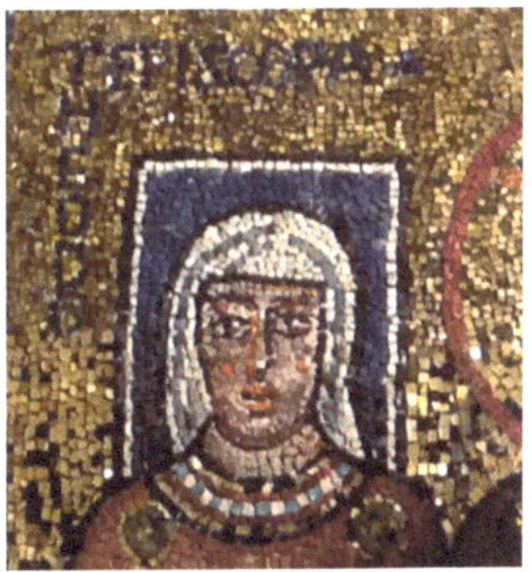

Theodora, the mother of Paschal, S. Zeno Chapel, S. Prassede, ca. 817

Theodora wears a square halo to show she is blessed, but also that she is alive.

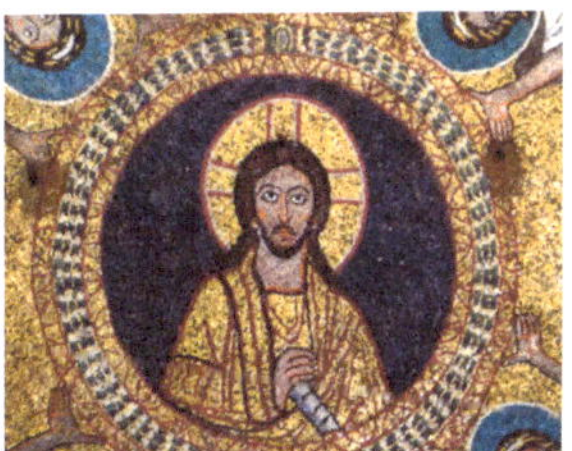

Christ in the centre of the vault, S. Zeno Chapel, S. Prassede, ca. 817

Christ is dressed in rich gold robes, holds a scroll and has a crossed nimbus or halo.

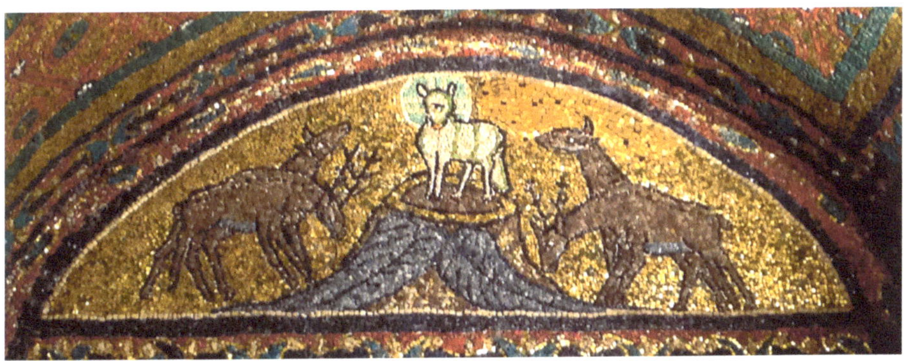

Christ imaged as a lamb standing above the four rivers of Paradise with deer drinking, S. Zeno Chapel, S. Prassede, ca. 817, a theme taken from Psalm 42: 1

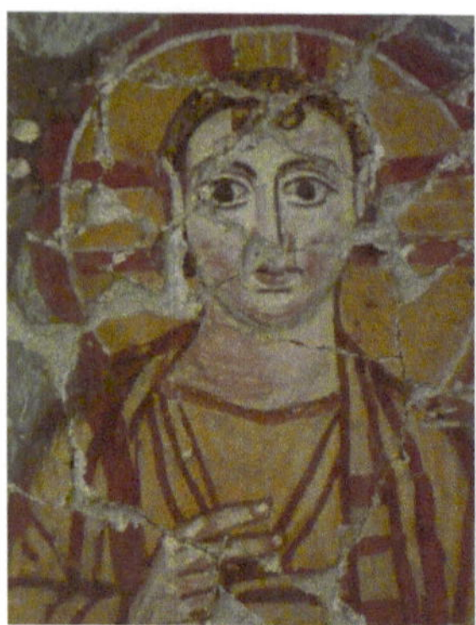

The Christ Child, S. Susanna, eighth century

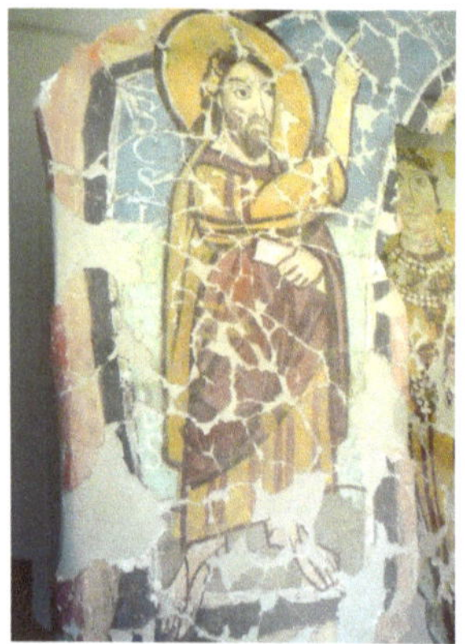

John the Baptist, S. Susanna, eighth century

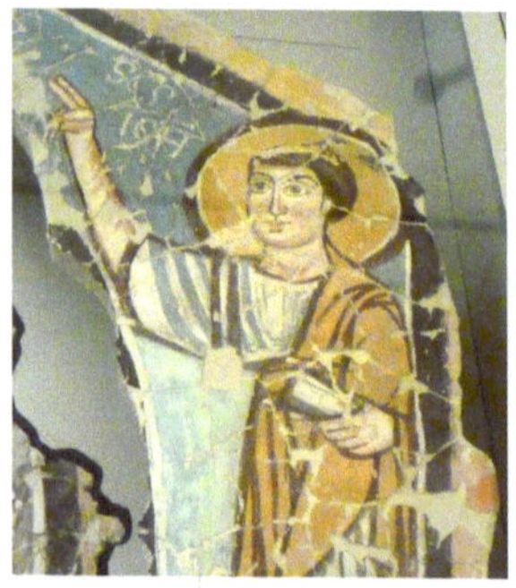

John the Evangelist, S. Susanna, eighth century

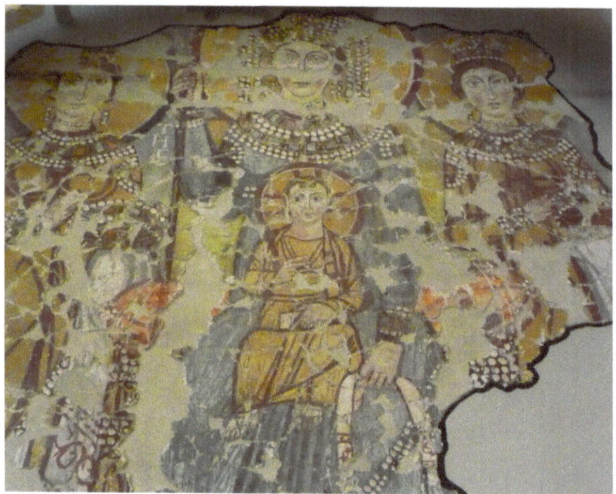

The Virgin and Child with SS. Agatha and Susanna, restored fresco, eighth century

Santa Susanna

History

This is one of the early titular churches of Rome (see box p. 70), and was founded in the fourth century on a site where Susanna was said to have been beheaded in 295. It was rebuilt ca. 796 under Pope Leo III (795-816) and remodelled later with a fine facade by Carlo Maderno, dated to 1603.

Fresco

In the sacristy (may be closed, but ask a nun to open during morning and afternoon opening times), there are remains of the early church excavated in 1991 and a remarkable fresco which was found in about 7,000 pieces and carefully reconstructed. It dates from the late eighth century and shows the Virgin and Child flanked by two saints, Agatha and Susanna (probably), with John the Baptist on the far left and John the Apostle on the far right. The Virgin appears in the *Maria Regina* type with a Byzantine style crown.

> ***Maria Regina***
>
> The term *Maria Regina* refers to the image of Mary crowned as queen (or empress) of heaven. It has been suggested that this form originated at the Byzantine court and was perhaps transferred to Rome by Pope John VII (705-7), who used Byzantine imagery in other works he patronised. Examples in Rome are found at Santa Susanna (this page), Santa Maria Antiqua (see p. 25), San Clemente (see p. 35), and in the icon at Santa Maria Trastevere (see p. 17).

CHAPTER THREE:

THE FORUM AND NEARBY

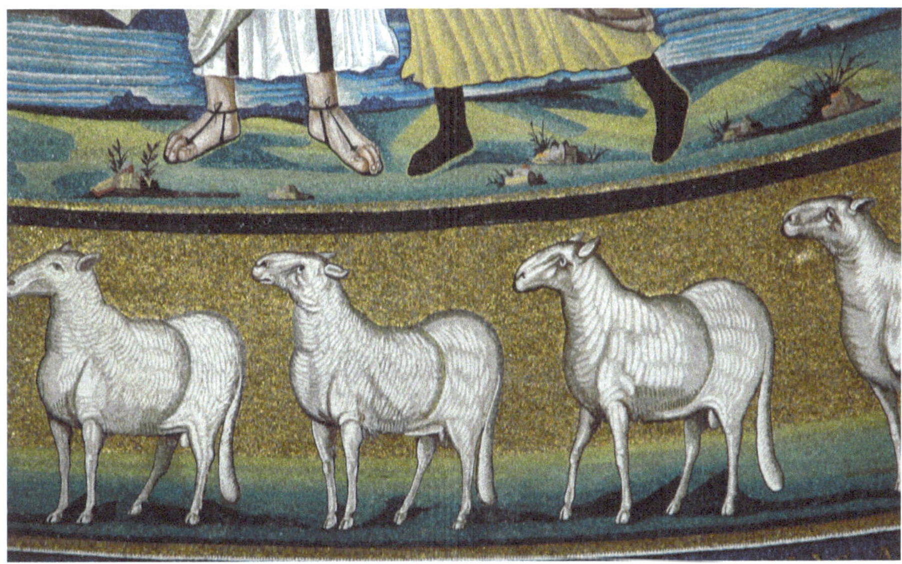

Sheep walking from the city of Bethlehem, apse, SS. Cosma e Damiano, ca. 527

San Marco, Santi Cosma e Damiano, Santa Maria Nova, Santa Maria Antiqua, Santa Maria in Aracoeli, San Teodoro, San Giorgio in Velabro

Introduction

The area around the forum is rich in early Christian buildings. San Marco, placed north east of the forum on the Piazza San Marco just beyond Piazza Venezia, was founded as early as 336 and has a ninth-century mosaic apse. Santi Cosma e Damiano, on the north edge of the forum, is from the sixth century and its apse confirmed the trend for those made in the eighth and ninth centuries. Adjacent to it is Santa Maria Nova, which holds one of the important early icons in the city. The most outstanding of these churches is Santa Maria Antiqua, in the heart of the Forum. It has been recently restored and is not necessarily open to the public. San Teodoro, on the Via di San Teodoro, is used by the Greek Orthodox community and is beautifully restored but is only accessible during Sunday services. San Giorgio in Velabro, close by, can be visited either here or while at Santa Maria in Cosmedin (see p. 54).

The **sheep** represent Christ's apostles and by extension the chosen followers of Christ. The figures are placed in Paradise with a verdant ground and little plants growing in front of the sky, lit up by Christ's Second Coming. The sheep are a common motif used in Early Christian decorations in both the east and west.

The imagery on the apse mosaic at **SS. Cosma e Damiano** was adapted and reused in many churches in Rome, adopting a central image of Christ flanked by **Peter and Paul** with key saints associated with the site. The theme is of Christ's Second Coming or ***Parousia*** and was particularly popular in the ninth-century so-called Carolingian renaissance.

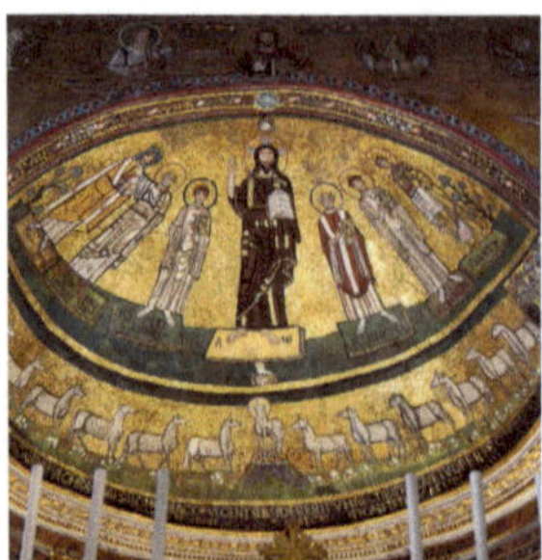

Christ with saints, apse, S. Marco, ca. 829

Beneath the figure of Christ is a representation of the **Lamb of God** in paradise with the twelve apostles as sheep leading from Jerusalem and Bethlehem. Above on the facade Christ is flanked by the ***tetramorph***, representations of the evangelists, and on the left, Paul, and on the right, Peter, each striding as if to reach Christ.

As is typical, the **inscription** records Gregory's patronage and asks St. Mark to ask God that he may go to heaven after a long life. It reads, 'the mighty footings of the vault rise upon their prime foundation and gleam like works of Solomon beneath the heavens. It is for you, Mark, and in your honour that Bishop Gregory, fourth of that distinguished name, brought this to completion. May you in turn beseech God that he may grant him a long life and conduct him after his death to the stars of heaven'.

Pope Mark only held papal office for eight months and 20 days, so one imagines, if indeed he did found this church, he would not have lived to see its completion.

San Marco

This ninth-century church is set back on the Piazza Venezia and was incorporated into the impressive Palazzo Venezia in the fifteenth century.

History

This is a wonderful place for seeing the remains of the churches built here on the site of a large house (late third to early fourth century). There were two earlier churches and the present church was built by Gregory IV (827-44), who was the cardinal priest at this basilica. The excavated areas can be seen by asking at the sacristy. They reveal the three stages of building, including the house's black and white mosaic floor. The lower walls and pavement as well as column bases of the first church are visible, dated to the mid-fourth century. This was perhaps built by Pope Mark (336) (as recorded in the *liber pontificalis*, see p. 82). It is thought that this church burned down. You can also see the *opus sectile* floor and parts of the *schola cantorum* of the second church, built sometime after the sixth century. This church was restored by two popes, Hadrian I (772-95) (who mentioned the narrative decoration in a letter to Charlemagne) and by Leo III (795-816). It was not long after, however, that it was in very poor repair and Gregory IV completely rebuilt it.

The apse

In the apse mosaic Gregory IV is pictured presenting a model of the church. He is on the far left, next to Saint Mark (the evangelist) and San Felicissimo. In the centre is Christ and to the right Pope Mark (336), Saint Agapitus and Saint Agnes. Felicissimo and Agapitus were deacons martyred in about 258. The design is typical of other churches in Rome with Christ centred amongst donors and saints. Gold ground sets off the figures. Unusually here, the figures stand on footstools with their names inscribed on them, including Christ's which is labelled with the letters Alpha and Omega.

The style of this mosaic is closely related to the three in Rome made under Paschal I (817-24), who was pope a few years earlier. Gregory was maintaining Paschal's tradition (see box p. 82). Pope Mark's remains were brought here in the twelfth century and placed under the altar.

The crypt

The crypt is open and contains the relics of two Persians, Abdon and Senen, barrel makers who protected Christians during the Diocletian (285-305) persecutions. It runs beneath the apse in a semicircle and is now undecorated.

Santi Cosma e Damiano

This church is accessed from Via dei Fori Imperiali. It is important for the style and iconography of many churches in Rome.

History

The church is dedicated to the twins Cosmas and Damian, two very important early martyrs who were healers. That their church is here was perhaps due to the pagan temple dedicated to Castor and Pollux (the Dioscuri), who were also twins, which was nearby. It was built in 527 by Pope Felix IV (526-30) using a preexisting round building on the edge of the forum and was the first church in the forum, the ancient heart of the city, and so marks the late takeover of Christianity here. Originally the church was entered from the forum through this building, which is now visible through the large window at the west end of the nave. Looking down gives a sense of the original height of the church.

The church

The proportions of the church have been changed and, in order to visualise its early appearance, the seventeenth-century baroque additions need to be imagined away and the floor pictured about seven metres lower. The apse has been made more narrow, and originally the church would have had side aisles that were later (according to Counter-Reformation requirements) made into separated chapels.

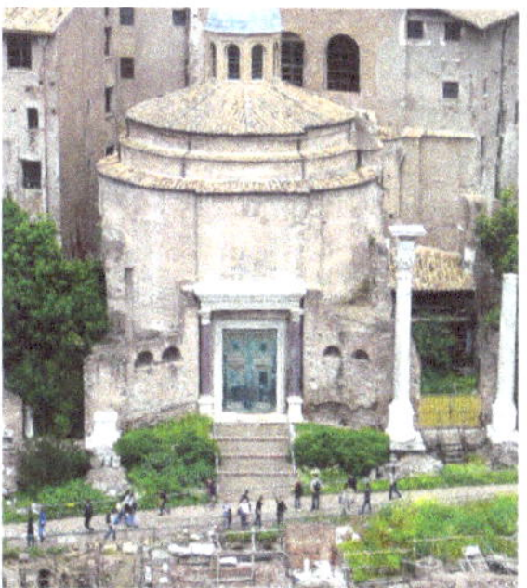

The building known as the Temple of Romulus as viewed from the forum, ca. 309

This fourth-century building was converted into the entrance of the church of SS. Comas e Damiano. The original **doors** are in place. It was possibly the entryway to the Forum of Peace but tradition holds it to be the Temple of Romulus, dedicated by Maxentius in 309 to his dead son.

The building is accessible from the forum and has interesting paintings, well worth seeing.

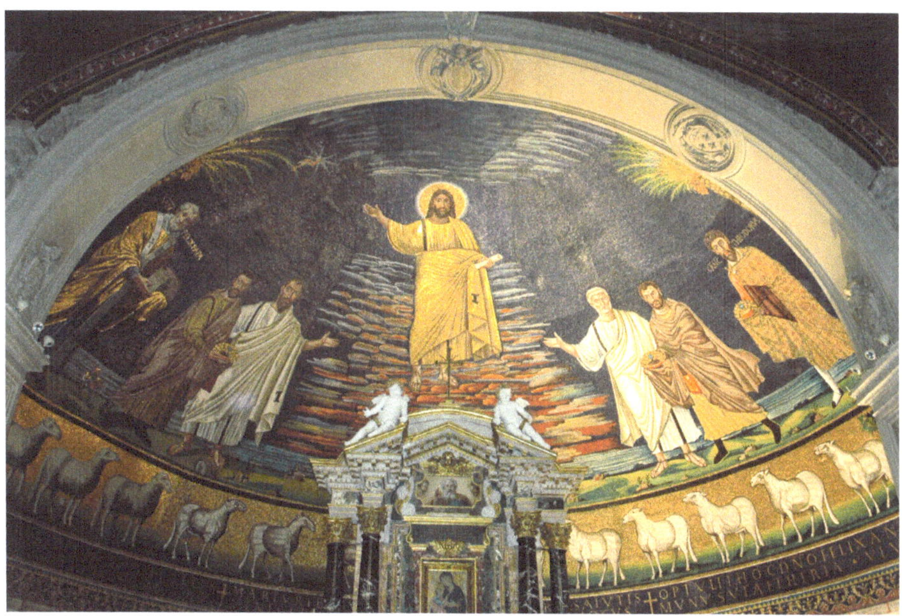

Christ's Second Coming, apse, SS. Cosma e Damiano, ca. 527

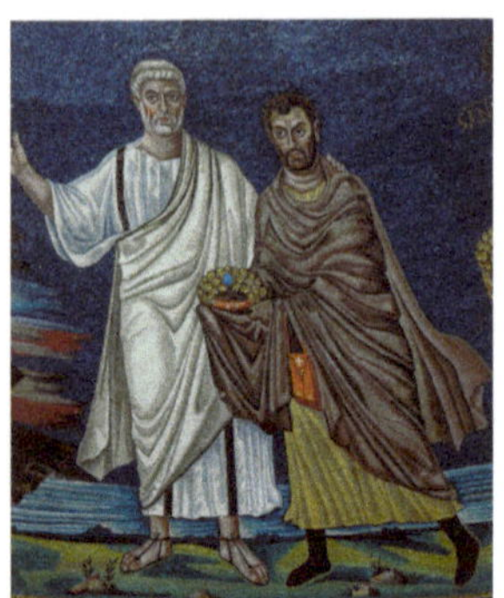

St. Peter with one of the doctor martyrs, apse, SS. Cosma e Damiano, ca. 527

Cosmas and Damian were martyred in about 287 during the rule of Diocletian. They were from Cilicia in Turkey, twins and doctors and are known as the *anargyroi* (not mercenary) in Greek as they refused any payment for their healing. They are generally pictured as identical and youthful with idealised beauty. However, here they are shown as mature men. The martyr on the right has a red medicine chest, an attribute of his profession.

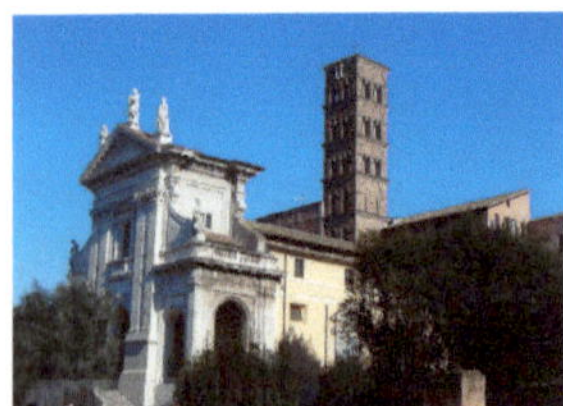

The temple of Venus and Roma with the church of S. Francesca Romana behind, Roman Forum

By tradition the early oratory at S. Francesca Romana was built on a site where Peter knelt to pray, and the marks of his **knees** were left in two stones from the Via Sacra, now visible through a grill in the south wall. **Simon Magus** was a sorcerer who converted and then offered Peter money in order to have power over the Holy Spirit. (Acts 8.9-24).

The apse

The apse depicts Christ's Second Coming and the martyrs being presented to him by Saints Paul (on the left) and Peter (on the right). On the far right is Saint Theodore and on the far left Felix. The sky has a stunning appearance with tiny clouds lit up in reds and blues. This theme is picked up in many later Roman churches, such as those built by Paschal I (see box p. 82). Various parts of the mosaic have been heavily restored.

Santa Francesca Romana (Santa Maria Nova)

This church is accessed from the Via dei Fori Imperiali by some steps. It is by the massive Basilica of Maxentius and Constantine built in the early fourth century, and behind the temple of Venus and Roma, which was closed as a temple in 391.

History

The earliest Christian building was an oratory dedicated to Peter and Paul which was incorporated into the temple in 757-67. The important church of Santa Maria Antiqua was damaged in 847 and its role as a diaconate church (see box p. 26), given to the oratory, then named Santa Maria Nova (new as opposed to ancient). In 1161 it was extended and the apse decoration depicting the Virgin enthroned with saints, and the campanile added. It was rededicated to Santa Francesca Romana after the saint of that name (1384-1440).

Icon

It holds a rare sixth-century icon of the Virgin and Child. The image was covered by a twelfth-century painting, also of the Virgin and Child, which was separated in 1950 and is now above the altar. The early one is held in the sacristy. If no one is present to show it, ring at the convent. It is occasionally also to be found at Santa Maria Antiqua, its original location.

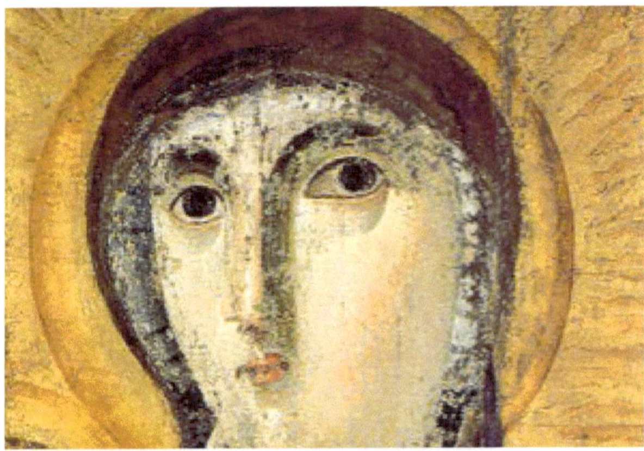

Icon of the Virgin and Child, detail, S. Maria Francesca

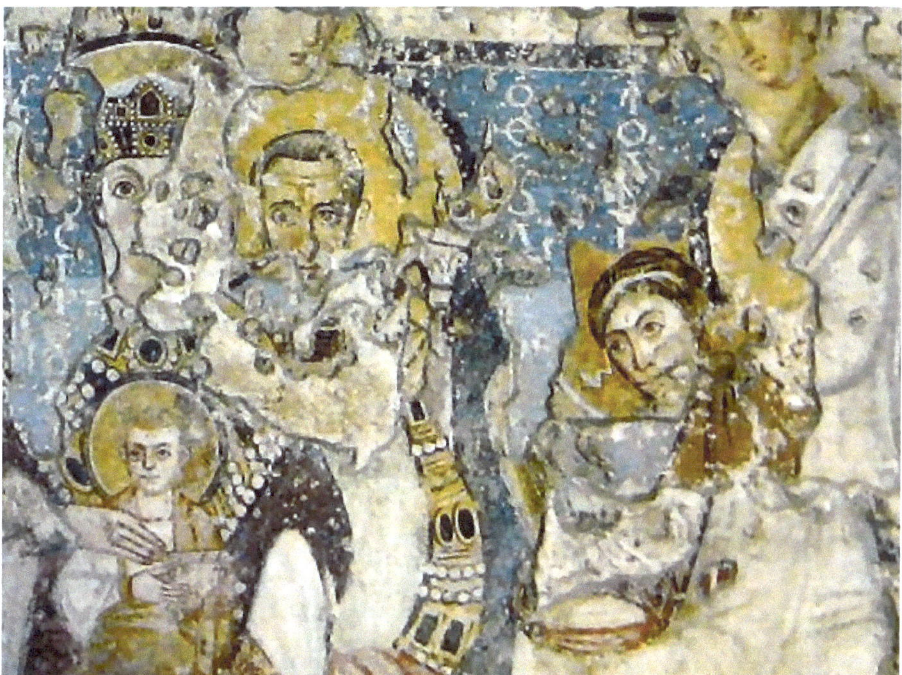

'Palimpsest' wall, triumphal arch, S. Maria Antiqua, sixth to eighth centuries

Santa Maria Antiqua

This is a very unusual building, situated in the Roman Forum and, if open, accessible with the Forum ticket. It has the most important early paintings to be found in Rome. If it is not open, ask for special permission to visit .

History

It was originally built in the first or second century C.E. In the sixth century, after being used as a guardroom for the (Byzantine) governor's palace on the Palatine Hill, it was inaugurated as a church. It fell into disuse in the ninth century and has recently been restored.

Oratory of the Forty Martyrs

To the left of the entryway is the Oratory of the Forty Martyrs. It is dedicated to forty soldiers who died in a freezing lake in Sebaste (modern Sivas, Turkey) in 320. They are depicted in wonderful eighth-century frescoes in the apse.

The church

To the right, across the atrium, which was used as a burial ground, is the entry to the church. The narthex leads into the central nave which has low walls with paintings on them, part of the *schola cantorum* (the area for the choir) erected by John VII

On the 'palimpsest' wall (where later work is superimposed on earlier work) there are **five layers** of painting in total, but three are more easily detected. The earliest is the crowned Virgin holding the Christ Child and the head of the angel to the right (at the height of the Virgin's shoulder) (sixth century). The next in date is an Annunciation (early seventh century). The head of the Virgin can be seen to the upper right of the crowned Virgin and the Angel Gabriel is above the other angel. The third layer depicts church fathers such as the head directly to the right of the crowned Virgin's (705-7).

The very lovely seventh-century Annunciation is in a style known as '**Hellenistic**', which tends to look back to the painting of antiquity, using fleeting brush strokes and naturalistic representations.

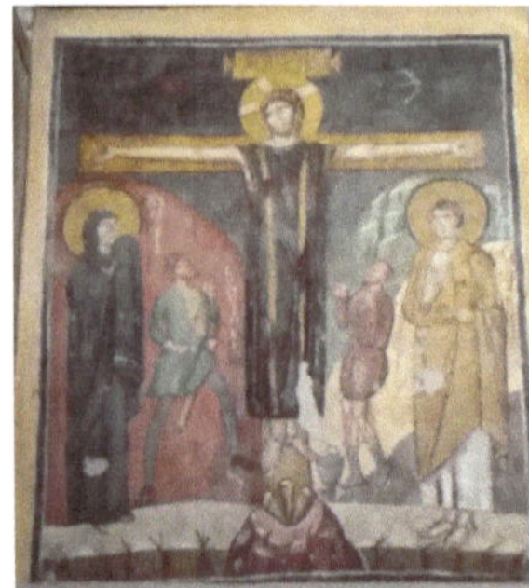

Crucifixion, Theodotus Chapel, S. Maria Antiqua, 741-52

The **Virgin** stands on the left and **St. John** on the right. Christ wears a long robe, known as a ***kolobion***, a style which is used in eastern depictions from the sixth century. In later representations, he wears a loincloth.

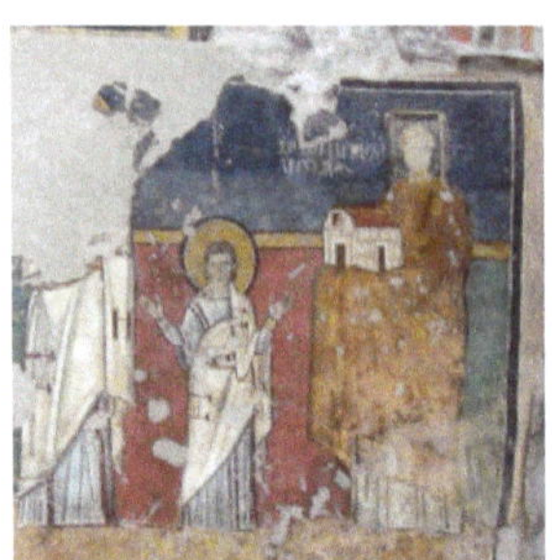

Theodotus offering the chapel, Theodotus Chapel, S. Maria Antiqua, 741-52

This scene is below the Crucifixion. Theodotus has a square halo to show he is living and his hands are covered as a sign of supplication to the Virgin.

(705-7). Much of the painting in the church is from the same period. The image in the apse is slightly later, painted under Paul I (757-67) and shows Christ flanked by the *tetramorph* (the symbols of the Evangelists). The triumphal arch has fascinating paintings from various periods, including the earliest in the church, a representation of the Virgin as *Maria Regina*, to the right of the apse (see p. 20). This was painted before the apse was inserted in the wall.

There are extensive frescoes on many of the walls with scenes from the Gospels and many saints and church fathers. The church has several images of children and adolescents, including youthful martyrs, such as the Maccabee family (from the Old Testament), the Virgin, Christ, and John the Baptist as babies with their mothers, and the child martyr, Saint Quiricus, as well as donor children in the Theodotus chapel.

Theodotus Chapel

The Theodotus chapel, to the left of the apse, was painted in 741-52. It has a series of paintings about Saints Julitta and Quiricus. Quiricus was a three-year-old boy who was martyred with his mother. On the end wall is a Crucifixion. An interesting family portrait is on the right wall, showing the donor of the

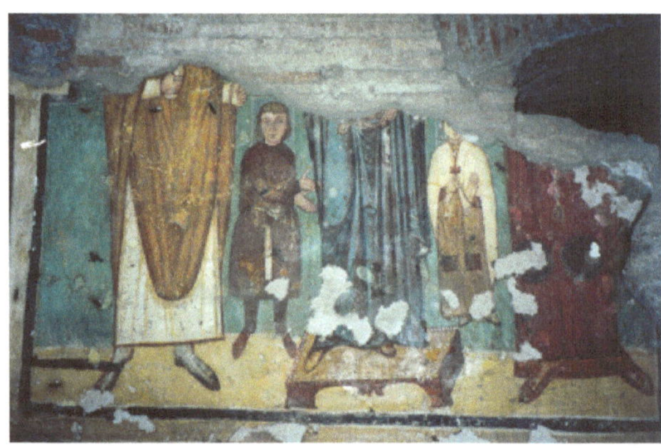

Theodotus with the Virgin and his family, Theodotus Chapel, S. Maria Antiqua, 741-52

Diaconia

Santa Maria Antiqua and San Teodoro were *diaconiae*. These were churches designated to take care of the poor and stem from the insistence of Gregory I (the Great, 590-604) to do this. Giving of alms was inherited from civil Roman practice and it was traditional to do so near the forum. Funding for the alms came from lands owned by the church or by gifts from wealthy members of the church, and the person in charge, the *dispensator*, would receive these donations on behalf of the church. Theodotus, the patron of the Theodotus Chapel in Santa Maria Antiqua, was one of these *dispensators*.

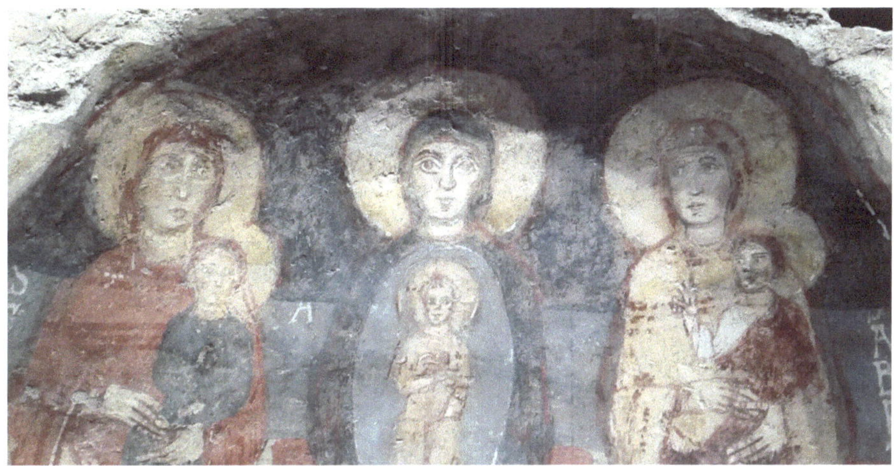

The three holy mothers, Anne with the child Mary, the Virgin Mary with Christ, Elizabeth with John the Baptist, S. Maria Antiqua, 757-767

portraits, Theodotus, who held a responsible position at the church. He stands on the far left with a young boy next to him, the Virgin is in the centre, and then a young girl and a woman stand to the right, presumably his son, daughter and wife. Square haloes frame the heads of both children, a feature which suggests they are living.

The painting of the **three mothers** is placed on the right hand wall of the nave in a niche. It appears to have been a special shrine probably associated with child bearing.

Chapel of the Healers

The chapel to the right of the apse has paintings of healing saints who carry their surgeon's boxes. Worshippers would spend the night in the chapel laying close to the saints, in prayer for a miraculous healing.

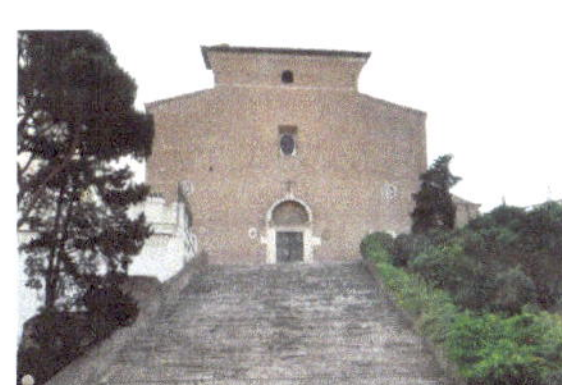

The stairs to S. Maria in Aracoeli

Santa Maria in Aracoeli

This church is placed adjacent to the Capitoline Museums on the capitol hill. Climb the staircase to the left of the stairs to the museums. It was built by the eighth century.

By tradition the church is built on the site where the Tiburtine Sybil told the emperor Augustus about the coming of Christ, saying 'Behold, the altar of God's firstborn', leading to the name of the church, the 'altar of heaven'.

Decoration

The interior has several interesting paintings, including ones on the columns. In the eastern chapel of the south aisle are paintings by Pietro Cavallini, with the Virgin and Child flanked by John the Baptist and John the Evangelist as well as representations of buildings and Christ with angels. In the north aisle (to the left of the altar) is an elaborate tomb to Cardinal Matteo di Acquasparta (d. 1302) with a further painting associated with Cavallini of the Virgin and Child with Saints Matthew and Francis, placed on high. The gabled tomb was made by the Cosmati family (see box p. 46). Two very fine *ambones* dated to ca. 1200 made by the Cosmati are in the centre at the east end. In the tympanum above the south door (exterior)

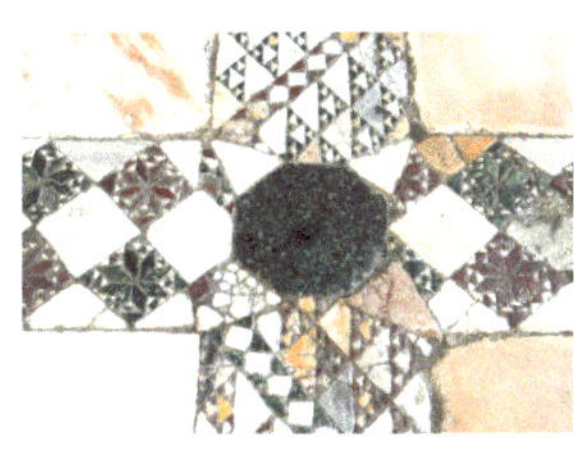

Cosmati floor, detail, S. Maria in Aracoeli. 1200

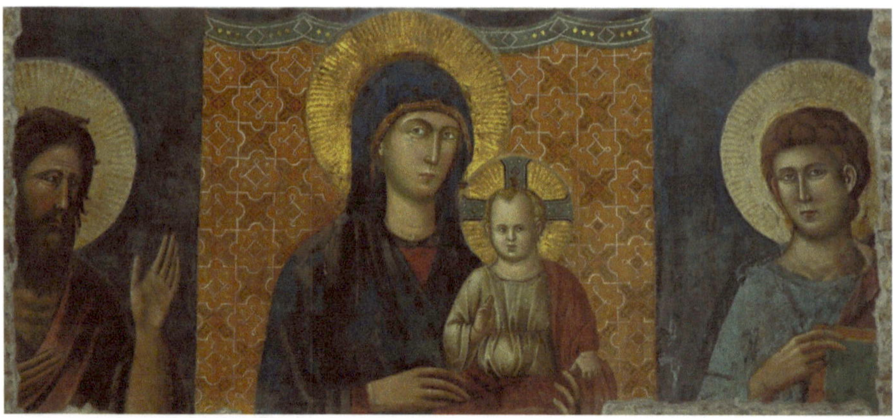

Virgin and Child with St. John the Baptist and St. John the Evangelist, Pietro Cavallini, east chapel, south aisle, S. Maria in Aracoeli, ca. 1290

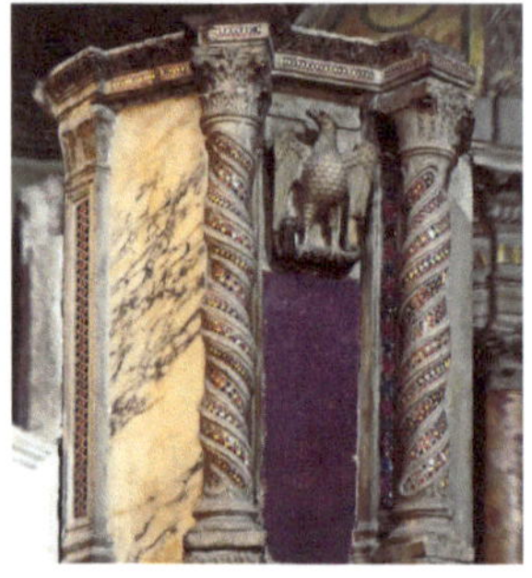

Ambo, Lorenzo Cosmati, S. Maria de Aracoeli, ca. 1200

is a mosaic, also connected with Cavallini's workshop, of the Virgin and two angels. Furthermore in the Savelli chapel in the south transept (east end), dedicated to Saint Francis is a Roman sarcophagus incorporated by Arnolfo di Cambio (1287) into a sepulchral monument for Luca Savelli.

Worth seeing also are two later works: the paintings by Pinturicchio (1454-1513) in the west chapel of the south aisle, and, also at the west end, at right angles to the west wall an erected pavement tomb by Donatello (1386-1466) of Giovanni Crivelli, the archdeacon (1432). This was originally placed on the floor, over his tomb, hence the wear you can see. Donatello's signature is visible.

San Teodoro

This small church is on the Via San Teodoro on the side of the Palatine Hill. It is usually only open for Sunday services, held by the Greek Orthodox Church, but is worth seeing for its sixth-century apse which was part of the early oratory associated with a *diaconia* (see box p. 26). The church was rebuilt in the fifteenth century. The mosaic shows Christ in the centre flanked by Paul (left) and Peter (right) with two martyrs, one who is probably Theodore Stratelates (right), a popular eastern saint. The other has been very heavily restored. It has been suggested that it is Theodore Tyron, another eastern saint, but this is by no means certain. The design of the mosaic is close to that at the church of Santi Cosma e Damiano (see p. 23).

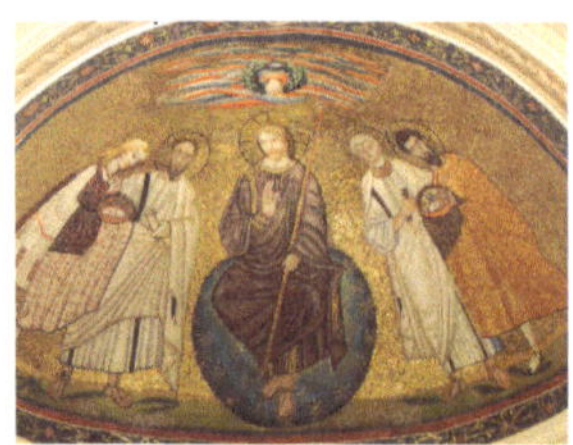

Christ with Saints, apse, S. Teodoro, sixth century

San Giorgio in Velabro

This seventh-century church built over an earlier *diaconia* (see box p. 26), has an apse fresco painted, probably, by followers of Pietro Cavallini. There are more paintings on the nave walls.

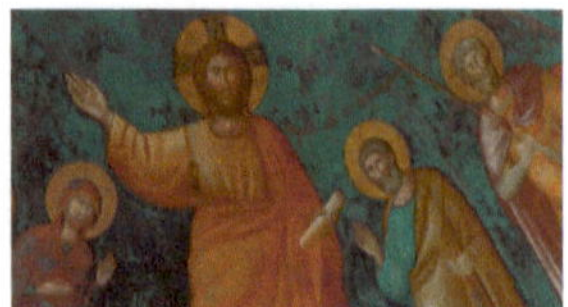

Attributed to Pietro Cavallini, Christ with Virgin and Saints, S. Giorgio in Velabro, ca. 1296, repainted

CHAPTER FOUR:

THE CAELIAN HILL AND NEARBY

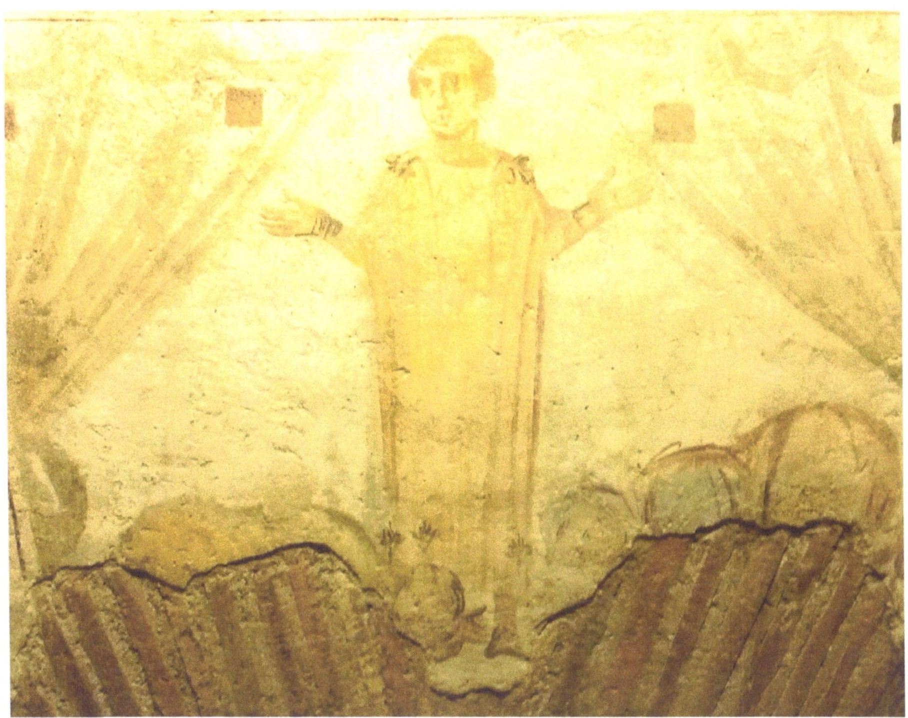

A man in prayer, with others bowing at his feet, *Confessio*, Case Romane del Celio, fourth century

San Clemente, Santi Quattro Coronati, San Giovanni in Laterano, San Giovanni a Porta Latina, Santo Stefano Rotondo, Santa Maria in Domnica, Santi Giovanni e Paolo, Case romane del celio

Introduction

Several of these sites can all be visited in one long day. However, most close at lunch. An early start can cover San Clemente, Santi Quattro Coronati and the baptistery at San Giovanni in Laterano before the lunch break. Generally the only site open all day is the Lateran basilica. The Case Romane del Celio is only open on certain days.

The Church of San Giovanni in Laterano, first built by Constantine I (306-37) in the fourth century, was rebuilt in 1644-55, but the site is worth seeing and the adjacent baptistery

In this painting, the young man is perhaps **Giovanni** or **Paolo**, the martyrs after whom the adjacent church is named. He is praying in the *orans* position with his arms held open. This is how early Christians prayed and is still used by certain communities. Curtains are drawn back on either side.

This technique used for this painting is fresco, one used to decorate Roman buildings and used throughout the medieval and periods. The water base paint is applied to wet plaster. It then bonds with the plaster and so preserves its strength and colour. When paint is applied to a dry surface, it is called secco.

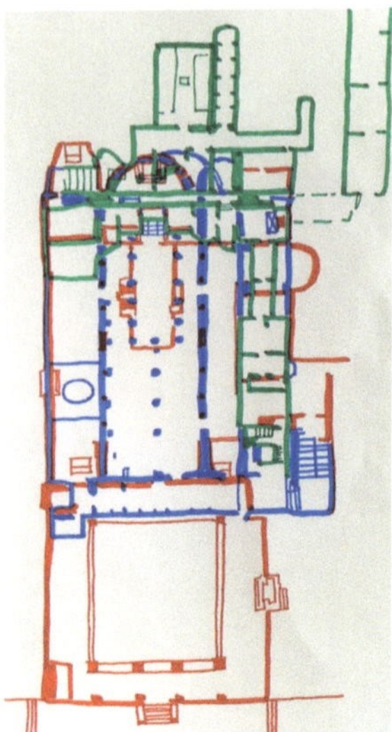

Sketch indicating the interrelation of the three main levels at San Clemente (after Leonard Boyle)

Green = Mithraeum/Roman level
Blue = Lower Church level
Red = Upper Church level

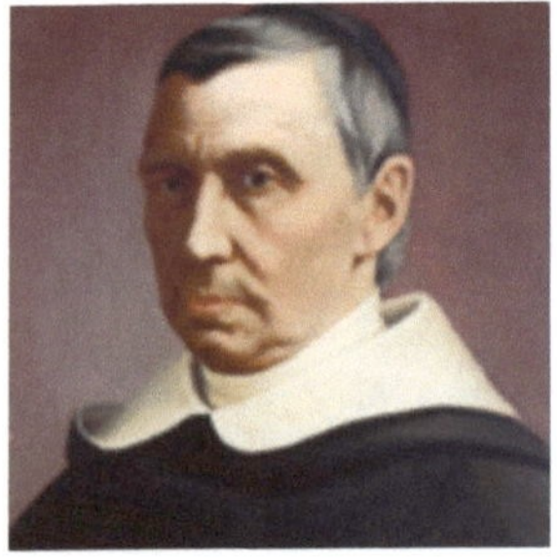

Father Mullooly (1812-80)

The old church was discovered in 1857 by Father Mullooly, prior of the Irish Dominicans, who had been given the site in the seventeenth century. He was responsible for the extensive excavations, revealing the lower church and the mithraeum and is buried beneath the main altar of the early church.

is a key early building with some surviving decoration. The old Lateran Palace contains the renowned *Scala Sancta*, sacred stairs, and the famous icon of Christ (see p. 17). A short but fairly steep walk away, the churches of Santo Stefano and Santa Maria in Domnica, one from the fourth, the other from the ninth century, are both distinctive. The church of Santi Giovanni e Paolo has some wonderful paintings from the thirteenth century, and the adjacent house, Case romane del celio, gives a rare view of a domestic building with paintings from various early periods.

San Clemente

This is one of the most extraordinary churches in Rome. It has Roman domestic remains, an underground stream, substantial elements of a Mithraic cult site, paintings from the seventh (probably) to eleventh centuries in the ruins of an early church (now below ground level) and, above, a twelfth-century church with a stunning apse mosaic.

History

The church is named after Clement, the fourth pope (90-99). It existed in the fourth century and was referred to by Saint Jerome. Clearly important, it was the site of two papal councils, in 417 and 499. The church was restored in the eighth century and again in the ninth, but was severely damaged when Rome was sacked by Robert Guiscard in 1084. After this it was no longer used, and in 1108 the new church was constructed over it under Paschal II (1099-1118). There is an attractive atrium to the west of the church, restored by Carlo Stefano Fontana ca. 1715.

Lower church

By choice, visit the lower archeological site before the main church so as to understand the chronology of the building. Walk through the twelfth-century church on the current ground level to a vestibule beyond the south aisle (on the right) in order to pay the small fee to visit the lower areas. From here descend the stairs to the level of the original church, first built in the fourth century.

The steps bring you down to the narthex or entryway ahead of you. The walls have been decorated with various parts of

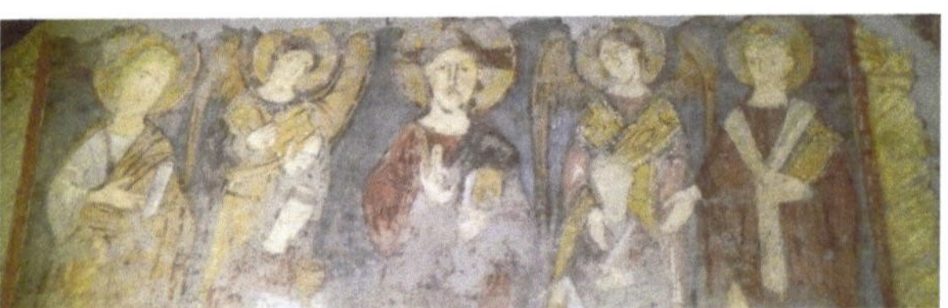

Christ in Judgement, west wall, narthex, S. Clemente, late ninth century

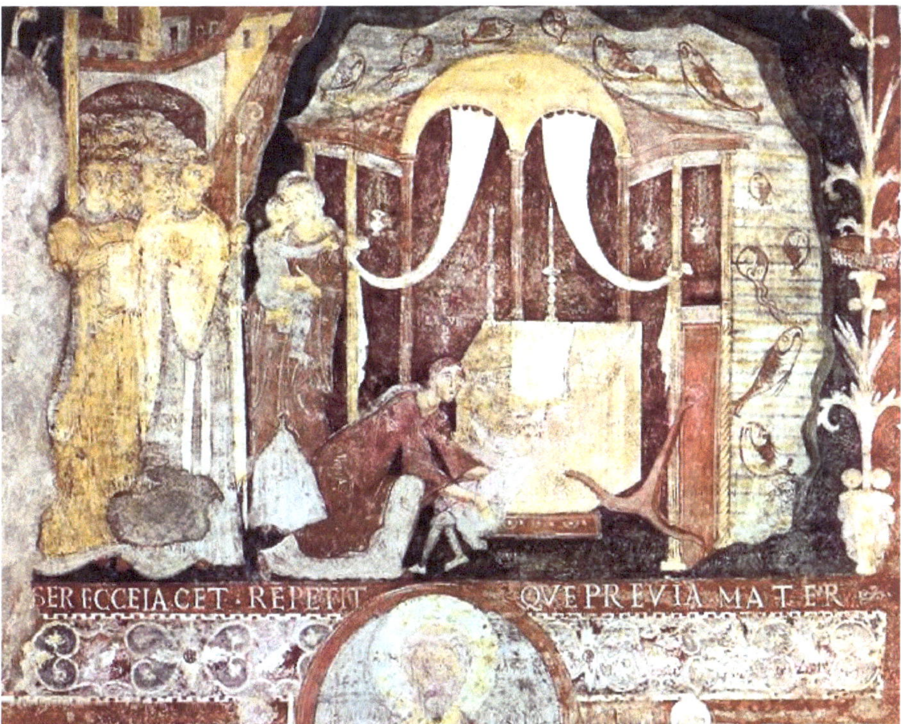

Miracle of St. Clement, fresco, narthex, east wall, ca. 1080

spolia from different periods found in the excavations (some are cast copies).

Lower church narthex: Christ in Judgement

In the narthex are three important frescoes. The earliest (ninth century) is on the west wall (to the left) just as you enter the narthex. It shows Christ in the centre with his hand raised flanked by the archangels Gabriel and Michael with Saint Andrew on the far left and Saint Clement on the far right. There are two indistinct kneeling figures, suggested to be Cyril and Methodius, brothers who were sent by the Byzantine emperor Michael III (842-67) to convert the Slavs. Methodius was the second of the brothers to die, in 887, so the painting may have been made shortly after then.

Lower church narthex: Paintings about Clement

The two other frescoes in the narthex are probably datable to ca. 1080 just before the church was destroyed. They are on the east wall (to the right). The first has two parts, the lower one showing portraits of the donors Beni and Maria Rapiza and their family. The upper is a delightfully illustrated depiction of a legend about Saint Clement.

Stories about the life of **Clement**, the fourth pope, arose in the fourth century and are illustrated in the church. Clement was banished to the Crimea under the emperor Trajan (98-117) and there, through miraculous events, converted many to Christianity.

He was killed by being thrown into the Black Sea tied to an anchor. **Angels** built a tomb for him in which his body was later found. Illustrated above is the story in which the sea **miraculously** revealed the tomb (looking like an elegant tent) each year and, on this occasion, a **child**, who was thought to have drowned, was discovered safe and sound in the tomb and given into the arms of his mother. There is a wealth of sea life encircling the tomb.

The portrait below the scene shows St. Clement blessing.

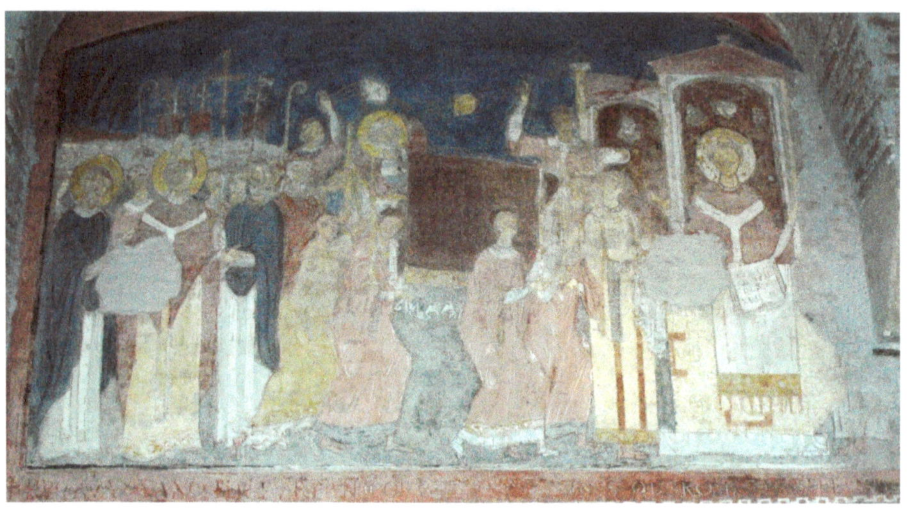

The Pope leading brothers Cyril and Methodius with the relics of St. Clement, narthex, east wall, S. Clemente, ca. 1080

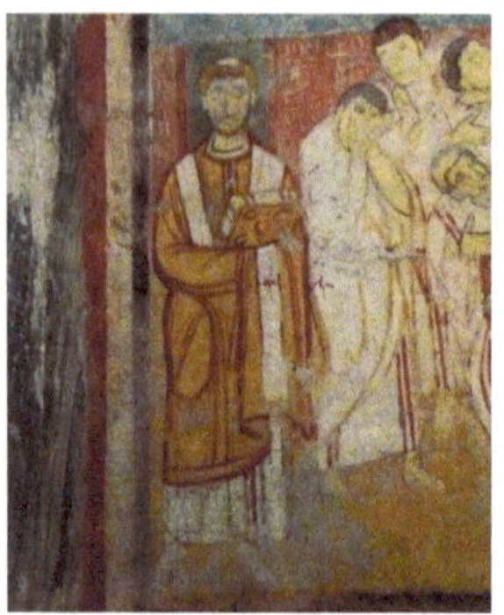

Pope Leo IV, west wall of nave, lower church, S. Clemente, ca. 847-55

The second painting, further down the narthex was also painted at the same time and shows the procession from the Vatican to this church when Clement's relics were brought here after Cyril and Methodius had delivered them from the Crimea.

Lower church nave: Ascension

Next, enter the main nave of the original church. Immediately on the left, on the west wall, is a rare painting from the ninth century. At the bottom is a painted dado, here imitating the cloth around an altar. Above there is an oval depression that would have held some kind of sacred object.

The date is identifiable from the pope, Leo IV (847-55),

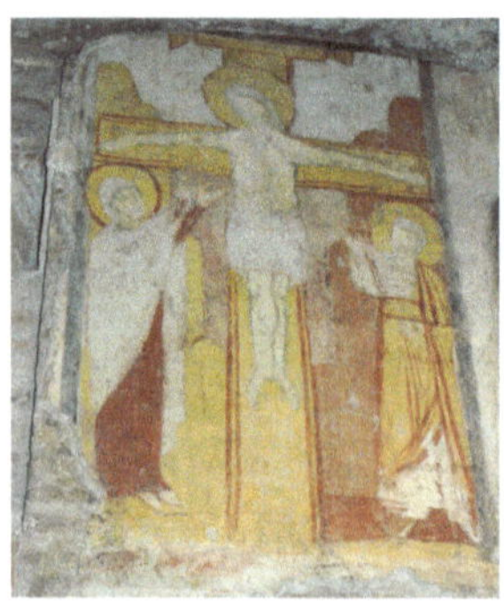

Crucifixion, west wall of nave, lower church, S. Clemente, ca. 847-55

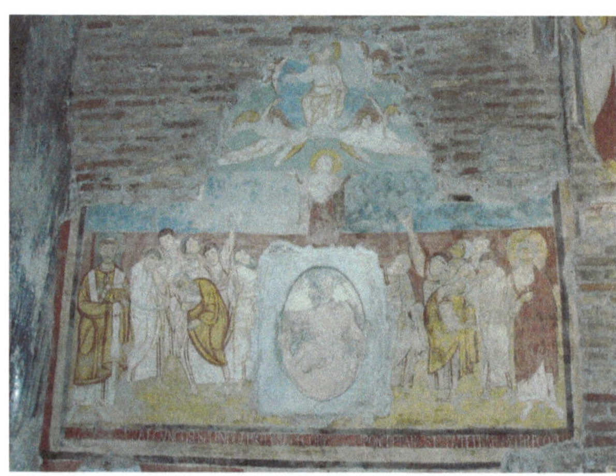

Ascension of Christ, west wall of nave, lower church, S. Clemente, ca. 847-55

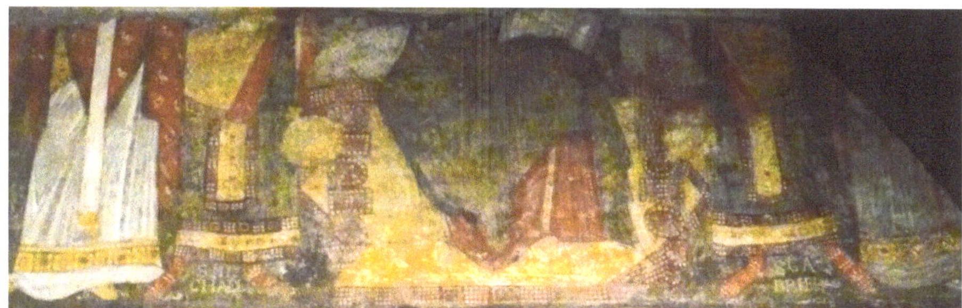

Pope Clement, the Archangel Michael, enthroned Christ, the Archangel Gabriel and St. Nicholas, lower church, north wall, S. Clemente, partially hidden by the twelfth-century church, ca. 1080

pictured on the far left, with a blue rectangular halo (showing he is alive). At the top is an Ascension scene with Christ lifted to heaven by angels. On the wall to the right is the Crucifixion.

Lower church nave: Alexis painting

Proceeding further into the nave are two paintings from the same period as the two about Clement in the narthex. At the first, look up to see the lower part of five figures, Christ enthroned, with the Archangel Michael and Clement on the left and the Archangel Gabriel and Saint Nicholas on the right. The angels are dressed in Byzantine imperial dress as was customary in Byzantine art. This gives a sense of the original height of the early church. The present roof was established at the beginning of the twelfth century when the new church was built above it.

The scene below shows a legend about a man named Alexis who wanted to be a religious ascetic, but to please his family he married and then withdrew to Edessa in Syria. After 17 years, he came home. He is shown as the figure with a halo and short tunic, greeting the man on horseback, his father, who does not recognise him; nor does his wife, pictured above looking out of the window. He takes a menial position at the house and sleeps under the stairs. After 17 more years, he dies (shown in a red cloak on a cocoon shaped bed). A piece of paper is found in his clenched hand. Only the pope (shown in a gold cope with halo and papal crown) can release it, to reveal his true identity. To the right, he is moved to a proper bed, surrounded by the pope and his mourning family.

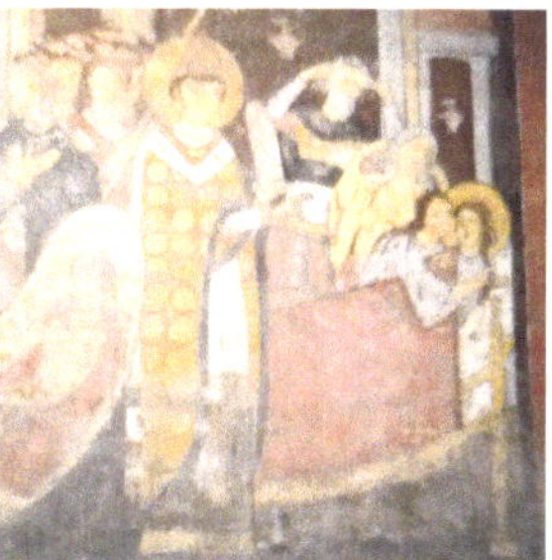

Deceased Alexis with mourning family, lower church, north wall, S. Clemente, ca. 1080

Lower church nave: Sisinnius painting

In the second painting, further along the nave, the cut-off figures above are Clement, in the centre, with his papal predecessors: Peter (42-67) next to him on the left, then Linus (67-78), and (Ana)Cletus (78-ca. 90) on the right. The scene below is a comical legend about Clement. In the centre he is saying mass. The woman on the right wearing a gold and a white headdress is Theodora, a Christian, who is followed to the mass

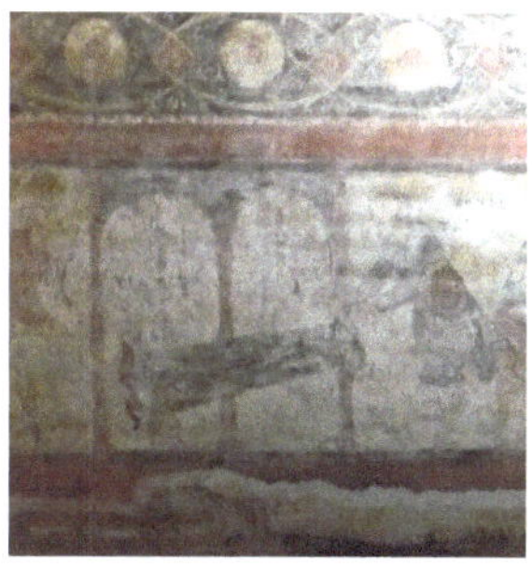

The jealous husband's servants seize a column rather than Clement, lower church, north wall, S. Clemente, ca. 1080

When Sisinnius orders his servants to grab Clement, the words he uses are the first surviving use of **local Italian** rather than Latin, which translates to 'Go on, you sons of harlots (fili dele pute), pull. Pull away Gosmari and Albertel. You, Carvoncelle, get behind with a lever'.

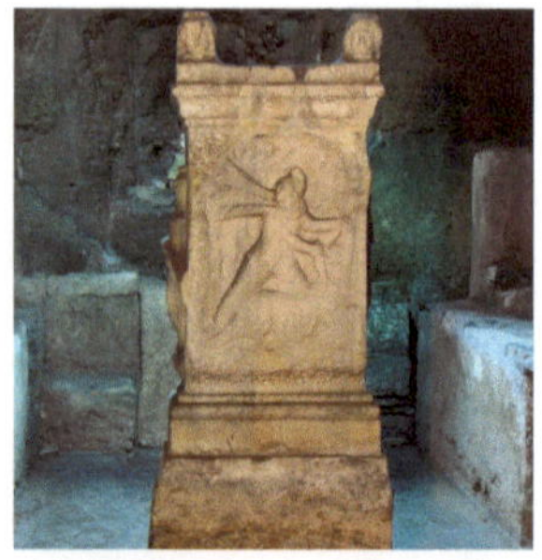

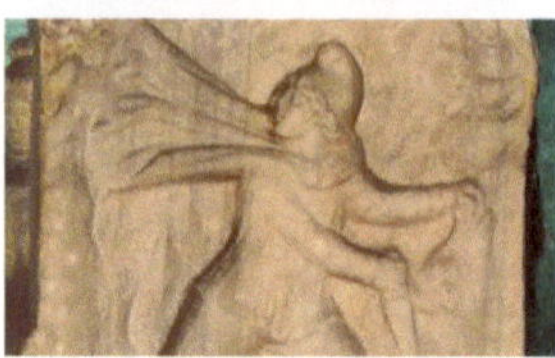

The cult statue/altar depicting Mithras slaying a bull, Mithraic centre, S. Clemente, 2nd -3rd century C.E.

The god **Mithras**, in a Phrygian hat with cape billowing behind him, slaughters a bull. He holds the bull down with his left leg as he grasps its muzzle with his left hand and thrusts in the dagger with his right.

The **altar** is now set in the banqueting room lined with stone benches where members of the cult would meet for ritual meals.

This **mystery cult** was very popular, particularly with the Roman army, from the first to the fourth centuries. Cult centres are found throughout the Roman empire from Britain to Dura Europus in eastern Syria.

Mithras derived from the **Persian god Mithra** but the Roman cult is distinctive in its practice. It rivalled Christianity in the early period and has some shared elements, such as ritual meals and the conflict between good and evil, symbolised by the **slaying of the bull** (tauroctony). However, there are few texts recording the beliefs and practices, which were kept secret.

A mithraeum is beneath Santa Prisca church (not usually open).

by her jealous husband, Sisinnius. Sisinnius is struck deaf and blind and so is led away. Later, Clement comes to their home and restores him to health, but Sisinnius is angry and orders his servants to seize Clement. However, they accidentally grab a column, which is shown in the lower panel. Later on Sisinnius converted and was martyred.

This painting was paid for by the Rapiza family. It has been suggested that it was made by the same artists as the two in the narthex and that the Alexis painting was done at the same time but perhaps by a slightly less skilled artist.

Lower church north aisle

Moving into the north aisle, to the left of the main nave, there is a sculpture of Mithras with his attribute, a bull. At the east end is a modern chapel dedicated to the brothers Cyril and Methodius, dating to 1929 and 1952. It is thought this was where Cyril was buried in 869.

Archaeological site below the lower church

Beyond here, steps (some of which date from the fourth century), descend to the earlier levels.

Mithraeum

Turning to the right is a vestibule of the Mithraic temple with a stucco ceiling made of fine ground gypsum modelled into delicate patterns, a popular form of decoration in the Roman period.

Opposite, at the far east end, is a grill through which is the Mithraic banqueting room. This was created within the courtyard of a first-century apartment block and is thought to have continued in use until the fourth century. It is set up with two long carved benches with a table in the centre and the cult statue at the far end (the statue may well have been in the vestibule originally), showing Mithras killing the bull. At the end of the corridor is a room referred to as a Mithraic school since it has seven niches that are thought to represent the seven stages one would pass through to attain the inner mysteries of the cult.

House and palazzo

The very wide straight wall to the west of these rooms is part of the remaining end wall of the original house, the *Titulus Clementis*, known to exist by 200 C.E., on which the church was built. It was owned by someone called Clement (not the saint), and was an early place of Christian worship.

The doorway cut in this tufa wall leads to a first-century palazzo. Following the sound of running water, turn to the right and go through several rooms, with herringbone patterned floor and *opus reticulatum* walls (in which square bricks are inset into the wall in a diamond pattern). In the far corner is the stream which

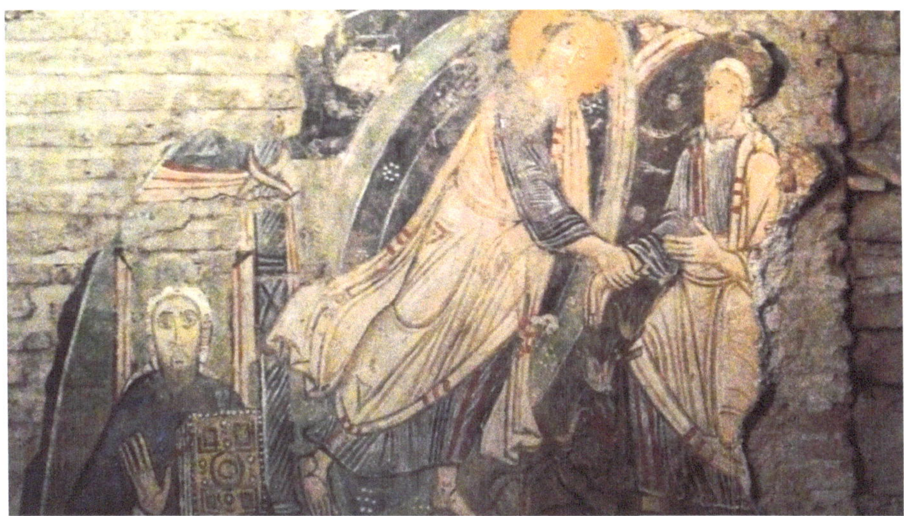

***Anastasis*, west end of south aisle, S. Clemente lower church, ninth-century**

would have provided fresh water for the house and fed the lake which was beneath the church until restructuring in 1912-14.

Lower church south aisle: Maria Regina

Returning up to the level of the early church turn back into the south aisle. About half way down, on the right, is an important painting of the Virgin, presented in a form known as *Maria Regina* (see p. 20). Further along are fragments of other paintings.

Lower church: Anastasis

In order to catch a further painting, go back up the aisle to where the modern stairs are that brought you from the lower areas and walk into the narrow aisle that runs south of the nave. Go to the end to see a ninth-century painting of the *Anastasis* (Resurrection) with Christ in an almond-shaped mandorla reaching down to Hades to bring Adam up from the dead. The figure on the left dressed as an eastern monk and holding a gospel is possibly Cyril, who was buried in this church, perhaps here rather than in the north aisle.

San Clemente upper church

This church was begun in 1108 by Paschal II (1099-1118). It was restored between 1702 and 1715, so to visualise the twelfth-century church, take away the chapels in the side aisles, the eighteenth-century frescoes and the heavy ceiling, and imagine alternating round and elliptical windows rather than the large rectangular ones. Despite these features, it is a remarkably authentic twelfth-century structure, which itself was modelled on the earlier church and incorporates elements from it.

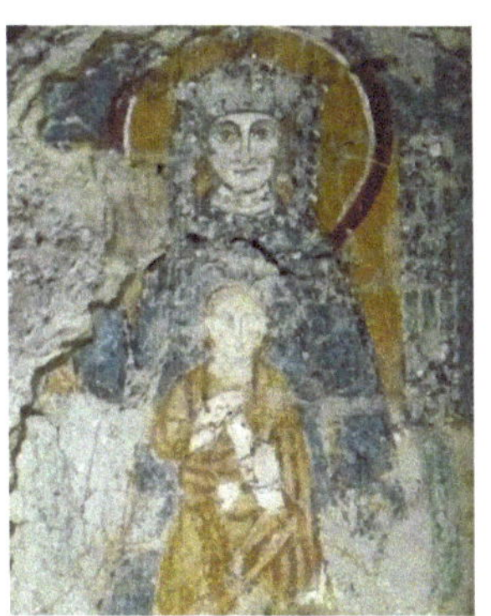

Virgin and Child, south aisle, lower church, S. Clemente, seventh or eighth century

The **Virgin** is placed in a niche flanked by Saints Euphemia and Catherine. She wears an elaborate crown with hanging *prependulia* (strings of hanging jewels), a typical feature of Byzantine crowns. The Christ Child is dressed in gold and holds a scroll. Although, the Virgin is dressed as a **Byzantine empress**, this type of image is not found in Byzantium but may have originated there.

Euphemia and Catherine are two early martyr saints, both killed for their faith in the early fourth century.

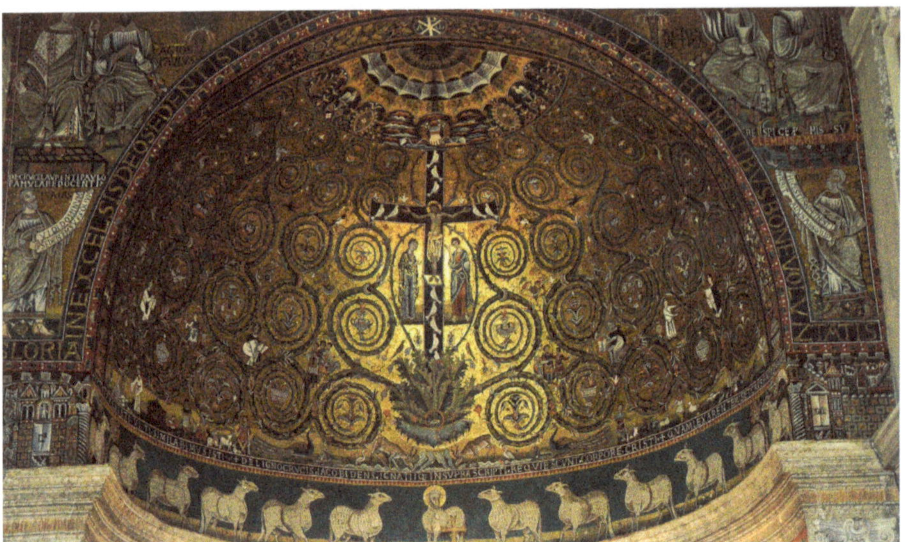

Apse, S. Clemente, upper church, ca. 1108

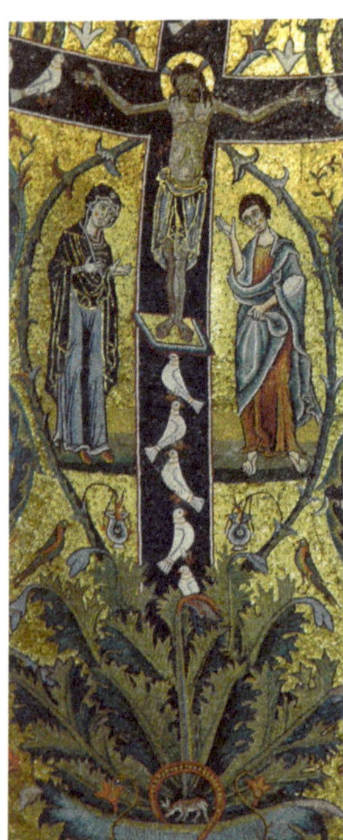

The central image of the apse, S. Clemente, upper church

A **hart** drinks from the fountain of life at the foot of the cross.

Elements from the early church

To consider first those parts that are from the early church, the most striking feature is the *schola cantorum*, the marble structure in the centre of the nave, used for the choir and the celebration of the liturgy. This was a feature of Early Christian basilicas. The marbles were given by Pope John II (533-5), and his monogram can be seen on the chancel screen to the right of the altar. The ambo (pulpit) on the right is original, and the one on the left (with the paschal candlestick next to it) is from the twelfth century. In the early church the ambo was used in liturgical processions with singing and readings. The baldacchino over the altar is partly from the sixth-century church and partly later.

Later elements

To the right of the altar is a wall tabernacle which may have been made by Arnolfo di Cambio (or his circle) at the end of the thirteenth century. Behind the baldacchino is a semi-circular row of seats for the clergy and in the centre the throne for the bishop. Above this are twelfth-century paintings of Christ, the Virgin and the apostles.

The apse

The highlights of the church, however, are the mosaics. These may be modelled on those in the early church and much of the iconography is typical of the fifth and sixth centuries, although the image of Christ on the cross is more typical of the twelfth. The central motif is the cross as the Tree of Life, planted in Paradise and watered by its four rivers. Christ is on the centre of the cross with twelve doves, representing the apostles, and the

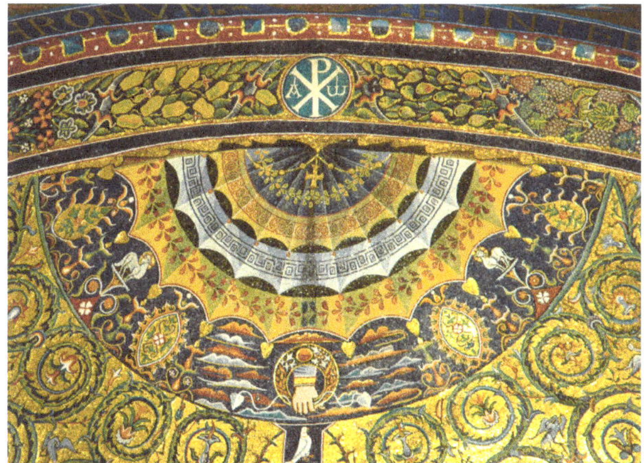

The apex of the apse, S. Clemente, upper church, ca. 1108

Virgin stands to the left and Saint John to the right. The entire apse is covered in delicate acanthus tendrils which sprout from the base of the cross.

Part of the inscription running above the lambs reads in Latin, 'Let us liken the Church of Christ to this vine'. This idea is exemplified by small details inhabiting the tendrils, various animals, birds and people, some important early theologians of the church and some ordinary folk in everyday activities. The theologians, dressed in black and white, are each named, Augustine, Jerome, Gregory and Ambrose. The inscription goes on to say that relics of the True Cross and of Saints James and Ignatius are in the mosaic of Christ's body, thus the apse itself acts as a reliquary.

At the apex of the apse is a representation of the heavens with the hand of God symbolising his omnipresence. The monogram at the top has a X (chi) and P (rho) superimposed, the first two letters of Christ's name in Greek, plus the first and last letters of the Greek alphabet, the A (alpha) and the Ω (omega), referring to his presence from the origin and eternally.

The triumphal arch

The imagery on the triumphal arch refers to the four living creatures in the Book of Revelation (4:7-14), who are interpreted as the four evangelists. At the top on the left is Saint Laurence with his feet on the grid on which he was martyred sitting next to Saint Paul, and below is the prophet Isaiah with his book in the form of a scroll above the city of Bethlehem. At the top on the right is Saint Clement sitting next to Saint Peter, and below is the prophet Jeremiah and the city of Jerusalem.

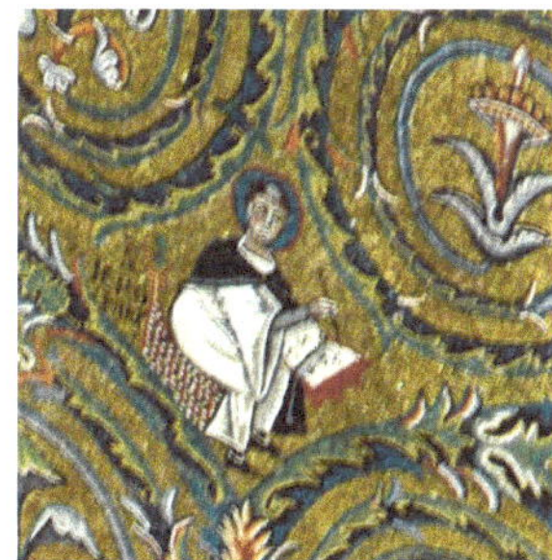

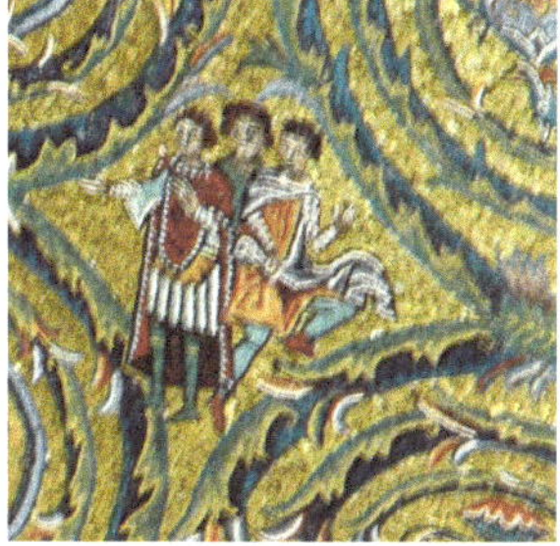

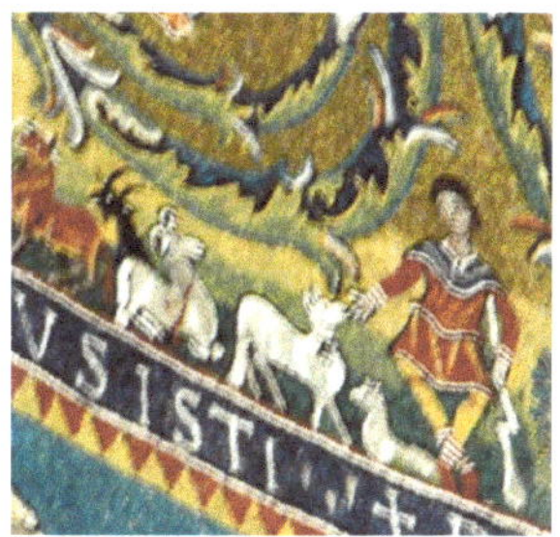

Details from the left side of the apse, theologian, young men, shepherd, S. Clemente, upper church, ca. 1108

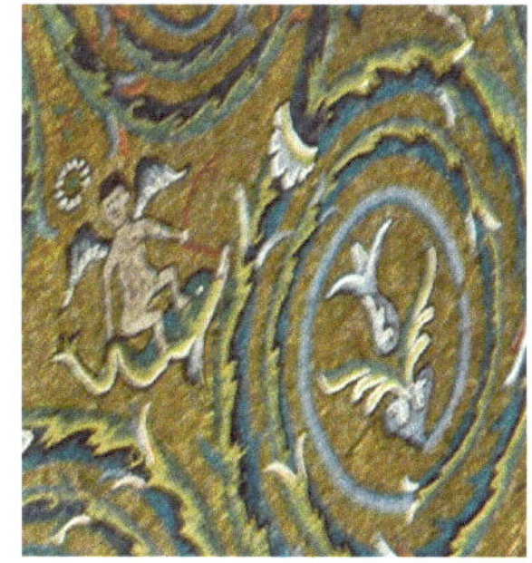

Detail from the right side of the apse, *putto*, S. Clemente, upper church, ca. 1108

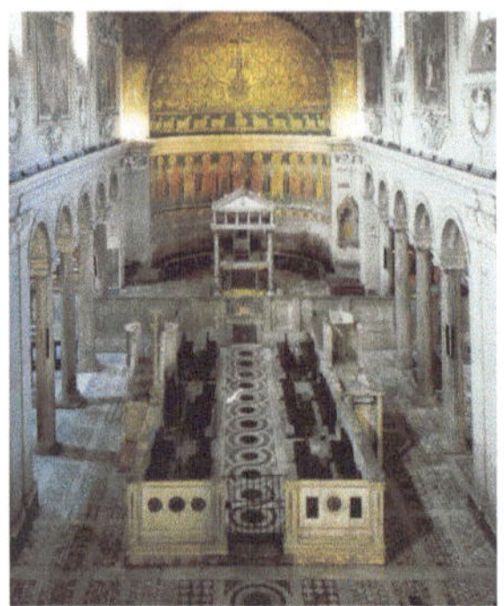

San Clemente upper church, ca. 1108, (image: Marcantoni Architects)

The ***schola cantorum*** is placed in the nave with the *ambones* on either side. At the far end, under the apse, is the baldacchino. The *opus sectile* floor is stunning from this view.

***Pluteus*, marble panel, 553**

This panel is from the early church and has been reset on the right hand side of the chancel screen. It shows the monogram of pope John II (553).

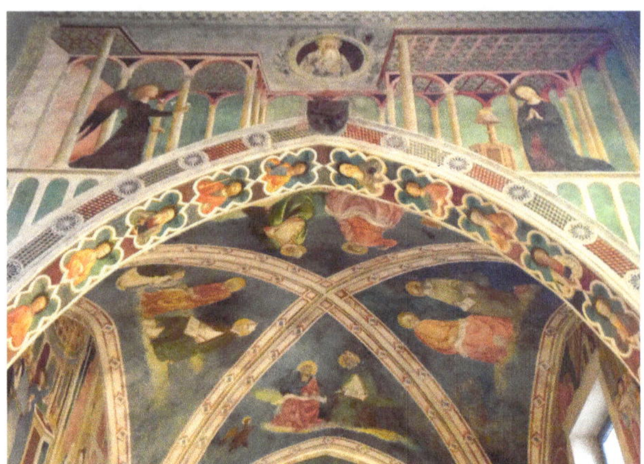

Annunciation, St. Catherine's Chapel, S. Clemente, upper church, external wall, ca. 1428-30

Chapel of St. Catherine

Another significant part of the church is the Chapel of St. Catherine, which while not within the time period covered here, is unmissable. The chapel was painted by Masolino da Panicale (ca. 1383- ca. 1447), with possibly the help of his younger assistant Masaccio (1401-29). The most captivating images are those based on Saint Catherine's life on the north wall. Catherine was a wealthy Christian girl living in Alexandria who was persecuted for her faith by the emperor Maxentius in the early fourth century. On the adjacent wall to the right are underdrawings from the portrayal of Saint Christopher and the life of Saint Catherine. Underdrawings are rarely visible and these indicate what may lie beneath many early paintings.

Santi Quattro Coronati

Reached via the street of the same name, the entry is up narrow stairs turning back on the street.

History

The history of the early church is not quite clear but it was certainly built by the sixth century and destroyed by the

The Donation of Constantine

This document is the source of the paintings at Santi Quattro Coronati. It was forged, perhaps in the eighth century, and includes details such as Constantine's leprosy, healing and profession of faith as well as him giving the pope authority over Rome and the western part of the empire. It was useful for the popes, especially in the thirteenth century, and particularly at the time when Innocent IV (1243-54) wanted to impose his precedence over Frederick II (1220-50), who had taken over some of the papal states and was excommunicated in 1245. The document was recognised as a forgery in the fifteenth century.

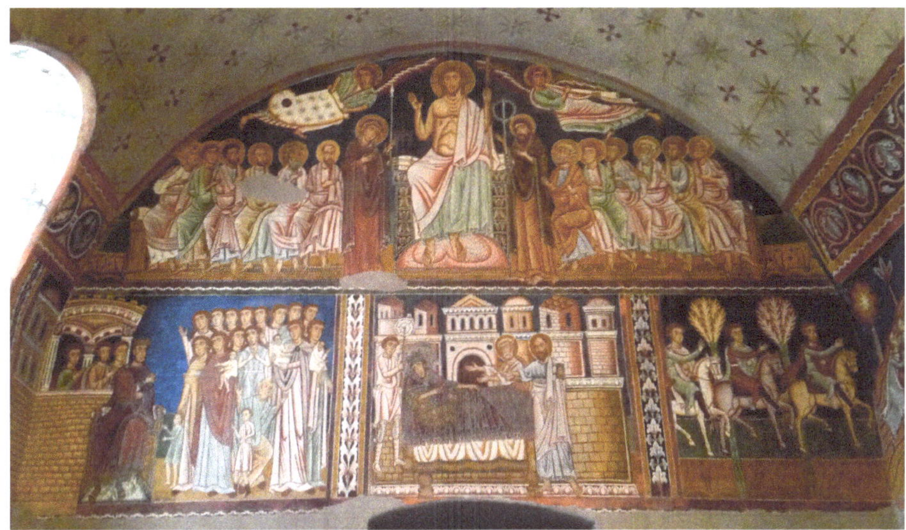

Scenes from the life of Constantine, interior of S. Sylvester Chapel, SS. Quattro Coronati, 1246

Normans in 1084. It was rebuilt in 1110 by Paschal II (1099-1118), as also was San Clemente. The dedication is to four martyrs, originally unknown and simply named 'crowned' referring to their martyrs' crowns. They were killed under Diocletian (284-305) and later identified with Claudius, Nicostratus, Simpronianus and Castorius.

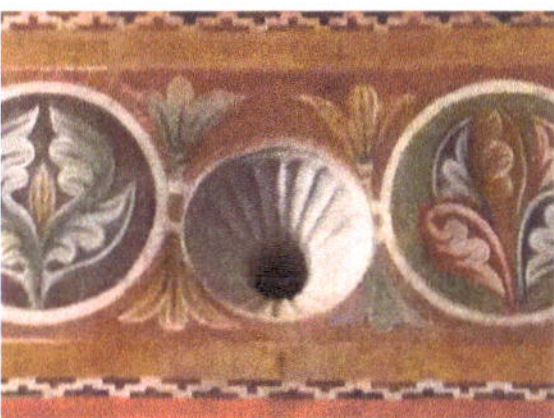

Peep hole in the wall, S. Sylvester Chapel, SS. Quattro Coronati, 1246

This hole was used to privately listen to activities in the chapel. Voice tubes lead to the Gothic Hall above. Note the beautiful painted flowers.

The courtyards

Of the two courtyards, the one furthest from the church is entered under a ninth-century campanile (the oldest in Rome), and has a guard tower. The second courtyard or atrium is from the twelfth-century rebuilding (the original church was much larger and extended to here). The entrance foyer of the convent is on the right, known as the *Stanza del Calendario*, because of a thirteenth-century liturgical calendar painted on the wall.

San Sylvester Chapel

From here access a highlight, the San Sylvester chapel which is part of the Cardinal Palace and dates to 1246. It has wonderfully preserved paintings about the supremacy of the pope over the emperor. In the entrance foyer to the convent, knock at the grill on the left. An Augustinian nun will take a small fee and hand over a key if the chapel is locked (this is sometimes done using a turntable so the nun has no contact), although often the chapel is open with successive groups visiting (it is good to go in at a quiet time).

Above the doorway, in the upper register, Christ is depicted flanked by the Virgin, John the Baptist and the apostles. Below, the legend concerning Constantine begins on the left and moves

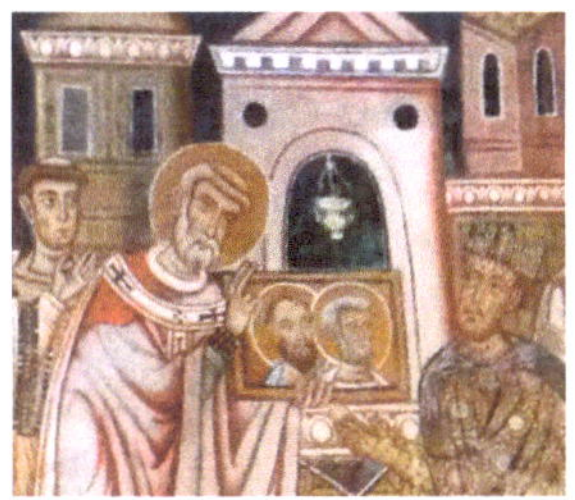

The pope shows Constantine (on the right) an icon of Paul and Peter, S. Sylvester Chapel, SS. Quattro Coronati, 1246

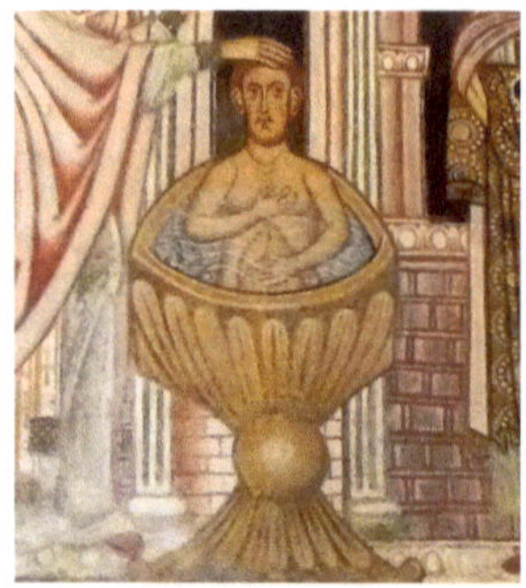

Constantine is baptised, S. Sylvester Chapel, SS. Quattro Coronati, 1246

Constantine is pictured submerged in a **baptismal font.**

When the paintings were made, the resident of the palace was Cardinal Stefano Conti, Pope Innocent III's nephew, who held great power.

clockwise around the building. He is pictured enthroned but with leprosy, shown by the spots on his face, then in bed dreaming that the saints Peter and Paul visit him and tell him to get help from the pope, Sylvester (314-35). Note the lovely city scape behind. Three messengers leave on horseback. Turning to the next wall, they climb the hill to where Sylvester is on retreat. The next scene is in Rome, with Sylvester showing Constantine an icon of Peter and Paul to prove the apostles' identity (the icon is held to represent the true likenesses of the saints), at which point Constantine converts, is baptised in a font and cured. The next scene is the really crucial one, for Constantine hands the imperial tiara to Sylvester thereby giving him authority over the emperor. Note the attendant holding the parasol over the tiara. Then Constantine, in a subservient position, leads the pope on horseback. Moving across to the facing long wall, Sylvester brings back to life a bull, pictured vertically.

The next image concerns the visit of Helena (Constantine's mother) to Jerusalem where she discovers the cross on which Christ was crucified. The next scene is largely lost.

Gothic Hall (Aula Gotica)

Important thirteenth-century paintings by a Roman artist were discovered in 1995 in a hall on the first floor of the main tower, used by the cardinal for banquets and ceremonies. It has secular iconography of the twelve months of the year and the Liberal Arts and seasons. These are now occasionally open to the public and well worth seeing if possible.

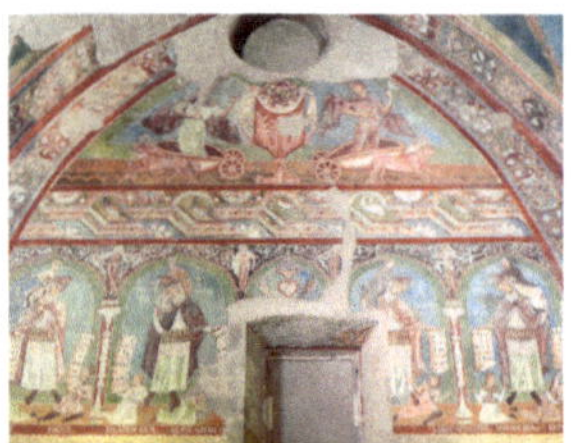

The *Aula Gotica*, SS Quattro Coronati, thirteenth century

The Gothic Hall has a pointed arch between two aisles. It is some 17 metres long.

The church

The church has some fourteenth-century paintings. The relics of the Santi Quattro Coronati are in urns in the ninth-century crypt.

Cloister

A door in the north aisle on the left leads to the lovely thirteenth-century cloister (there is a bell on the right if you need admission). A chapel off the cloister (to the left) is dedicated to Saint Barbara and was originally part of the church. Some ninth-century painting survives over the south apse and the remainder is fourteenth century. The Symbols of the Evangelists are in the vault, a Virgin and Child with Saints in the main (east) apse, and also visible are a bishop and scenes from Saint Barbara's life.

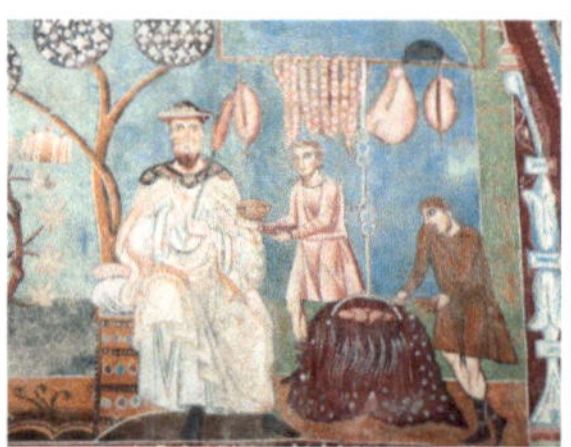

The *Aula Gotica*, SS Quattro Coronati, thirteenth century

Here the two-headed Janus represents the month of January.

San Giovanni in Laterano

This was the first basilical church built in Rome by Constantine I (306-37). He chose a site in part owned by his wife Fausta and in part used by the imperial horse guards, within the city walls but away from the historical centre. The site was presented to the pope and probably built 314-18 and dedicated in 324 as the cathedral of Rome, the seat of the Bishop of Rome, the Pope. It was originally dedicated to the Redeemer (Christ) and only later to Saint John the Baptist and then to Saint John the Evangelist. The early plan was similar to the present one, a five-aisled basilica (a nave with two aisles on each side) with an apse, here at the west end. It was restored in the fifth and eighth centuries and rebuilt twice in the fourteenth century. The present structure was designed by Borromini (1646-9). Little of the medieval building remains except in the cloister, baptistery and palace. However, the main bronze doors are Roman and come from the Curia (the Senate House). Also, in the centre of the north aisle (to the right of the altar), there is a painting, perhaps by Giotto, from 1300.

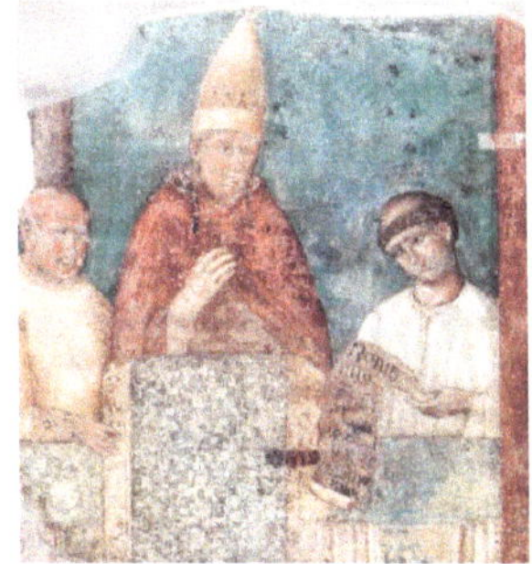

Giotto (?), Pope Boniface VIII (1294-1303) announcing the Jubilee of 1300, north aisle, S. Giovanni in Laterano, ca. 1300

The **Jubilee** of 1300 was the first to be declared. It was a special year for the remission of sins and pardons. Pope Boniface issued plenary indulgences to Romans who visited the Basilicas of SS. Peter and Paul at least once a day for 30 days. Outsiders only needed to go for 15 days.

Cloister

This has a small entrance fee and is accessed from the south side of the church (to the left of the apse). It was made in 1222-32 by Pietro Vassalletto and his son, marble workers rivalling the famous Cosmati family (see box p. 46). A porphyry slab is an ancient relic purported to be the stone on which the soldiers threw dice to win Christ's clothes. The well in the middle of the cloister is from the ninth century and around the walls are various sculptures from the early building, including an early tomb by Arnolfo di Cambio, made about 1276, an ancient papal coronation throne and the measure of the height of Christ.

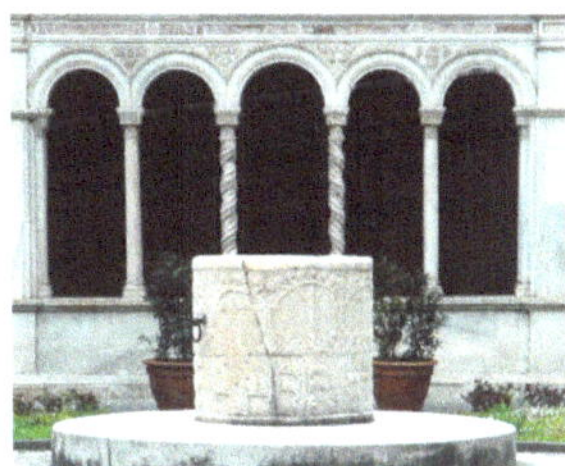

Well in the centre of the cloister, S. Giovanni in Laterano, ninth century

Museum

In the museum, just to the right of the cloister, is an exceptional fourteenth-century cope made in England The fine embroidery is known as *opus anglicanum* (English work).

Baptistery

The baptistery has a separate entrance and more restricted opening hours than the basilica. A baptistry was built at the time of the fourth-century church. It was rebuilt in the fifth century under Sixtus III (432-40) using much *spolia*, material from earlier buildings, and is now octagonal in shape. This is typical of many early baptisteries, but it may have originally been circular. The central font is not the original but gives a sense of its size and placement.

There are four chapels. To the right of the entrance is one dedicated to John the Baptist, founded by Pope Hilarius (461-8). If you can move the doors, they have a musical sound. Across from the entrance is a chapel dedicated to Saints Cyprian and Justina. This was the narthex or entryway to the fifth-century building. Looking up to the left, some of the original mosaic, and the oldest in the building, survives in the apse with vine tendrils against a brilliant blue ground. Beyond is a courtyard, well worth going into in order to look back and see the fine entryway with ancient columns and reused Roman architrave. Returning inside, the next chapel is dedicated to Saint Venantius,

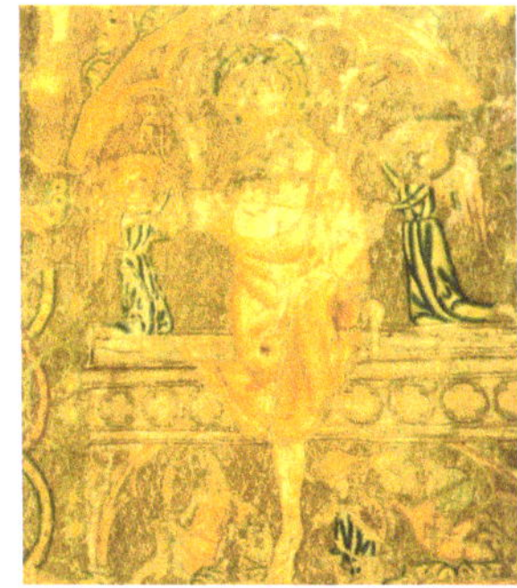

Christ's Resurrection, cope, English, Museum, S. Giovanni Laterano, 1330-40.

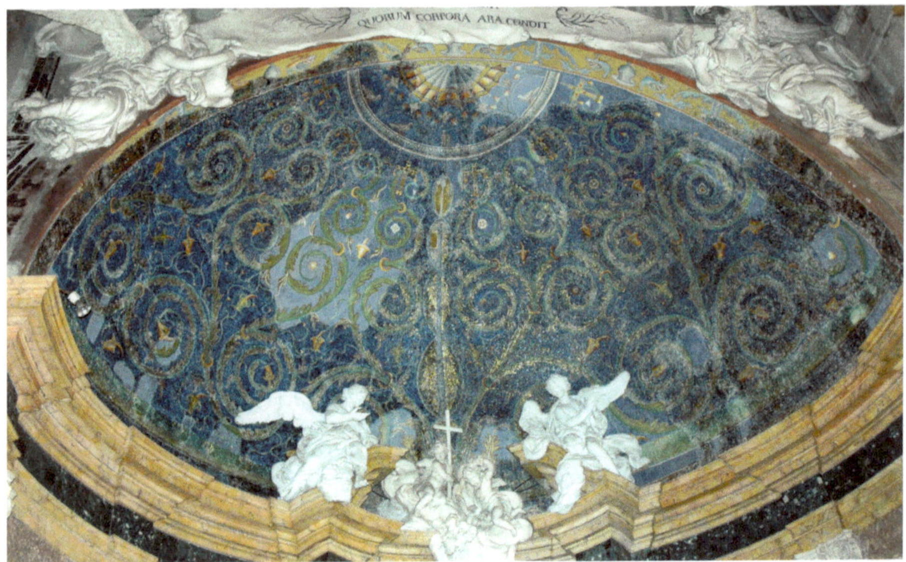

Mosaic decoration in the narthex apse, baptistery, S. Giovanni in Laterano, fifth century

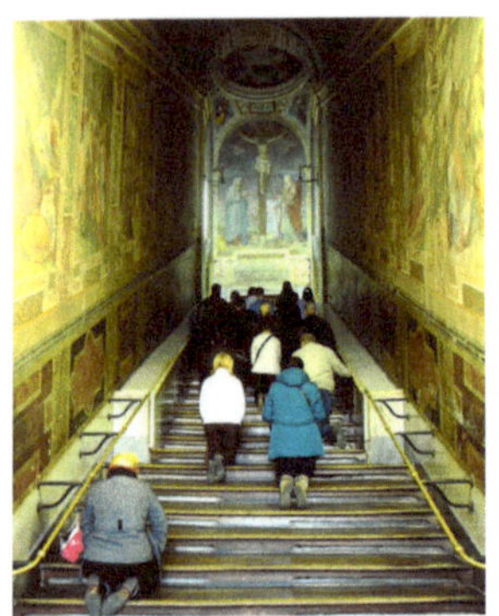

The *Scala Sancta*, Lateran Palace

It is now traditional for pilgrims to climb the steps on their knees. This act of devotion has been associated with the granting of indulgences.

dated to 640, with mosaics from 642-9 showing Christ with angels and the Virgin with Pope Theodore (642-9) and saints as well as representations of Bethlehem and Jerusalem. Finally, the chapel dedicated to Saint John the Evangelist has fifth-century mosaics showing Christ as a lamb, with birds and flowers. The bronze doors date to 1196.

Lateran Palace

The palace was first built by Constantine and survived until the beginning of the fourteenth century when it was severely damaged just before the popes moved to Avignon in 1309. They came back to Rome in 1377, but from then on made the Vatican their central location. The present building dates to 1589 and was designed by Domenico Fontana (1543-1607). However, parts of the old palace remain within.

Scala Sancta

The staircase has been described since the sixteenth century as the one brought from Pilate's house in Jerusalem by Helena, Constantine's mother. Christ is thought to have gone down them after he was condemned.

Baptism

In the Early Christian period, baptism took place once a year, on the eve before Easter Sunday. The ceremony was presided over by the bishop. The catechumens (who had been prepared to become Christian), wearing white robes, were fully immersed in a central font before entering the cathedral in procession. Fourth-century Ambrose of Milan described the ritual in detail.

Sancta Sanctorum

At the top of the stairs the famous icon of Christ, known as the *Sancta Sanctorum Icon*, is on display. It has been repainted and is covered with silver casing (see pp. 16-17). The private chapel of the popes, also called the Chapel of St. Lawrence and the Sancta Sanctorum was rebuilt in 1278 by Pope Nicholas III (1277-80). It has brilliantly coloured paintings, a Cosmati floor, and used to contain relics. The paintings in the chapel show Pope Nicholas III being presented to Christ and the deaths of significant early martyrs, Paul, Stephen, Lawrence and Agnes, as well as events from the life of St. Nicholas, the pope's namesake. It is not known who painted them. The relics in the altar safe behind the grate were sealed centuries ago. The safe was only opened in 1902, the first time since 1521, to examine the head of Saint Agnes kept there. Three years later the extensive collection of reliquaries made of precious metals, enamels and rich fabrics were studied and moved to the Vatican. The bronze doors were alleged to have been given by Constantine to Pope Sylvester (314-35).

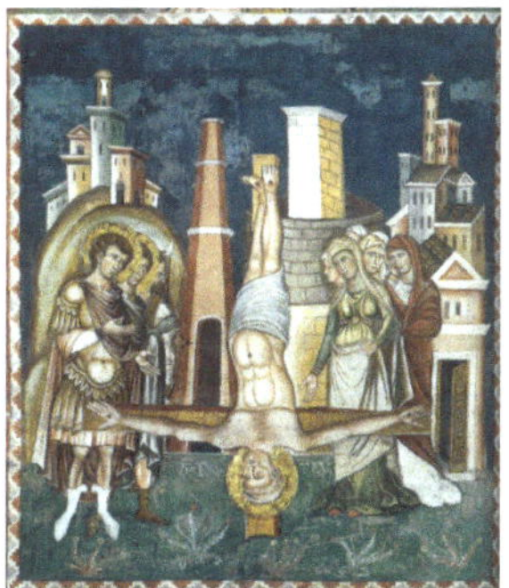

Crucifixion of St. Peter, Sancta Sanctorum, Lateran Palace, 1278-79

By tradition, Peter was crucified **upside-down**. The paintings are in excellent condition with vivid colours and are well worth seeing.

San Giovanni a Porta Latina

This lesser-known church lies two kilometres from the Lateran. Initially built in the fifth century, it was rebuilt by Hadrian I (772-95) and again by Celestine III (1191-8). There is an eighth-century well head by the entrance and significant twelfth-century paintings in the nave depicting Old and New Testament scenes.

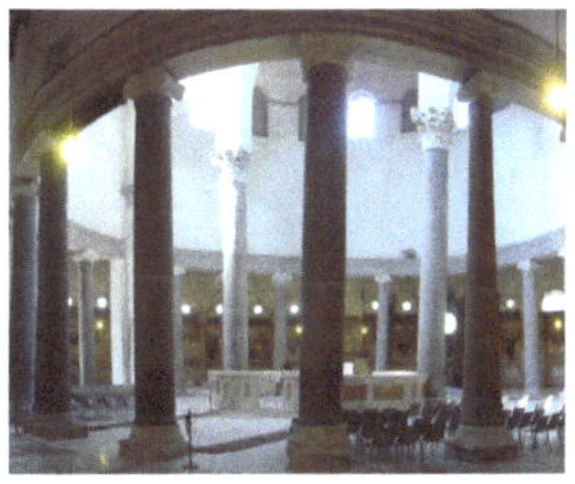

S. Stefano Rotondo, interior, fifth century

Santo Stefano Rotondo

This is an important early church, also known as Santo Stefano al Monte Celio, located at the top of the Via della Navicella on Via Santo Stefano Rotondo. It is not always open.

History

Saint Stephen was the first Christian martyr, and this building was dedicated to him by Pope Simplicius ((468-83). It was even larger then than now, with an ambulatory all around the current structure. This was intersected by four chapels, one in each quarter. It has been suggested that the design is related to the fourth-century Rotunda in Jerusalem, which was circular in form and built over the site of Christ's tomb and resurrection (the Holy Sepulchre). The outer ambulatory was pulled down in 1450. The gruesome frescoes of martyrs are sixteenth century.

Mosaic decoration

In the northeast is a chapel with an apse, decorated in mosaic in the seventh-century by Pope Theodore I (642-9). He installed in the altar here the relics of Saints Primus and Felicianus, two brothers martyred in the late third century. They are depicted in mosaic flanking a *crux gemmata* (jewelled cross).

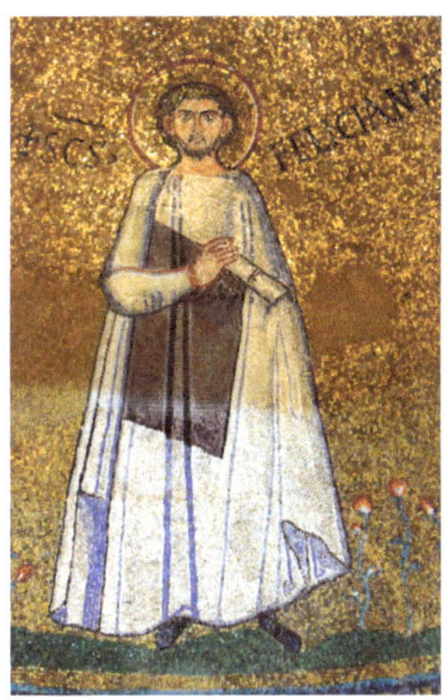

S. Feliciano, S. Stefano Rotondo, 642-9

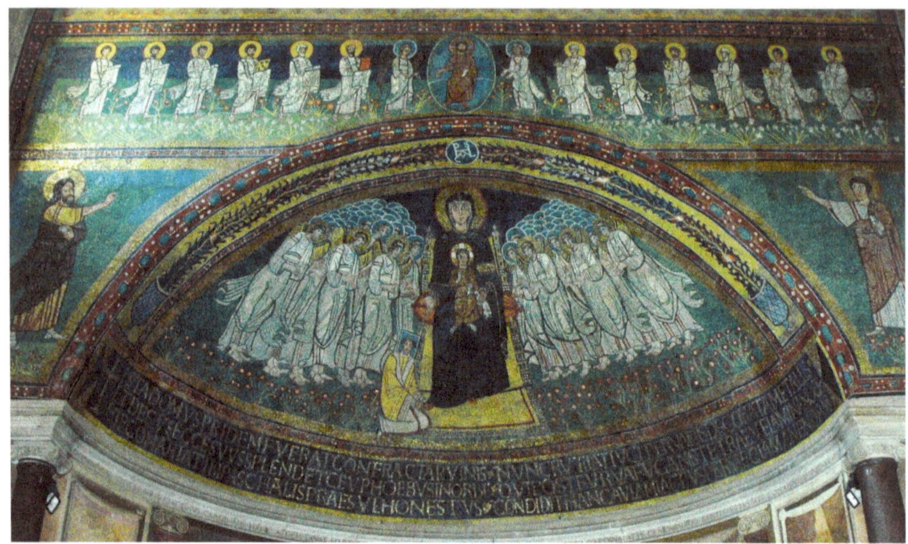

Virgin and Child flanked by Angels with a kneeling Pope Paschal, Apse, S. Maria in Domnica, 817-24

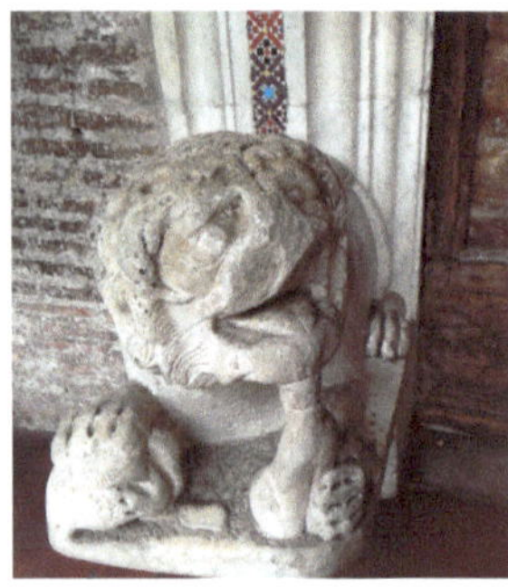

Lion flanking the entrance, SS. Giovanni e Paolo, date uncertain

Many churches had lions guarding their entrances as symbols of authority.

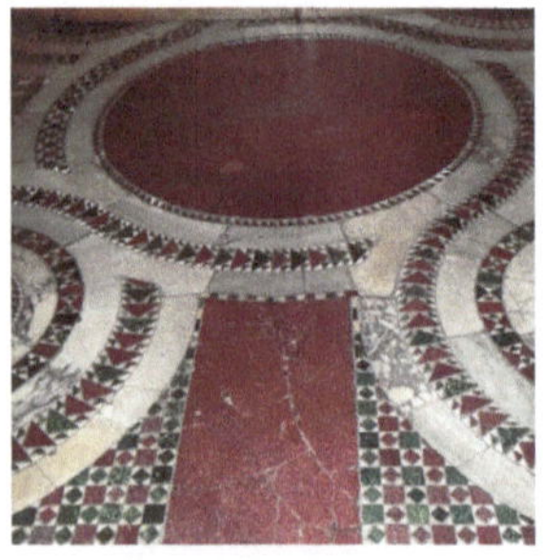

Cosmati floor, SS. Giovanni e Paolo, thirteenth century

Santa Maria in Domnica

Situated on the Via della Navicella, near to Santo Stefano, this is one of the three churches built in Rome by Pope Paschal I (817-24) (see box p. 82).

Apse and triumphal arch

The apse design is very similar in style to those at Santa Prassede and Santa Cecilia (see pp. 18, 52), but here the emphasis is on the Virgin, who is enthroned in the centre flanked by a host of angels and with Paschal kneeling and touching her red slipper. Above are Christ and the apostles and, to the left and right, Elijah and Moses, the two prophets present in the Transfiguration.

The colours are stunning, and the simplified design using repetition is very forceful. The somewhat stylised forms are typical of the adaptation of Early Christian models in the ninth century.

Santi Giovanni e Paolo

The present church and campanile were built under Paschal II (1099-1118) and Hadrian IV (1154-9). The colourful ceramic plates set into the campanile are copies of the original Islamic ones (now in the museum in the Case romane del Celio).

Paintings

A highlight of the church is the painting of Christ and the Apostles behind the altar. It is dated to 1255 and, although by a Roman painter, it shows the strong Byzantine influence and

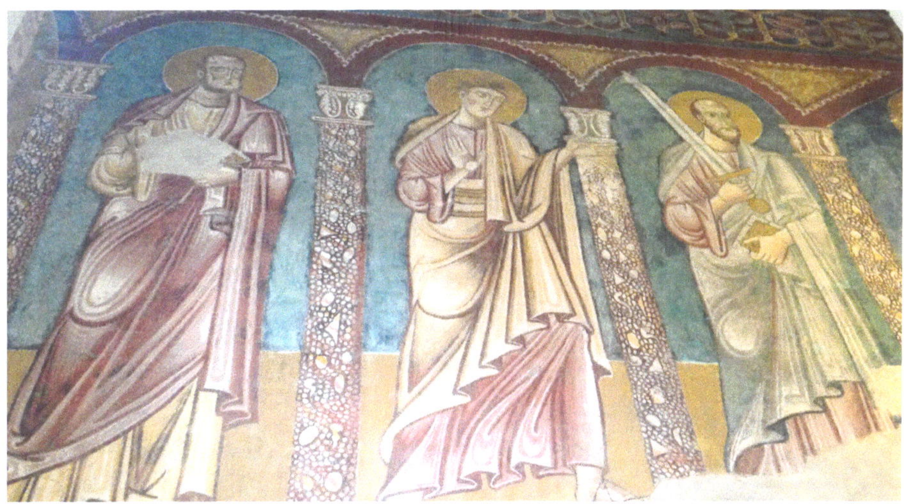

Apostles, frescoes behind the altar, SS. Giovanni e Paolo, ca. 1255

looks Romanesque in style, although dated later. The apostles are each framed within a colourful marble columned arcade and have active energetic poses with drapery showing strong contours and dynamic movement. Ask the sacristan to see the paintings as the room is not normally open.

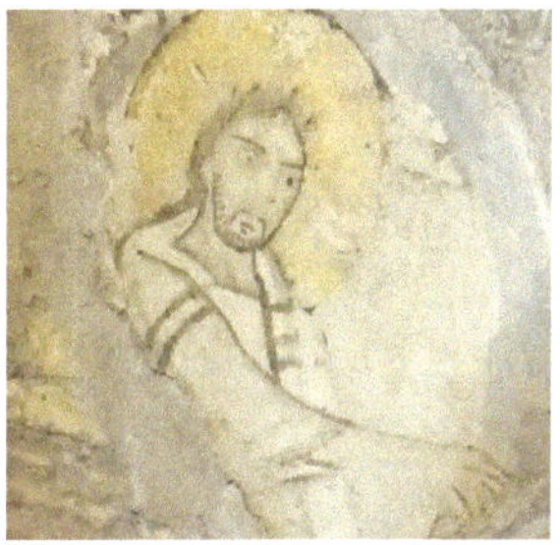

Detail of Christ, *Anastasis*, Case Romane del Celio, ninth century

Case Romane del Celio

This is a fascinating series of buildings, just below the church of Santi Giovanni e Paolo, said to have been the home of two martyrs killed in a short period of pagan domination in the fourth century under the emperor Julian the Apostate (361-3). Remains can be seen of two Roman apartment houses and shops, a larger Roman *domus* (house), a house with Christian decoration as well as an oratory (a place of worship), and there are paintings from the various periods.

Paintings

One outstanding fresco is on a wall from the Roman garden and shows Persephone and nereids. Christian paintings include ninth-century paintings in the oratory (the room to the right as you go in) of the Crucifixion and the *Anastasis* as well as fourth-century frescoes in a small room at an upper level.

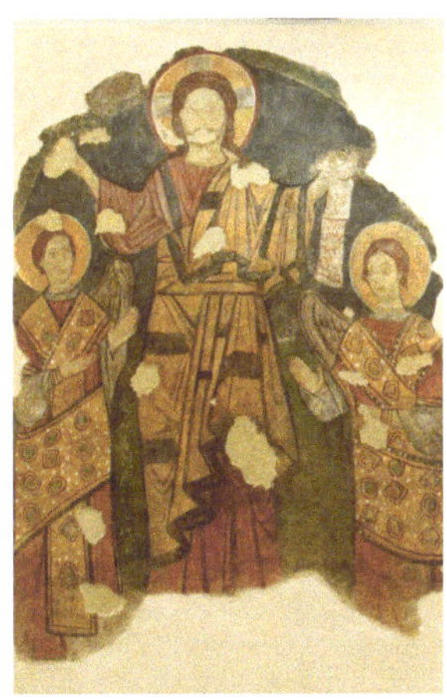

Christ and angels, Case Romane del Celio, antiquarium, twelfth century

Museum

The small elegant museum or antiquarium has various ancient pieces of sculpture and glass, important Islamic ceramics, examples of stamped Roman bricks, as well as a twelfth-century painting of Christ from the oratory of Santi Salvatore.

Cosmati work

The Cosmati family lived and worked in Rome in the twelfth and thirteenth centuries and were celebrated for their skill in *opus sectile*, cut stone work, principally used for making floors but also for sculptural and architectural features such as *ambones*, doors, tombs and cloisters. Working over four generations, there were seven principal members, starting with Lorenzo whose known production dates from 1190. Mainly found in Rome, their work extends elsewhere, such as to the two celebrated floors in Westminster Abbey, London, made in the second half of the thirteenth century.

The style originates in Roman work and was used widely in the Early Christian east and west, with a revival in Rome in the Carolingian period. The floor at the Benedictine Abbey of Monte Cassino (1066-71) was made by Greek artists in a related style, and Lorenzo is said to have studied with Greek artists, but to have then developed his own style.

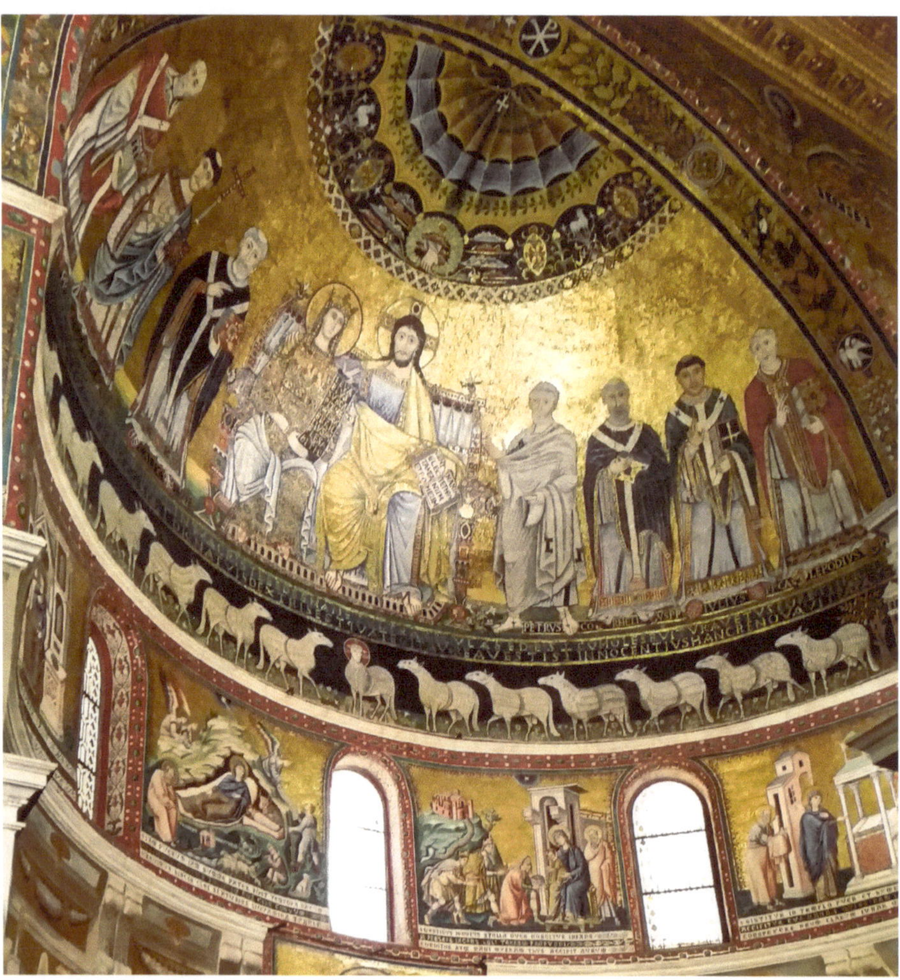

Apse, Santa Maria in Trastevere, 1140 and ca. 1291

CHAPTER FIVE

TRASTEVERE, THE AVENTINE HILL AND NEARBY

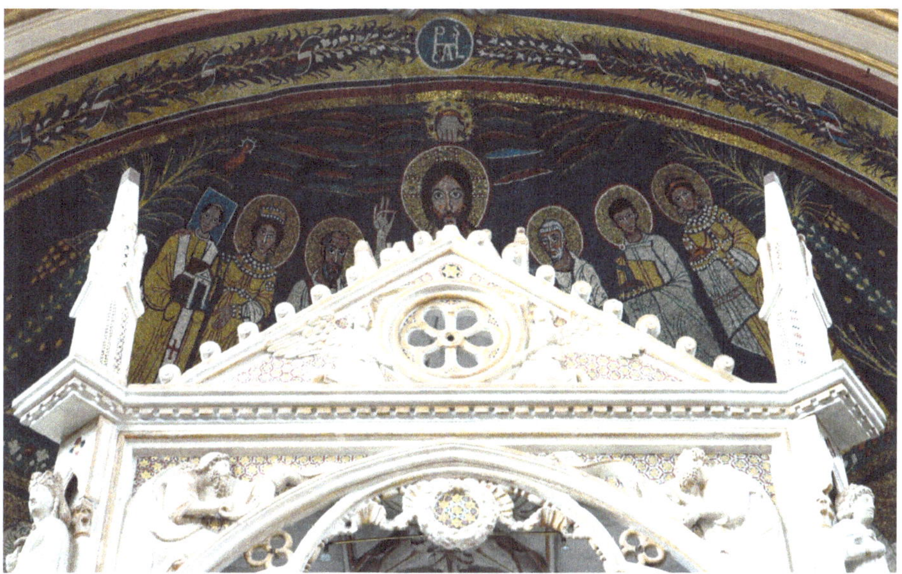

Ciborium by Arnolfo di Cambio, 1293, apse ca. 820, S. Cecilia

Santa Maria in Trastevere, San Crisogono, Santa Cecilia, Santa Maria in Cosmedin, Santa Sabina, San Saba

Introduction

Trastevere, meaning across the Tiber, maintains some semblance to a medieval town with narrow streets and rich character. In the early period it was the site of some lavish imperial villas and housed seamen and many immigrants, including a large Jewish population. It has three very old churches whose mosaic and painted decoration is extraordinary.

On the opposite side of the Tiber lies the Aventine hill and the very early church of Santa Sabina, which still has its remarkable fifth-century wooden doors. At the foot of the hill is the unusual church of Santa Maria in Cosmedin with many medieval elements. San Saba is further away but very interesting.

The churches covered here can be visited in a day. They are arranged in an order which allows one to walk from one to the other beginning with Santa Maria in Trastevere.

Arnolfo di Cambio (1240 -ca. 1310) was a sculptor who was in Rome at the end of the thirteenth century. He had worked with **Nicola Pisano** in Siena and absorbed the elder man's use of models from ancient Roman sculpture. He employed and introduced to Rome Gothic architectural motifs. He also used polychrome glass decorations, as can be seen here.

His work is in many churches in Rome, including in S. Clemente, the Lateran, S. Maria in Aracoeli, St. Peter's, S. Paolo fuori le Mura, and in a celebrated *presepio* (a nativity scene), in the Museum at S. Maria Maggiore.

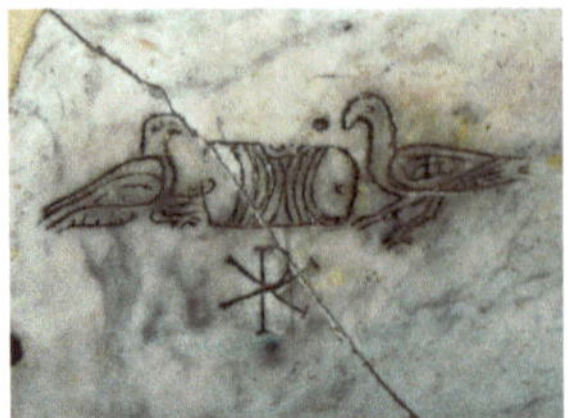

Early Christian carving of doves and chi rho, portico, S. Maria in Trastevere, ca. third century

The portico was designed by **Carlo Fontana** in 1702 and incorporates architectural fragments. The chi rho here is a Christian symbol created from the first two letters of Christ's name in Greek.

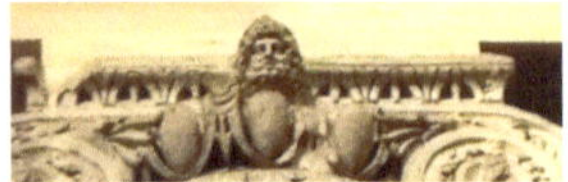

Head of Serapis on a capital (212-17), S. Maria in Trastevere

This capital is to the south of the nave at the west end. Several of these, showing **Serapis and Harpocrates** were taken from the Baths of Caracalla in about 1140 when the church was rebuilt.

Santa Maria in Trastevere

This church is in the heart of Trastevere on the neighbourhood square. It was probably the first official Christian place of worship to be built in Rome. According to legend, it was founded by Pope Callixtus I (217-22) in the third century, when Christianity was still a minority cult, and finished by Julius I (337-52). The site was renowned for a miraculous flow of oil which first occurred in 38 B.C.E. and was supposed to be a portent of the coming of Christ. Other accounts say it ran for a whole day in the year he was born. The patron of the present church was Innocent II (1130-43), who started rebuilding it in 1138.

The church is based on Early Christian designs with a trabeated nave (a horizontal entablature over supports–columns here), although Gothic architecture was being invented in the north when it was built. Most of the churches at this time have arcades.

The Cosmatesque floor of the church was remade in the 1870s, but gives a good idea of the original *opus sectile* (cut stone) floor of the thirteenth century. The ornate gold ceiling was designed by Domenichino in 1617.

The apse

The main remaining features of the medieval church are the mosaic decorations in the apse. In the twelfth century, the Pope's intention was to look back on the great history of the church and its early art: it has some features taken from early decoration. However the central motif in the semi-dome of Christ and the Virgin enthroned is novel. Above them is the hand of God bearing a wreath. On the right stand Saints Peter, Cornelius, Julius, and Calepodius; on the left Saints Callixtus and Laurence, and Pope Innocent II with a model of the church.

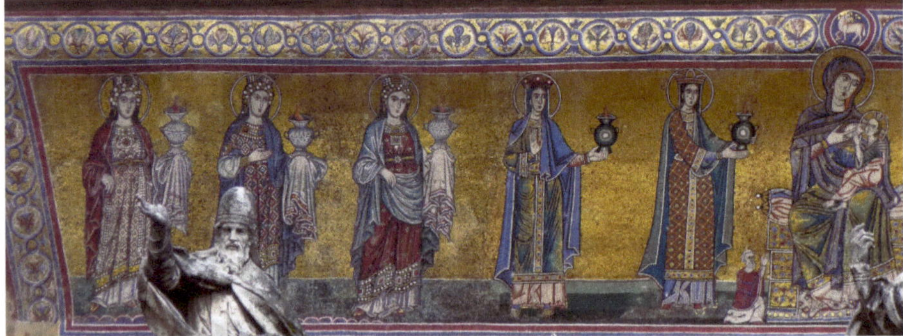

Women holding lamps and Virgin and Child, facade, S. Maria in Trastevere, 12th century and restored

The facade has twelfth-century **mosaics** that are hard to decipher. They would appear to represent the **five wise and five foolish virgins** of one of Christ's parables, standing offering oil lamps to the Virgin and Child. However, the number of burning lamps is inconsistent with the story. Eight of the lamps are lit, perhaps symbolizing virginity. The veiled women whose lamps have gone out are perhaps widows. The Virgin is feeding her child and two donors kneel at the foot of her throne.

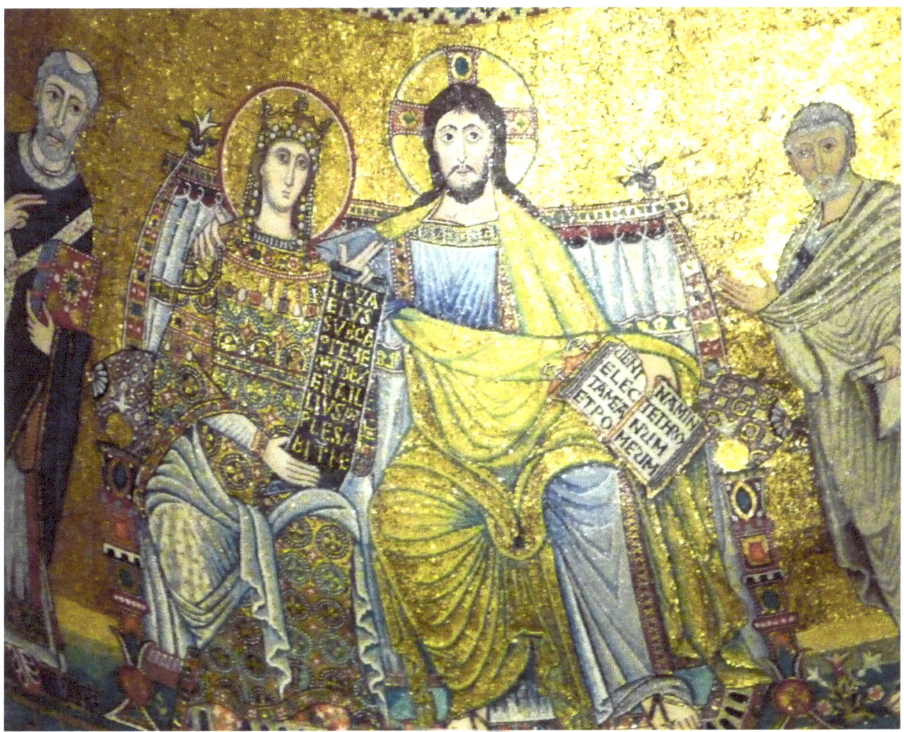

Christ enthroned with the Virgin, S. Maria in Trastevere, ca. 1140

Christ places his right arm around the **Virgin's** shoulder, and they share the throne. This image has been associated with the liturgy of the Feast of the **Assumption of the Virgin**. The text in Christ's hand reads: Veni electa mea et ponam in te thronum meum, 'I shall place thee on my throne.' The text held by the Virgin is from the Song of Solomon and reads: Leva eius sub capite meo et dextera illius amplesabitur me, 'O that his left hand were under my head, and that his right hand embraced me'. This is an early example of this iconography. **Christ's bride**, the Church, is identified with the Virgin his mother.

Spolia

Spolia is the term applied to the reuse of material. It is a form of recycling. *Spolia* can include material used to build (a column, a capital, a building block), or to decorate at key spots (such as doorways, windows). It is debated whether the use of *spolia* was due to lost skills, to convenience, to a lack of new material, or to aesthetic choice and a desire to have a variety of materials on a building. Probably *spolia* were used for several and various reasons.

In many medieval buildings in Rome, there are reused parts of ancient buildings. These are sometimes uniform but often mismatched, giving an interesting and varied appearance. Likewise, some material from the medieval period is reused in later buildings.

Spoliation of public buildings in Rome began in Antiquity and was countered with protective legislation. However, fourth-century laws gave the emperor responsibility for public monuments and their decoration, and this lasted in Rome until the end of Byzantine rule in the eighth century. This allowed the emperor Constans II (641-68) in 663 to strip the Pantheon of its bronze to send back to his capital Constantinople.

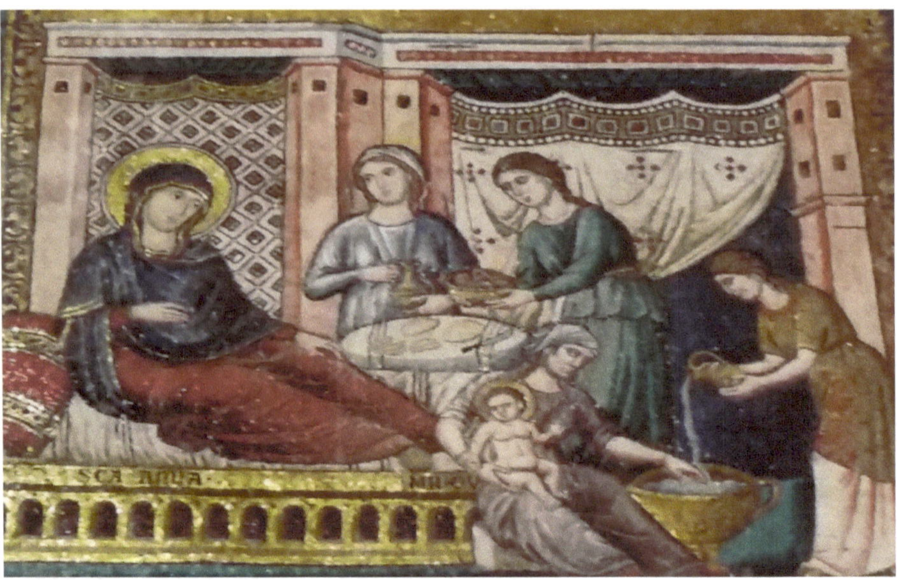

Pietro Cavallini, The Birth of the Virgin, S. Maria in Trastevere, ca. 1291

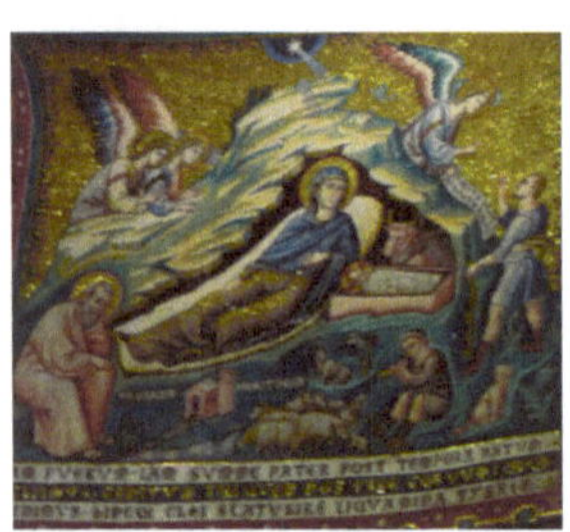

Pietro Cavallini, The Nativity, S. Maria in Trastevere, ca. 1291

The triumphal arch

The theme of the triumphal arch is the Apocalypse. A cross with the symbolic alpha and omega is between the seven candlesticks, which represent the seven early churches, and the symbols of the apostles. At the sides are the prophets Isaiah and Jeremiah, with a caged bird, symbolising Christ imprisoned because of the sins of man. Below, twelve lambs represent the twelve apostles with the cities of Bethlehem and Jerusalem.

Beneath the apse

The panels in the apse beneath the semi-dome are by Pietro Cavallini and dated to ca. 1291. They show scenes from the life of Mary and start from just to the left of the apse with the Birth of the Virgin. They continue around the apse with the Annunciation, the Nativity, the Adoration of the Magi, the Presentation in the Temple, and end with the Dormition of the Virgin on the right side. The iconography of the mosaics and to a certain extent the style, are based on Byzantine models, such as in the Nativity (set in a cave) and the Dormition. Cavallini made these mosaics at about the same time as he was painting the walls at Santa Cecilia (see pp. 53-4).

In the centre beneath the scenes from the life of the Virgin is a rectangular mosaic with Saints Peter and Paul presenting the donor, Bertoldo Stefaneschi, to the Virgin.

In the chapel to the left of the altar is a famous icon, la Madonna della Clemenza, perhaps presented by Pope John VII (705-7). Unfortunately the inscription around the image is not decipherable.

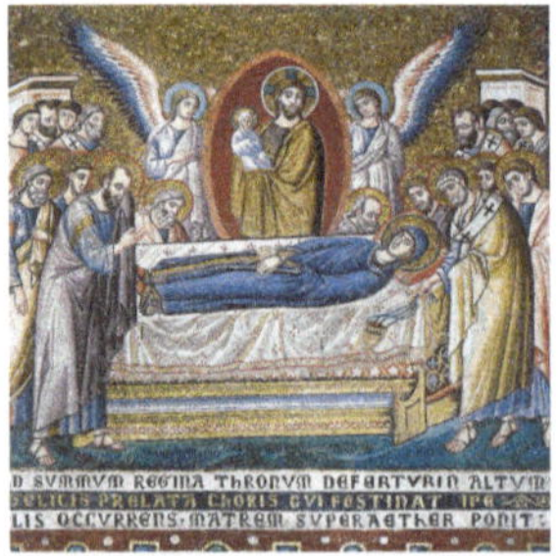

Pietro Cavallini, The Dormition of the Virgin, S. Maria in Trastevere, ca. 1291

Christ holds the Virgin's soul in the form of a baby before it ascends to heaven.

San Crisogono

This very old church is well worth a visit to see the unusual wall paintings in the lower church.

History

It is named after a saint who died ca. 304 and the church is mentioned as early as 499. The current building was erected over the original one in the twelfth century by a cardinal named Giovanni da Crema.

The church

This basilica has retained its original twelfth-century form and has a beautiful thirteenth-century Cosmatesque pavement (see box p. 46). The columns and ionic capitals are reused Roman ones and the baldacchino also has ancient alabaster columns. Housed in the altar is the twelfth-century reliquary of Crisogono. In the apse is a thirteenth-century mosaic, made either by Pietro Cavallini or by artists trained by him.

The lower church

This is accessed via stairs in the sacristy. There is a small fee. Descending to the fifth-century site it is possible to see the curved apse lying to the west (unusually), which is from the eighth century, built by Gregory III (731-41), and decorated with faux marble paintings. On walls in a stone corridor abutting the apse, originally part of the crypt where the saint's relics were, are paintings of Saint Crisogono and two saints who were martyred with him, Rufinus and Anastasia. They are framed by columns. In the room to the left of the apse is a baptismal font. In the south (left) aisle is a sixth-century altar and two marble sarcophagi. On the walls of the north aisle (to the right) are tenth-century paintings with the life of Saint Benedict.

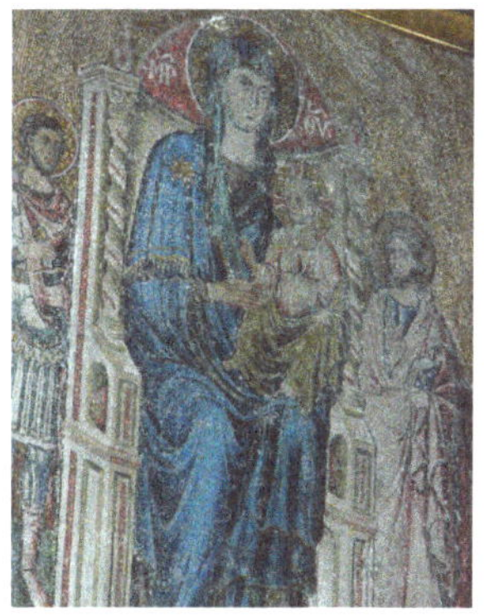

Pietro Cavallini or his followers, Virgin and Child with St. Crisogono (left) and St. James, mosaic, apse, S. Crisogono, ca. 1290

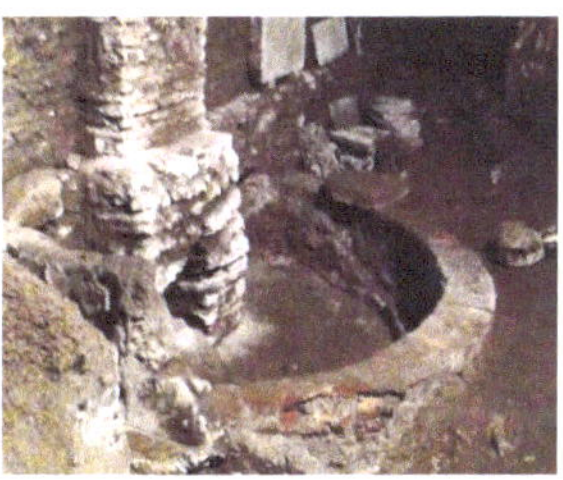

Baptismal font, S. Crisogono, lower church, baptistery to south of apse

The font was used for immersion baptism, hence its size.

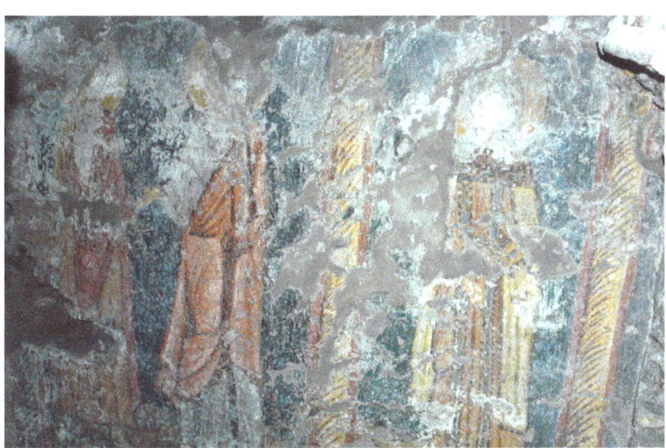

Saints Crisogono (centre), Rufinus and Anastasia, corridor in front of apse, lower church, S. Crisogono, eighth century (?)

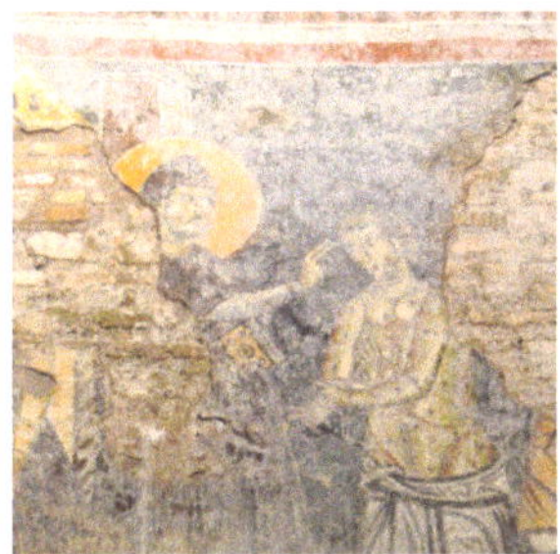

St. Benedict healing a leper, north aisle, S. Crisogono, lower church, tenth century

The leper's body is still covered with spots as Benedict, on the left, raises his hand to touch and bless him.

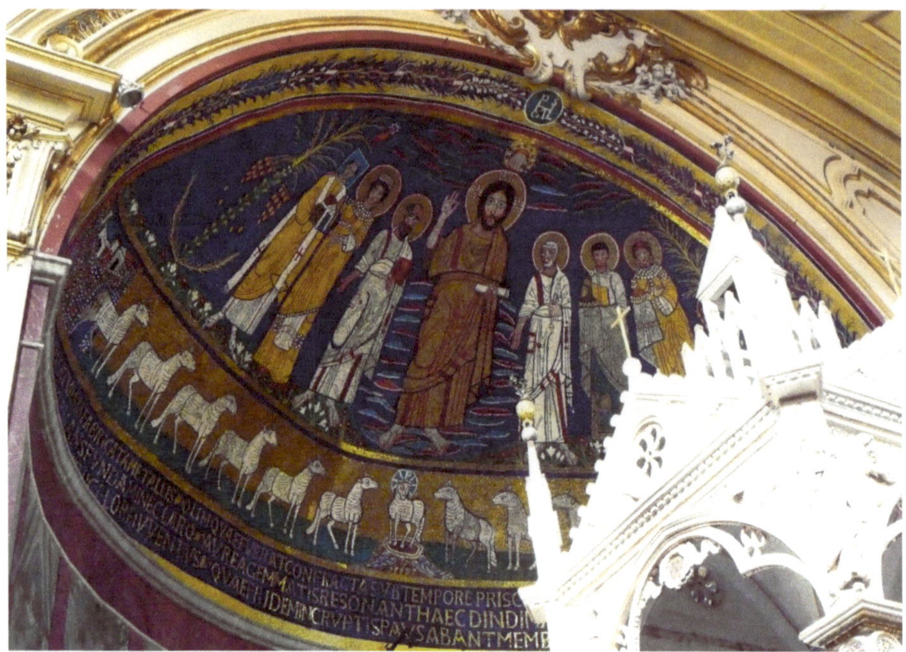

Christ, Paschal I with the saints Cecilia, Paul, Peter, Valerian and Agnes, apse, S. Cecilia, 817-24

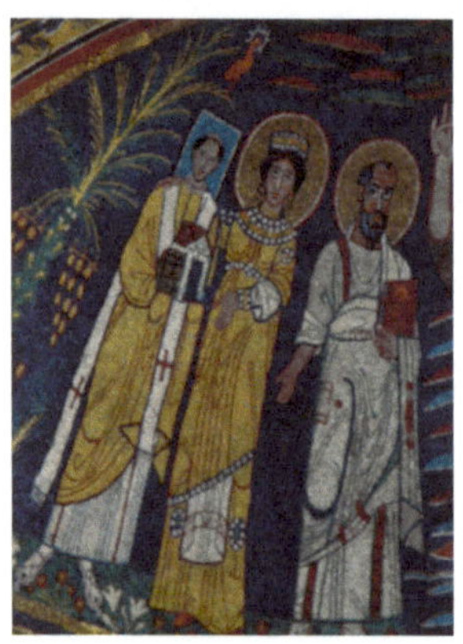

Pope Paschal I with S. Cecilia and S. Paul, apse, S. Cecilia 817-24

The **phoenix** above Paschal's head is a symbol of eternal life. It rests on a palm tree in paradise. Paschal's square halo indicates he is living. Paul is recognisable by his receding hair line and dark hair and beard. Peter usually has white hair and beard.

Santa Cecilia

This beautifully peaceful church is set back in Trastevere not far from the Tiber. It is a Benedictine convent. You enter the courtyard with its central fountain, designed around an ancient Roman vase, to see the early-eighteenth-century facade. The campanile and the doorway, made from reused ancient columns, are from the beginning of the twelfth century. The church itself contains ninth-century mosaics and thirteenth-century sculpture and rare paintings.

History

The church was built, by tradition, on the site of the house of Cecilia, a Christian, and her husband, Valerian. A *titulus* in the name of Cecilia is known from the fifth century. The basilica was built by Pope Paschal I (817-24). It was he who brought Cecilia's remains from the Catacomb of San Callisto and established the church in veneration of her. Cecilia's story is traumatic. She was martyred in 230 during the reign of Alexander Severus (222-35). She is said to have endured being scalded or suffocated in her own baths (on this site), then beheaded, and she survived for a further three days.

Sanctuary

As you approach the sanctuary, at the foot of the baldacchino is a very lovely statue by Stefano Maderno (1576-1636) of Santa

Cecilia as she was apparently seen in 1599 when her tomb was opened. The baldacchino is by Arnolfo di Cambio (1293) (see p. 47), and probably uses the black marble columns from a ninth-century construction. On the corners above the capitals are four figures, depicting Cecilia and Valerian, Tiburtius (Valerian's brother), who is on horseback, and Pope Urban I (222-230), who baptised them.

Apse

The earliest part of the decoration is the mosaic in the apse. Here, as at Santa Prassede (see p. 18) Paschal had himself depicted with Christ and the saints. He is on the far left with a square below halo standing close to Cecilia. Next to her is Paul, and Peter is on the other side of Christ. Valerian and Agnes are on the right. The familiar image of the Lamb of God in Paradise and the twelve apostles as lambs coming from the sacred cities of Jerusalem and Bethlehem is below.

The subterranean area

The lower areas beneath the church have fascinating remains from the second to fourth centuries and are accessed through the sacristy at the west end of the left aisle. Part of this is a Roman republican period house with paved floors and an imperial second-century house. There is also a room with eight huge containers sunken into the ground, which are thought to have been used as silos for storing food. On view also are mosaic floors and some sarcophagi.

The crypt at the far end was rebuilt in 1899-1901 and is decorated in a colourful neo-Byzantine style. The remains of four saints, Cecilia, Valerian, Tiburtius and their associate Maximus, lie in sarcophagi behind a grill.

Cavallini Paintings

A further highlight is to be seen in the upper west end of the church. However, to access this, ring the bell at the door of the convent, which is up the stairs to the right (as you walk out) of the main church entrance. There is a small fee. The nuns escort you up via a lift to the nuns' choir. In about 1290 the entire west wall was decorated by the artist Pietro Cavallini in a style then radically new and innovative. The painting that survives was covered over when a nun's choir was installed and so preserved.

It shows the upper part of a Last Judgement with Christ in the centre, surrounded by a host of angels and flanked by the Virgin and by John the Baptist with the apostles on either side. The Last Judgement is typically placed on the west wall of a church, as here. Notice how the haloes have been formed in relief. There are areas such as the apostles's swords which were painted in silver and have tarnished. You can also see the *giornata*, the area painted in one day or painting session, by looking

The inscription in the apse records the founding of the church. It reads in translation: 'This spacious house, which in former times was shattered, is made with various enamels and sparkles. **Paschal**, a munificent bishop, has founded in the best way this hall of the Lord, establishing it on a brilliant foundation. These golden mysteries of the Church resound with gems. Rejoicing in God's love, he united here the holy bodies: here youth glows ruddy in its bloom for Cecilia and her companions, who formerly rested their blessed limbs in the cemeteries.'

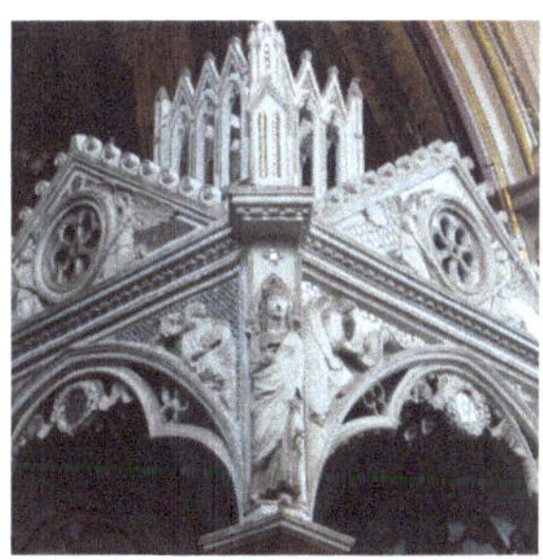

Arnolfo di Cambio, ciborium, S. Cecilia, 1293

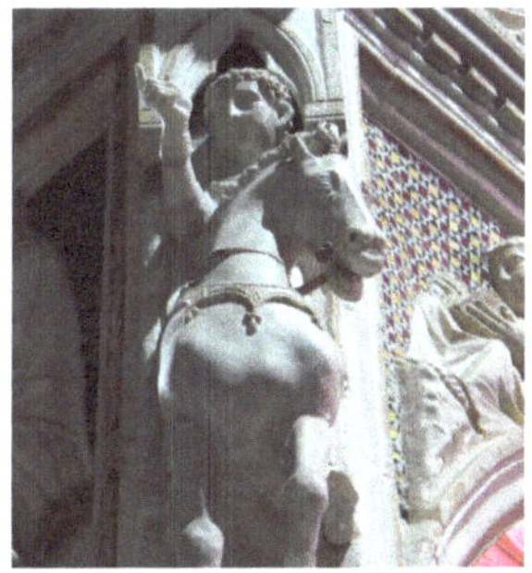

Arnolfo di Cambio, S. Tiburtius, corner of ciborium, 1293

The style of these figures clearly comes from **Roman sculpture**, particularly the facial features and use of the equestrian statue. The city in the thirteenth century must have had many remains from the Roman era easily visible, many more so than today.

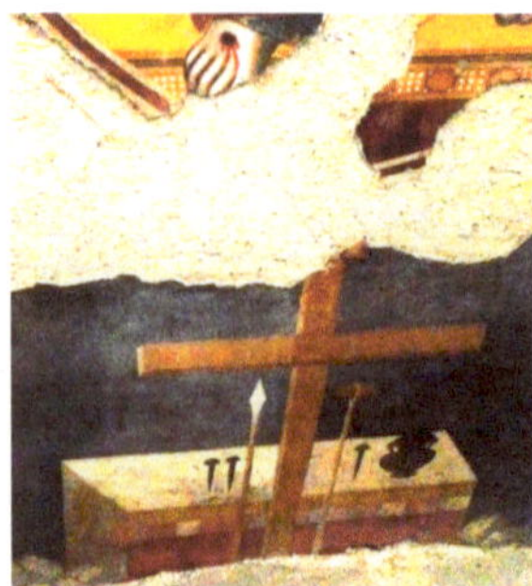

Pietro Cavallini, Instruments of the Passion, detail, Last Judgement, Santa Cecilia, ca. 1290

If you look down below the wooden pews, you can see the **passion relics** on an altar, including the nails that held Christ to the cross and the lance that pierced his side.

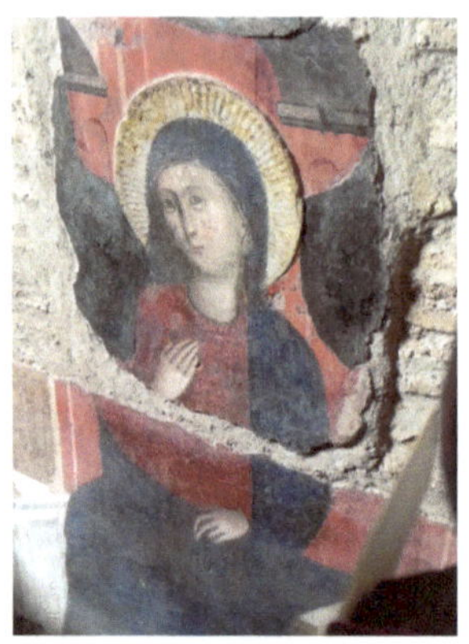

Pietro Cavallini, The Annunciation, detail, Last Judgement, Santa Cecilia, ca. 1290

If you go to the far left wall (as you face the apse), and look over the side, you can see the Virgin, originally part of an **Annunciation** scene.

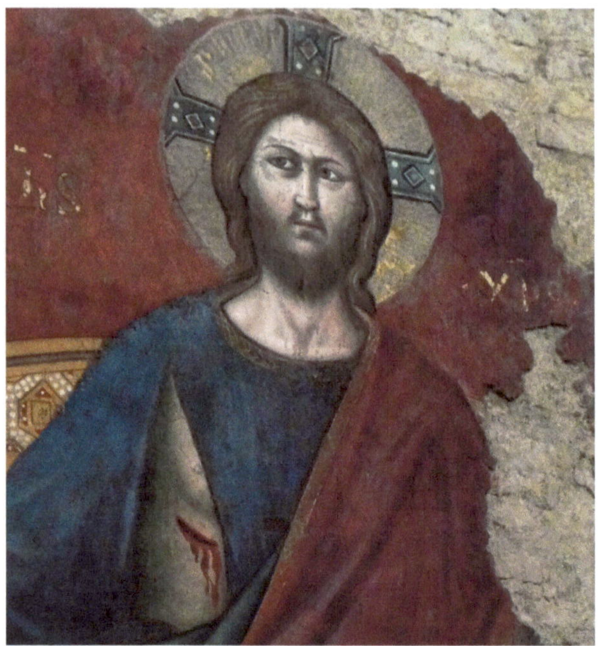

Pietro Cavallini, Christ, detail, Last Judgement, Santa Cecilia, ca. 1290

closely for changes in colour of the pigment in various areas.

Look down to the side wall on the far side for an Old Testament scene of Isaac blessing Jacob. Jacob has placed an animal skin on his forearm so his father will think he is the elder and hairier brother, Esau. In the same place on the wall on the opposite side is a very fine Virgin. One imagines that there was a series of narrative scenes from the Old and New Testaments, perhaps even decorating the whole church.

Santa Maria in Cosmedin

This is a short walk across the Tiber from Santa Cecilia. It has a fascinating past and has elements from throughout its history, a few of which make it worth a visit. It is a popular site for sightseers as it has in its entrance way the *Bocca della Verità* (mouth of truth), an old drain cover which is supposed to bite the hand of one who lies. Inside it is normally not crowded, though quite difficult to decipher.

Pietro Cavallini

Pietro Cavallini (ca. 1250 – ca. 1330) is thought to have come from Rome, as he signed his work *pictor romanus*. The naturalism in his work was taken up by artists of the fourteenth century in Assisi, Florence and Siena who contributed much to early Renaissance art.

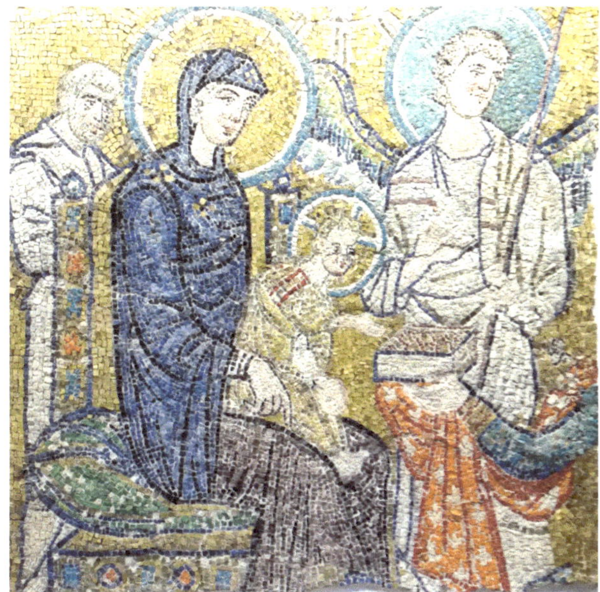

Adoration of the Magi, mosaic from Old St. Peter's, S. Maria in Cosmedin, 705-7

An important mosaic fragment of the **Adoration of the Magi** is kept in the sacristy, now a shop, on your right as you enter. It is hung on the far wall and is from an oratory in Old St. Peter's created by Pope John VII (705-7). It was originally part of a much larger scene showing the Pope with the Virgin and seven scenes from her life (see p. 64). In style it is very similar to a mosaic of the Presentation in the Temple from a Church dedicated to the Virgin in Constantinople, dated to the same period.

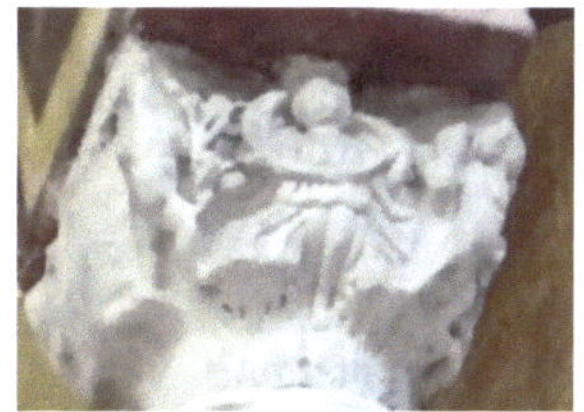

Capital with dancing figure, S. Maria in Cosmedin

History

The site of the church was formerly a temple dedicated to Hercules Invictus, against which a colonnaded loggia was built which was later turned into a Christian hall used as a *diaconia* (see box p. 26). Under Hadrian I (772-95) the hall was enlarged to make a basilical church with three apses. This was used by the Greek-speaking Christians who had come to Rome during Iconoclasm in the Byzantine east (see box p. 82). It must have been richly decorated as it took on the name 'in Cosmedin', which comes from the Greek word for decorated. It was rebuilt in 1123 under Pope Callistus II (1119-24). The twelfth-century campanile (bell tower) is over 34 metres high.

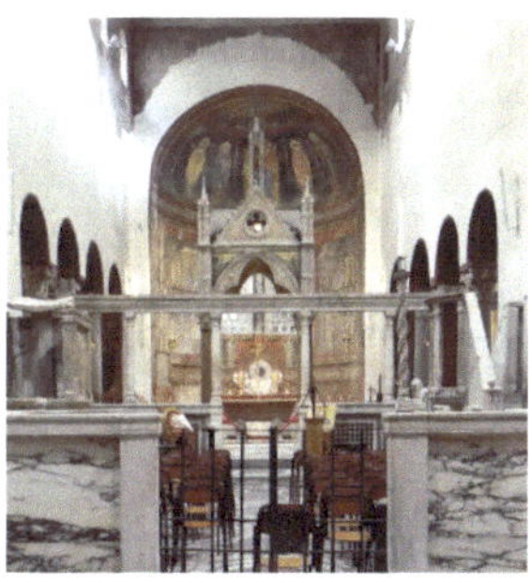

View of the *schola cantorum* and apse, S. Maria in Cosmedin (1123 in part)

Church

The columns and capitals are reused and of wonderful variety. Parts of the loggia's columns and arcades can be seen in the west end of the left aisle. The *schola cantorum*, the ciborium, paschal candlestick and floor are by the Cosmati (see box p. 46). The paintings in the apses are later imitations of twelfth-century ones.

The church has several elements that model an early church. The central marble structure, known as the *schola cantorum* (the area used by the choir), the paschal candlestick (lit on the night before Easter), the screen and the bishop's throne are from the twelfth century as well as the Cosmati floor.

Crypt

The crypt (entry to the left of the apse with a small fee) is designed like a small church with columns and dates from the time of Hadrian I. Here he housed relics that he had amassed from the catacombs; they would have been put in the small niches in the walls. This kind of space is unusual for Rome.

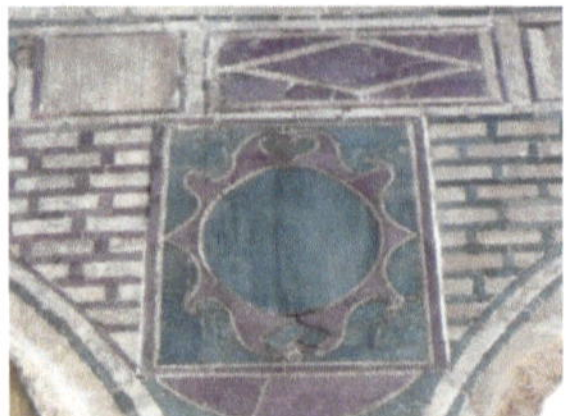

Opus sectile **work in the nave arcade, S. Sabina, ca. 430**

The **chalice** and sacrramental bread of the eucharist are in dark red porphyry marble.

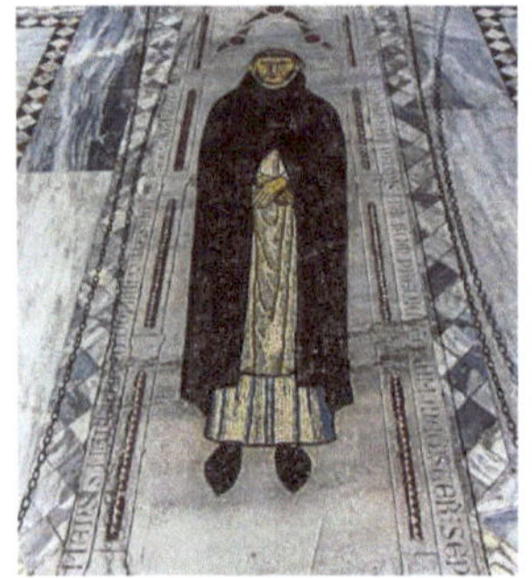

Tomb of Dominican Monk, ca. 1300

This tomb marker is set into the floor in the nave

Santa Sabina

The church of Santa Sabina is one of the most serene sites in Rome. It is a pleasurable, if uphill, walk from Santa Maria in Cosmedin. Note the lovely Parco Savello with an orange grove if you climb the stairs on the Clivo di Rocca Savelli from the Via di S. Maria in Cosmedin. Alternatively walk up from the Circus Maximus by the Via di Valle Murcia to see the Roseto, a rose garden. Set on top of the Aventine Hill, Santa Sabina has survived for nearly 1700 years and has been restored as close as possible to an Early Christian church as any in Rome. While much of its decoration is lost, it has some key elements that make it well worth a visit.

History

There is no saint named Sabina, but the name is taken from the *titulus* (see box p. 70) established on this site in the fourth century. The church itself was founded, as recorded by an inscription, by a presbyter (priest) called Petrus of Illyria (at that time Greece and the Balkans) in about 425-32. It was later restored several times but many of the restorations have now been removed, leaving it in a simplified form.

The church

The arcade is unusually uniform with twenty-four second-century fluted Corinthian columns made out of Proconnesian marble from an island in the Sea of Marmara (Prokonnesos). In the spandrels of the arcade is *opus sectile* work showing chalices and patens (plates) used in the celebration of the eucharist.

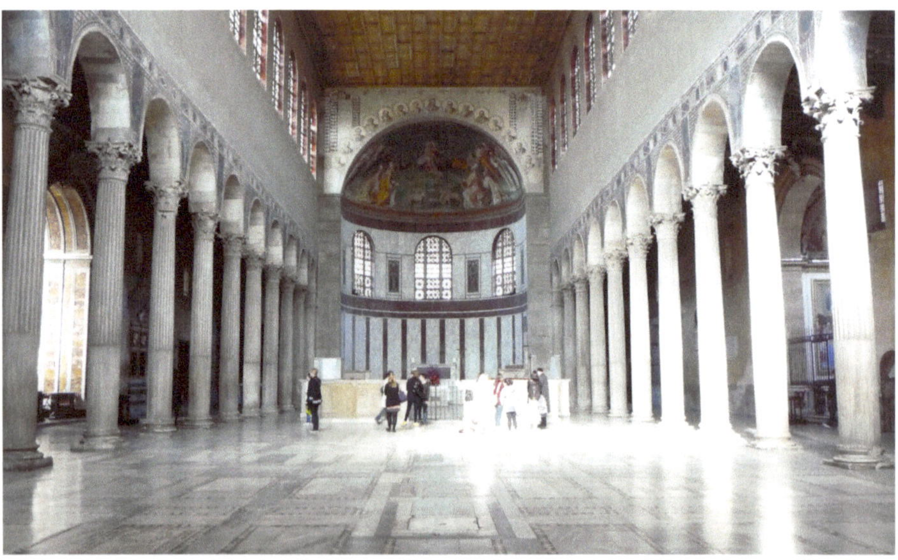

Nave facing east, S. Sabina, ca. 430

The early *schola cantorum* has been reconstructed along with the *ambones* and the bishop's throne. Above the west door are mosaics depicting personifications of the early church communities, the Jewish and gentile.

One of the finest features of the facade is the fourth-century wooden doors. These are visible from outside the west facade. It is remarkable that they have survived and though some panels are lost (the lower ones), it is largely complete. Some of the scenes are hard to decipher. It importantly shows one of the very earliest depictions of the Crucifixion. It has been suggested that some scenes may derive from a passion play performed outside the city walls, but this is hard to prove.

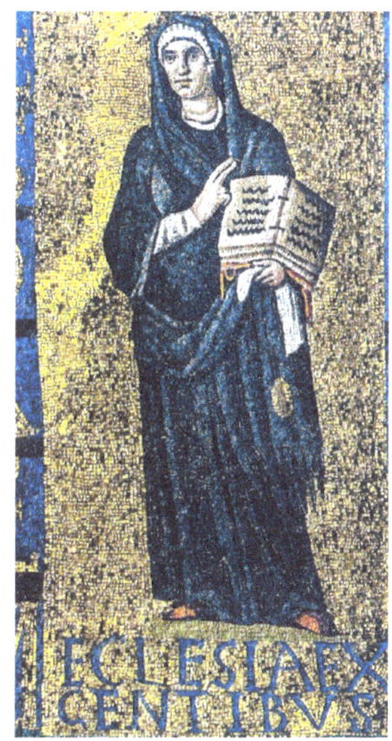

***Ecclesia*, mosaic, west wall, S. Sabina, ca. 430**

The inscription reads **Ecclesia** ex gentibus (the Church of the gentiles). This female figure represents the Church of those converted who were not Jews. The adjacent panel represents the Church of those who were **Jewish converts**, *ex circumcisione* (the circumcised).

Crucifixion	Empty Tomb	Adoration of Magi	Christ with Peter and Paul
Raising of Lazarus, Multiplication of Loaves and Fishes, Miracle at Cana	Moses in the Desert, Feast of Quail, Feast of Manna, Miracle of Water from Rock	Ascension of Christ	Second Coming of Christ
Three Women at the Sepulchre	Christ appears to Two Women	Prediction of Peter's Denial	Rescue of Habakkuk
Calling of Moses	Homages to a praying man (?)	Exodus from Egypt, Drowning of Pharaoh, Aaron and Serpents	Ascension of Elijah
Pilate washing Hands			Judgement of Christ

Suggested iconography of panels in wooden west door, S. Sabina, ca. 430

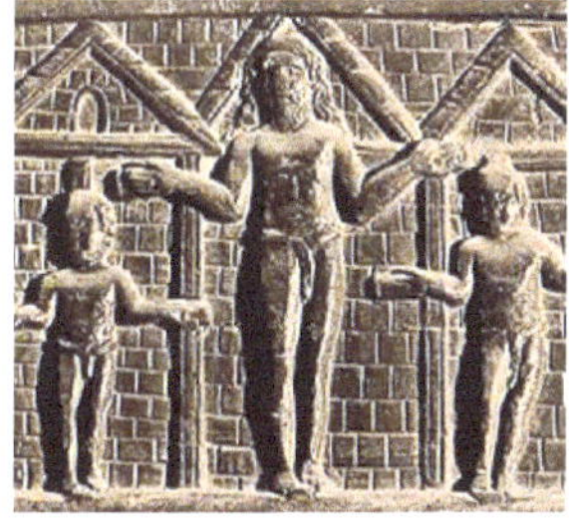

Crucifixion, wooden west door, S. Sabina, ca. 430

Christ is pictured flanked by the Good and the Bad Thief. The **crosses** may be represented by the structure behind which looks like the frames of three entry ways placed on a wall. Or are the three men shown in prayer?

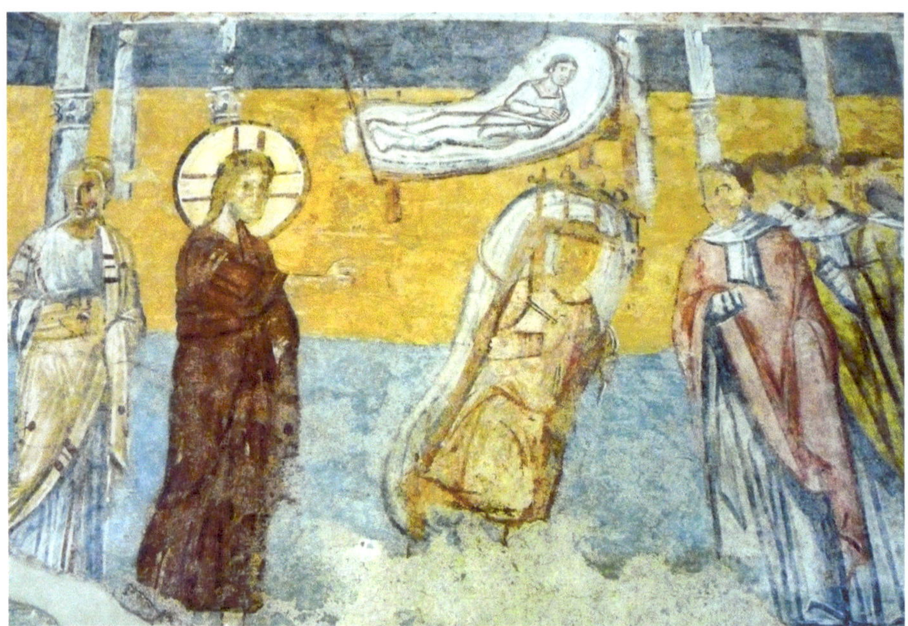

Christ healing the palsied man, from the oratory, S. Saba, first half of eighth century

This painting is the earliest known use of blue lapis lazuli pigment on a wall in the west. It shows Christ healing a man who had palsy (Mark 2.1-12).

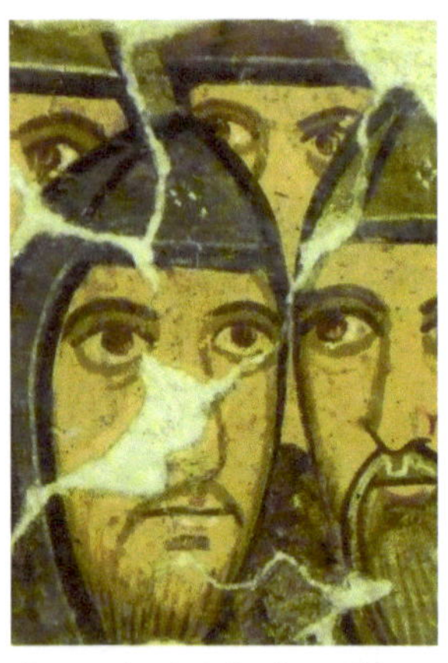

The monks, S. Saba, from the oratory, S. Saba, date uncertain

This powerful image indicates the unity shared by a group of monks. The remaining fragment shows seven of them.

San Saba

This church is a 15-minute or so walk south east of Santa Sabina. It has some significant early frescoes from the eighth century and later.

History

The house on this site was turned into an oratory by monks from Palestine. They came in the seventh century from the celebrated monastery of San Saba (Mar Saba), fleeing Islamic invasions. In the tenth century it was taken over by the Benedictines and later by the Cluniacs. The present church has been rebuilt several times.

Oratory and paintings

The floor is Cosmati work (see box p. 46). The oldest part of the church, the oratory is reached by stairs in the portico (ask for access). Early paintings have been moved from the oratory to panels on the sacristy corridor, accessed through a door in the right aisle. The lower parts of the wall or dado is painted to look like curtains. Later paintings from the thirteenth century are in the far left hand aisle, and a fourteenth-century Crucifixion is in the apse.

CHAPTER SIX

THE VATICAN AREA

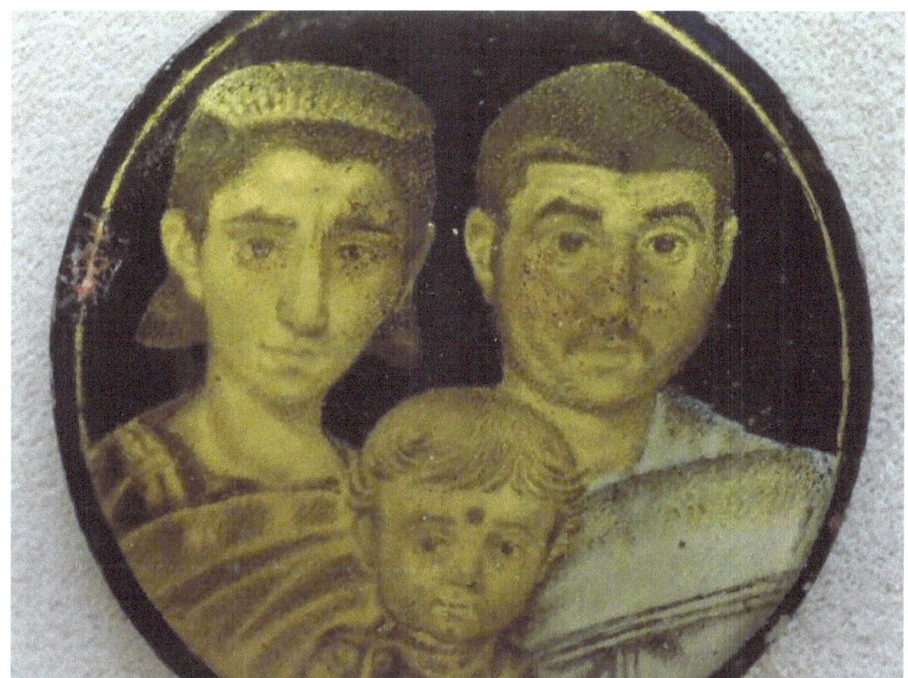

Family group, gold glass, Museum of Christian Art, Vatican, fourth century

Saint Peter's, Saint Peter's Treasury, Necropolis/*Scavi*, Vatican Museums

Introduction

Saint Peter's Church is on the site of a necropolis that was adjacent to the Circus of Nero where, by tradition, Peter was martyred in 64 C.E. Constantine I (306-37) chose this site as the location of a massive building, really a funereal hall with a martyr's shrine, dedicated to Peter, and by the sixth century it was being used as a church. This building is known as Old Saint Peter's. It was rebuilt in the sixteenth and seventeenth centuries.

Peter's primacy among the apostles made this a central place of pilgrimage, and it was an immensely lavish and splendid building. From early times the papal palace was at the Lateran, and it is only since 1377 when the papacy moved back from Avignon, that the Apostolic Palace by Saint Peter's became the residency of the popes. Surprisingly little survives from the early period and much that you can see today is from the renaissance

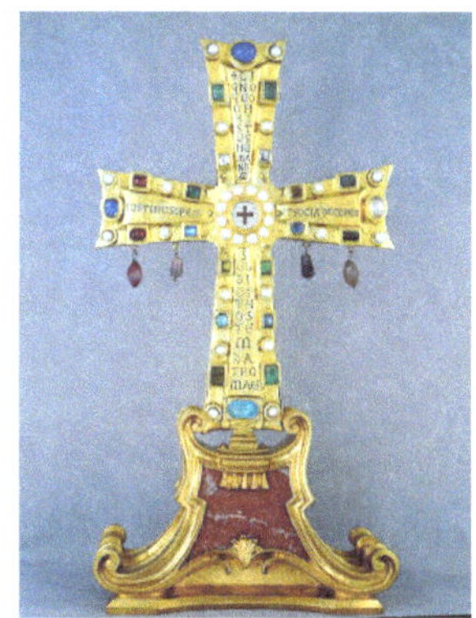

Cross of Justin II, front, Treasury of St. Peter's, 568-74

The inscription records the imperial donors' gift to Rome.

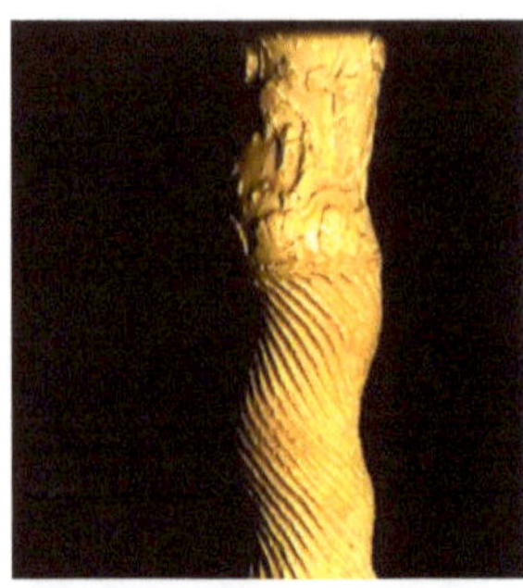

St. Peter's, spiral column, Vatican Treasury

This column is from the row of twelve in Old St. Peter's which stood in front of the ciborium, depicted on the *Pola Casket* (see box pp. 68-9).

Six of them were **reused** in the present St. Peter's in the balconies above the niches of the piers supporting the cupola in the centre of the building. Six are later reproductions. The idea arose in the thirteenth century that the columns of the **Temple** in Jerusalem were twisted like this, but there was no such connection in the fourth century.

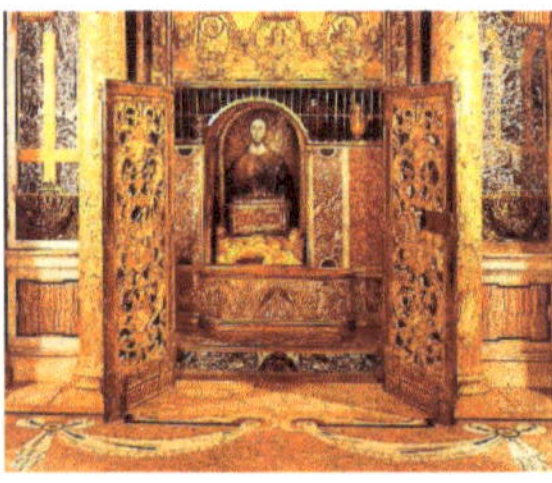

Niche of the Palliums, *Confessio*, St. Peter's

In the Niche of the Palliums, beneath the altar, is an eighth-century **mosaic** of Christ, which is quite heavily restored. The name of the niche comes from the woollen stoles or **palliums** kept there, which are woven with wool from lambs that are blessed each year on **St. Agnes' day**.

and later. Beneath the basilica, the Vatican Grottoes house the tombs of the popes, and select Christian objects are in Saint Peter's Treasury, well worth seeing.

The *Scavi* or archaeological site beneath the basilica may be visited by special arrangement and gives a fascinating view of the necropolis and suggested evidence for Peter's burial.

The extraordinarily rich papal collections are displayed in the Vatican Museums (a series of museums and galleries created over time and housed together).

Part of the massive wall that circles some of the Vatican area like a medieval fortress dates from the thirteenth century, although most is from the seventeenth. Vatican City was only created as a sovereign state in 1929.

Saint Peter's Basilica

The present Saint Peter's is very much worth visiting, but the medieval vestiges are few. The treasury makes it unmissable (see box pp. 68-9 for a description of Old Saint Peter's).

The main church

As you enter, look in front of the central doorway at the east end (you enter at the east) to find a circular porphyry disk which was originally placed in front of the altar in the Old Church. It was here that Charlemagne and his successors were crowned.

The present baptistery (the original was built by Pope Damasus in the fourth century and was at the end of the north transept) is the first chapel in the left aisle. The font is made from a fourth-century sarcophagus that is said to have belonged to the Prefect Probus. The lid is from the tomb of Otto II in the Vatican Grottoes. Pope Gregory the I's (the Great) (590-604) coffin is in the Clementine Chapel, the fourth chapel in the left aisle.

The papal altar is marked by a vast baldacchino designed by Gian Lorenzo Bernini in 1633-4. It shelters the twelfth-century altar of Callixtus II (1119-24), which is over the altar of Gregory the Great (ca 600), and beneath this, at a lower level, is the shrine of Saint Peter. In front of the altar is a sunken crypt (known as the *Confessio* in memory of Saint Peter's confession of faith) which has an early mosaic.

In the central bay supporting the dome, the left hand pier at the far west end, known as the Pier of Saint Veronica, contains the relics of the Passion which are displayed in Holy Week. The name comes from one of the relics, a cloth said to bear the image of Christ's face, imprinted when he wiped his face at Calvary. The others are the spear of Longinus (he pierced Christ's side at the Crucifixion), and a piece of the True Cross (see box p. 61).

In the far left corner is the Chapel of the Column which has a fourth-century sarcophagus with the remains of several early

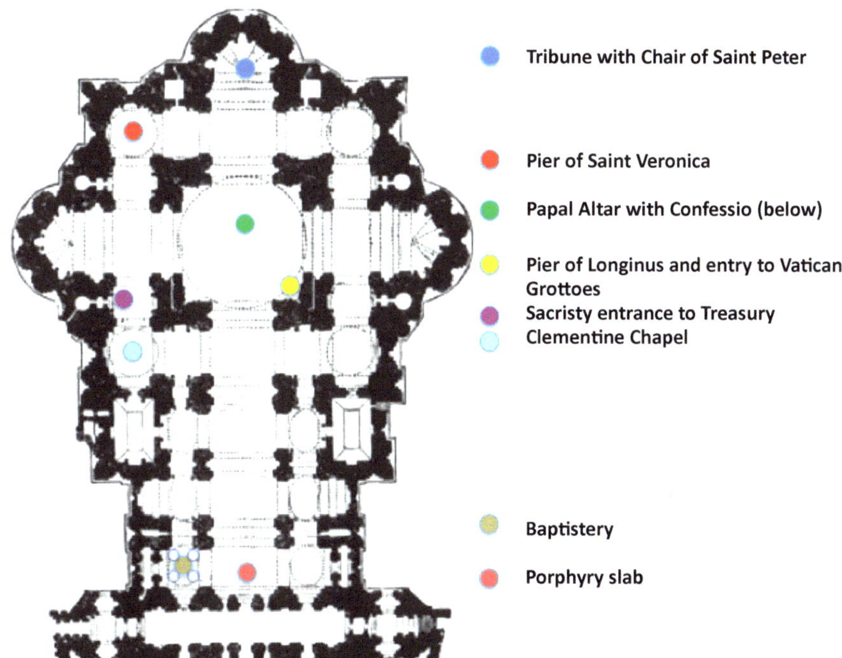

Plan of St. Peter's with locations of key sites

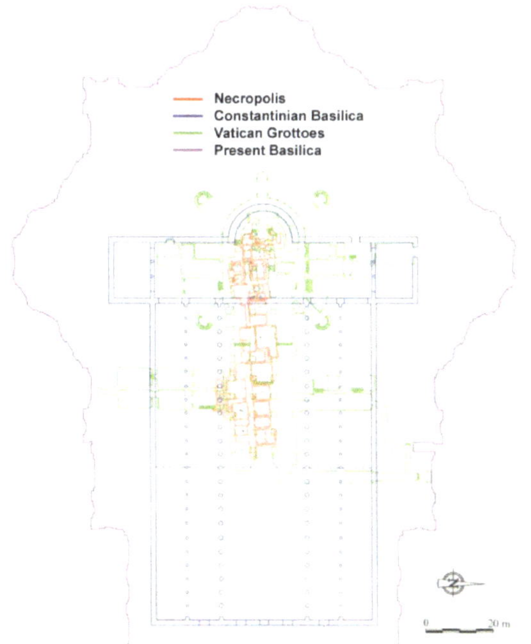

Plan showing the plan of Old St. Peter's overlaid with the Vatican Grottoes and the present church

The True Cross

This term is applied to relics of the cross on which Christ was crucified. By tradition, it was found by Helena, Constantine's mother, during her travels to the Holy Land in ca. 326-8. In about 350 Cyril of Jerusalem said that it was found during the reign of Constantine. However, the Helena story only originated as far as we know about 390. As is commonly said the amount of True Cross relics would take a forest to supply. There was one such relic at an altar dedicated to Simon and Jude in the nave of Old St. Peter's.

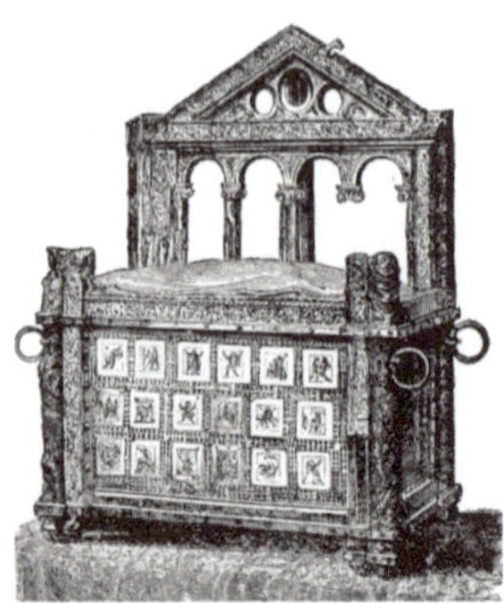

Representation of St. Peter's Chair, 875

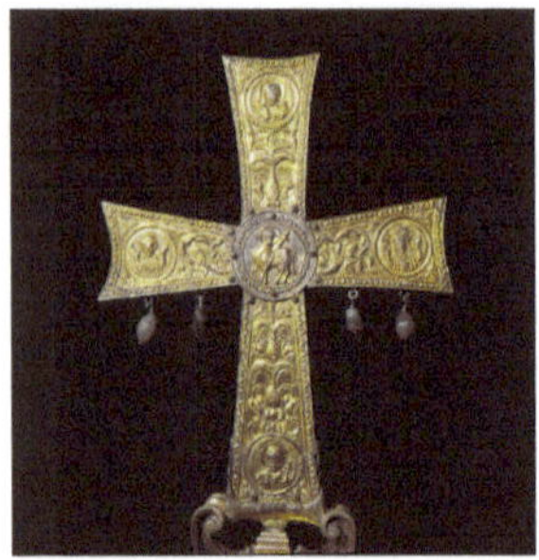

Cross of Justin II, reverse, Treasury of St. Peter's, 568-74

This cross was probably presented to Pope John II (561-74). It is made of gilded silver over a bronze central core. It represents the *Crux gemmata* which marked **Golgotha** in Jerusalem.

The inscription on the front (image on p. 59) reads, 'Justin and his Consort give to Rome a glorious treasure in the wood by which Christ subdued the enemy of mankind'. Rome was suffering from incursions by the Barbarians and so this may have been given in support of the people of the city.

On the back, Christ appears three times: in the centre as the Lamb of God, above holding the Gospels, and below holding a cross. To the left is **Justin** and to the right **Sophia**, both with arms raised in prayer and wearing Byzantine imperial crowns with *prependulia* (hanging gems).

popes. At the far end of the building is the gilt bronze casing for the Cathedra or chair of the bishop of Rome, the wood and ivory chair given in 875 given by Charles the Bald to mark his coronation (you can see a copy in the Treasury). The casing was made by Bernini 1(647-53). By the Pier of Longinus is a bronze statue of Saint Peter by Arnolfo di Cambio, (ca. 1300).

Treasury of Saint Peter's

The entry to the Treasury (small fee) is half way down the left aisle. The collection's display is dark and atmospheric. A few highlights are mentioned here.

The first room houses a column from Old Saint Peter's, one which, by tradition, Christ leant against when teaching in the Temple of Jerusalem. The second has some very fine objects. The large gold cross, studded with gemstones dates to the reign of Justin II (565-578) and was given by him and his wife Sophia. It contains in the centre a fragment of the True Cross (the small cavity holding it is a later replacement). The back is decorated in repoussé (relief hammered from the reverse). The stunning ecclesiastical garment, known as the 'Dalmatic of Charlemagne' is in fact a fourteenth-century *sakkos*, worn on feast days by Byzantine patriarchs. The decoration on the front shows a variation of the Last Judgement, on the back is the Transfiguration, and on the shoulders the Communion of the Apostles with Christ serving the Eucharist.

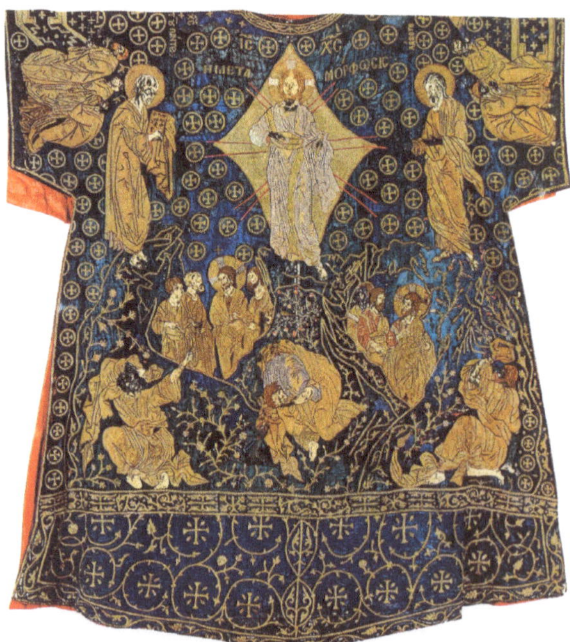

Vatican *Sakkos* also known as the Dalmatic of Charlemagne, Treasury of St. Peter's, fourteenth century

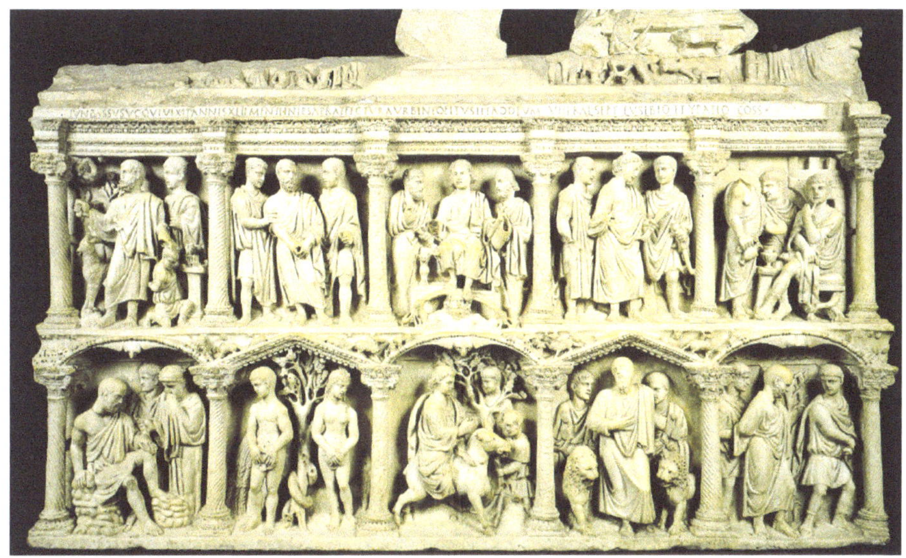

***Sarcophagus of Junius Bassus*, front, Treasury of St. Peter's, 359**

The scenes shown are from the Old and New Testaments and, running left to right, top to bottom are: Sacrifice of Isaac, Arrest of Peter, Giving of the Law to Peter and Paul, Arrest of Christ, Christ before Pontius Pilate, Job on the Dunghill, Adam and Eve, Entry to Jerusalem, Daniel in the Lion's Den, Arrest of Paul. There are further scenes acted out by sheep above the lower set of columns.

The *Sarcophagus of Junius Bassus* at the end of the Treasury is one of the finest to survive from Late Antiquity. The inscription dates it to 359 and explains that the prefect Junius was baptised just before he died: 'Junius Bassus, a man of the highest rank, who lived 42 years, 2 months, in his own prefecture of the city, newly baptised, went to God, on the 8th day from the Kalends of September, Eusebius and Hypatius being consuls' (25 August 359).

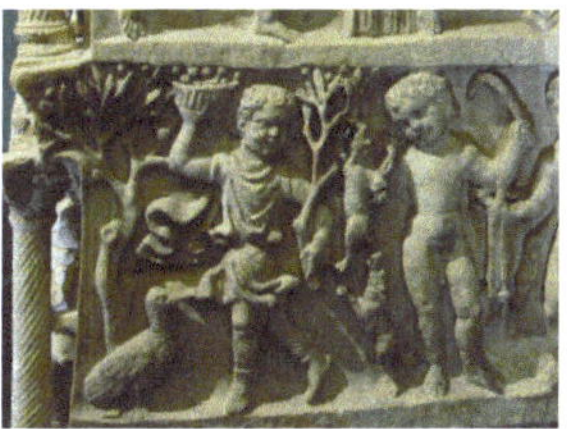

***Sarcophagus of Junius Bassus*, right end, Treasury of St. Peter's, 359**

The ends of the sarcophagus have scenes which may represent the **seasons** personified by children. The cyclical nature of the year can be linked to regeneration and so **resurrection**. This type of imagery comes from the Roman world. Here small hunters and gatherers are shown with a shepherd's crook and hare, fruits and a duck-like bird.

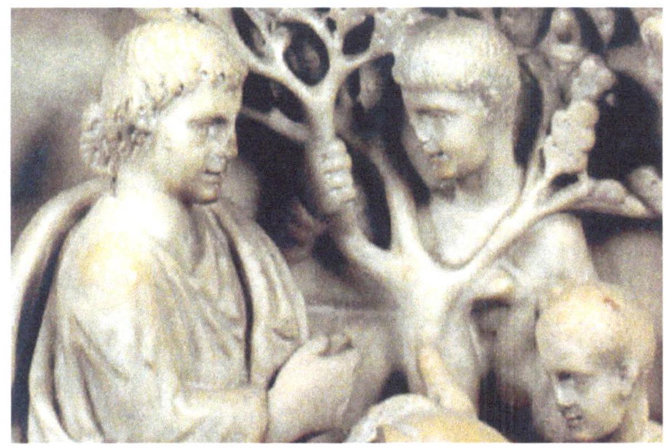

***Sarcophagus of Junius Bassus*, Entry to Jerusalem, detail, Treasury of St. Peter's, 359**

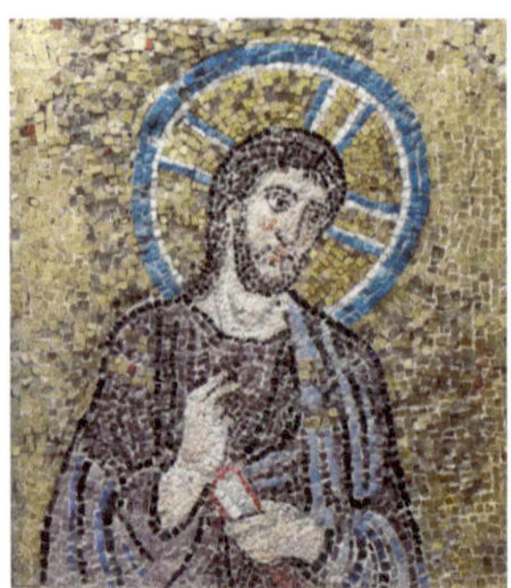

Christ, from the Entry into Jerusalem, formerly oratory of John VII, Vatican Grottoes, 706

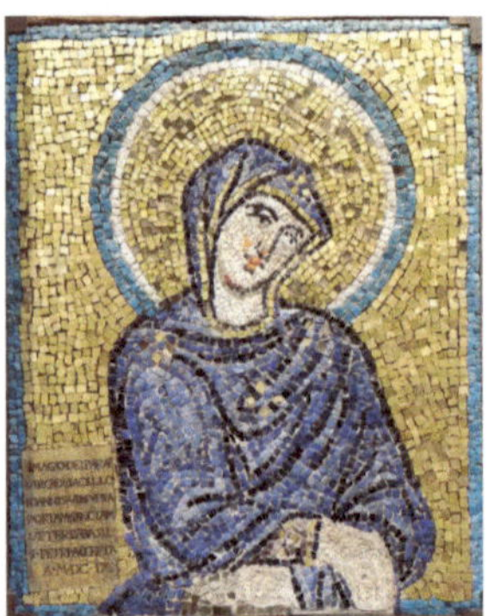

The Virgin, from the Nativity, formerly oratory of John VII, Museo d'arte sacra di Orte, 706

This section is no longer in Rome.

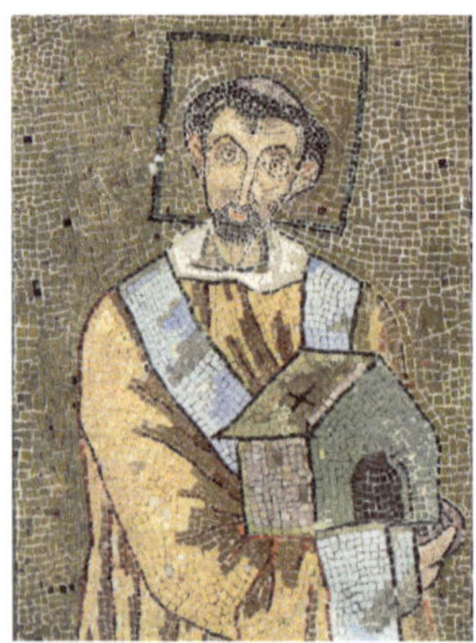

Pope John VII, presenting the chapel to the Virgin, detail, formerly oratory of John VII, Vatican Grottoes, 706

The Vatican Grottoes

The entry is in the Pier of Saint Longinus which is diagonally opposite the Pier of Saint Veronica. The exit takes you out of the basilica, so make sure you are ready to leave.

This is an interesting visit to an area principally designed in the sixteenth century to house and display the tombs of the Popes but which also has some important remains of the early church. It lies over the floor level of the Old Church and beneath the New and is a rather austere space.

You enter to the right side of the crypt dating from the sixth century. The semicircular west end lies directly over the Shrine of Saint Peter. If you enter the Clementine Chapel at the west end, peek inside the grille above the altar to see the two later altars above the so-called Trophy over the shrine of Saint Peter, where he is said to have been buried.

A highlight is the mosaics which are in a corridor that leads to the north annexe on the right side. They are from an eighth-century oratory dedicated to the Virgin which was at the east end of the north aisle of the Old Church. It was built by Pope John VII (705–707) and destroyed in 1605.

The central image on the east wall was of the standing Virgin, Queen of Heaven and it was surrounded by scenes from the life of Christ, fragments of which survive.

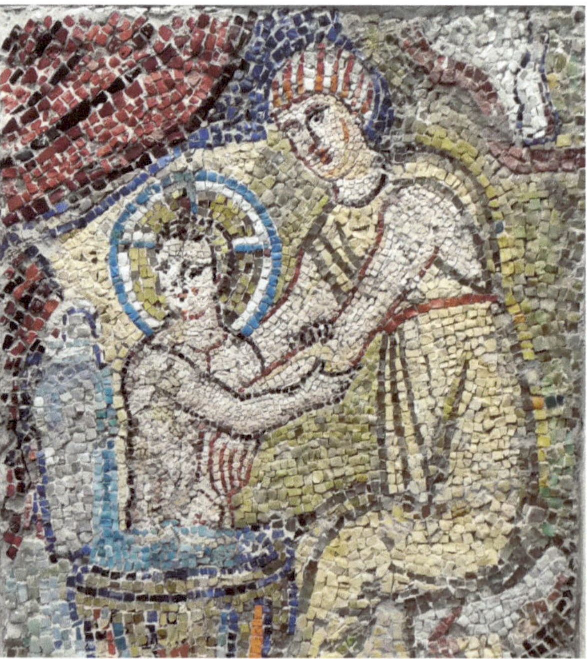

Midwife washing the Christ Child, from the Nativity, formerly oratory of John VII, Vatican Grottoes, 706

Scavi/Necropolis

It is necessary to book in advance to visit here through the Vatican (Excavation Office), and all tours are guided. This extraordinary area was secretly excavated from 1940-50 under the orders of Pope Pius XII (1939-58). The Roman necropolis had just been rediscovered and the intention was to reveal the burial place of Saint Peter. After Peter's martyrdom, he (by tradition), was buried in the cemetery here, along with other Christians and pagans, and in the second century a shrine was set up to mark the spot. Peter's purported remains were transferred elsewhere on the Via Appia for safe keeping in the mid-third century and translated back here at some point, perhaps when the basilica was built.

Apart from the interesting narrative presented in the tour of the finding of Saint Peter's tomb, the mausolea in the necropolis are extensive and well preserved with impressive buildings and second- and third-century paintings.

In the mausoleum M, Julii, which is the only entirely Christian one, dated to the third century, unique mosaics were discovered in the sixteenth century. A lost inscription over the door recorded that the chamber was made by a couple for their son Julius Tarpianus, who died aged one year, nine months and 27 days. The inscription does not have any Christian references and may date to an earlier use of the room. The walls are covered in mosaic with vine leaves and feature a Good Shepherd, Jonah and the sea monster (whale), and a figure interpreted as Christ-Sol (Christ in the guise of a sun god), ascending on a two-horsed chariot. Rather than a halo, light beams radiate from his head and his cloak billows out behind him.

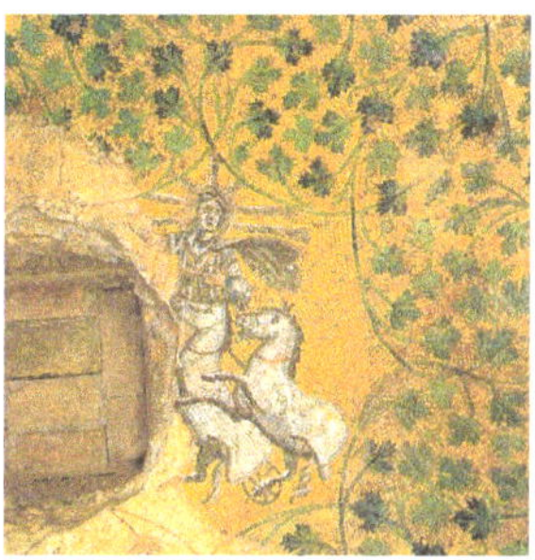

Christ-Sol, Mausoleum M, Julii, Necropolis, Vatican, third century

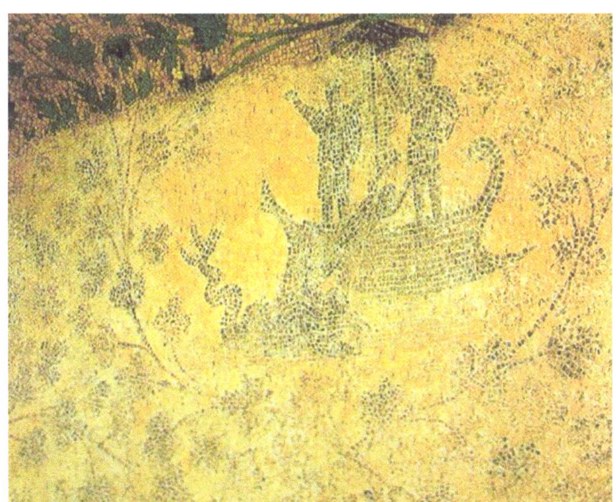

Jonah being thrown into the sea, Mausoleum M, Julii, Necropolis, Vatican, third century

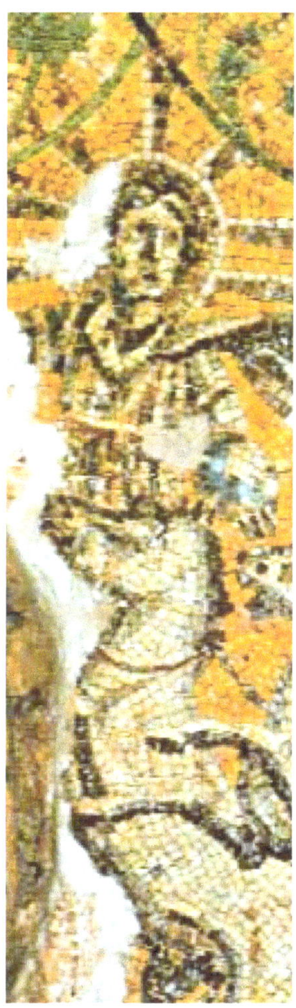

Christ-Sol, detail, of above

Vatican Museums

The museums are housed in the Apostolic Palace, which has been gradually added to since the twelfth century. It is very extensive and the various galleries and chapels have extraordinary collections of early Christian and medieval objects. Seeing them is not necessarily easy, largely because of the crowds on the enforced routes. The itineraries give precedence to the Sistine Chapel. At this time, the route takes you there via the west gallery (either including the Raphael Stanze or not). Two highlights en route are two fourth-century porphyry sarcophagi which may have belonged to Constantia, the daughter of Constantine I (306-37), and to Helena, his mother, situated in the Greek Cross Hall.

After emerging from the Sistine Chapel, you arrive at the Museum of Christian Art housed in a long corridor preceded by the Chapel of Pius V (1566-72). As you enter the Chapel, the case on your immediate left (easy to miss) holds some important reliquaries from the Sancta Sanctorum, the popes' private chapel. These include a, probably sixth-century, box known as the *Sancta Sanctorum reliquary* and the ninth-century *Paschal Cross*. As you proceed down the corridor, the cases contain medieval ivories, with some very fine French Gothic pieces, book covers and metalwork including Limoges enamels. In a room off to the left are the Roman Aldobrandini Wedding paintings and some exquisite Roman miniature mosaics. Proceeding down the corridor towards the exit, various objects from the catacombs include a very fine collection of gold 'sandwich' glass in cases

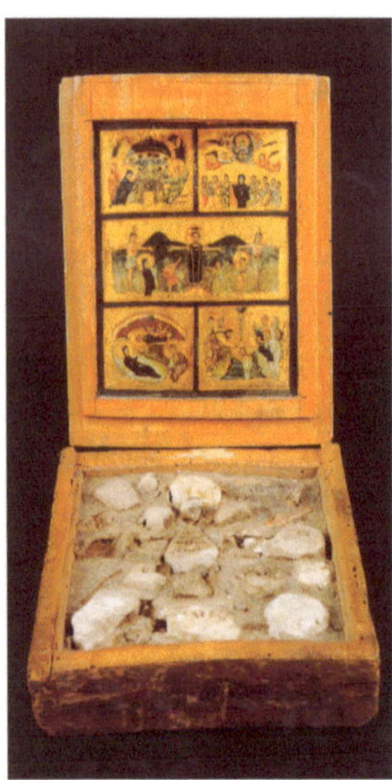

***Sancta Sanctorum Reliquary*, probably from Palestine, Museum of Christian Art, Vatican, sixth century**

This rare box contains stones from the **Holy Land** and the cover depicts the Nativity, Baptism, Crucifixion, the Marys at the Tomb and the Ascension. The scene shown to the right (Marys at the Tomb), probably depicts the ***Anastasis***, the name given to the building over the supposed tomb of Christ in the **Holy Sepulchre Church**, Jerusalem, and so is a useful document of how it looked in the sixth century.

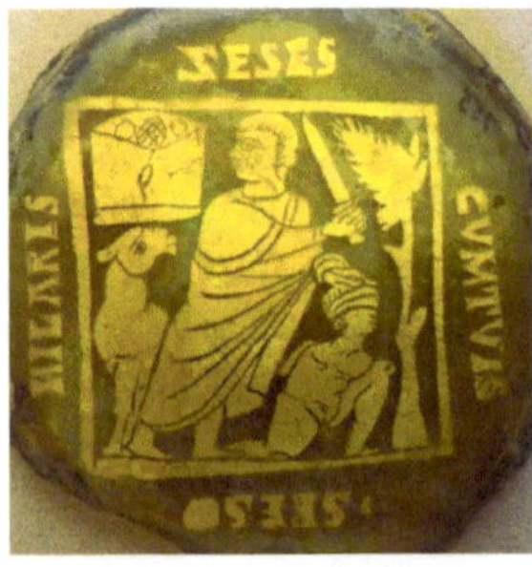

Sacrifice of Abraham, gold glass, Museum of Christian Art, Vatican, fourth century

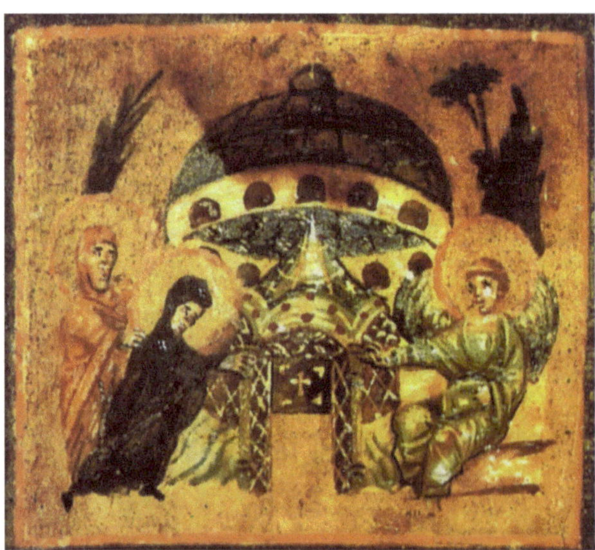

***Sancta Sanctorum Reliquary*, detail of the Women at Christ's Tomb, probably from Palestine, Museum of Christian Art, Vatican, sixth century**

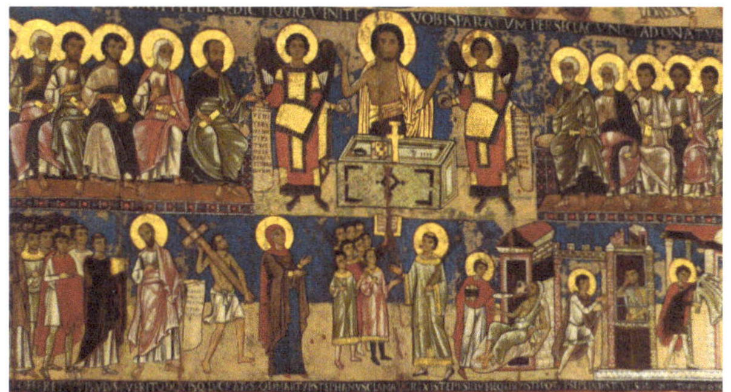

Nicolò and Giovanni, *Last Judgement*, from the Oratory of S. Gregorio Nazianzeno, Rome, Pinacoteca, Vatican, second half of eleventh or twelfth century

on the left side (gold leaf is between two layers of glass). The medallions were formally the bottoms of containers and were used in the catacombs as grave markers. When they are seen in museum collections, they usually have lost their appearance as containers and look like round images. It is thought that the majority of these were made in Rome. They often depict scenes from the Old and New Testaments (often associated with resurrection), but occasionally also show saints or portraits, and they often have inscriptions.

As you are nearly at the end of the itinerary look out for the Pio Christian Museum (entrance on your left), which has a vast collection of Early Christian marble sarcophagi.

You can visit the *Pinacoteca* (picture gallery) either when you arrive or before you leave. It is up some stairs from the open court beyond the Quattro Cancelli The first room has some important early paintings, including an eleventh- or twelfth-century *Last Judgement*, and in the second is Giotto's famous double-sided *Stefaneschi Altarpiece*, which was made for an altar in Old Saint Peter's.

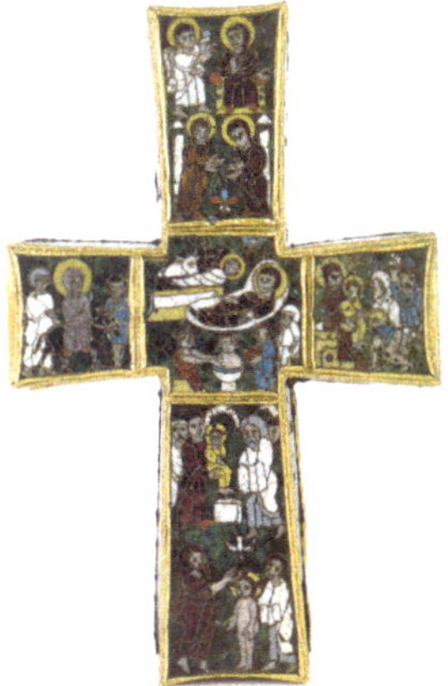

***Paschal Cross*, Museum of Christian Art, Vatican, 817-24**

This box contains fragments of the **True Cross** and was made for Pope Paschal I (see box p. 82). It has scenes from Christ's life up to his Baptism (bottom) and is made from cloisonné enamel.

This is a particularly fine and rare example of this enamel **technique**. The powdered glass is applied in a liquid and laid in between narrow gold strips, which are placed to form barriers between the colours. It is then heated in a kiln and afterwards smoothed and polished. The technique was being perfected at this time.

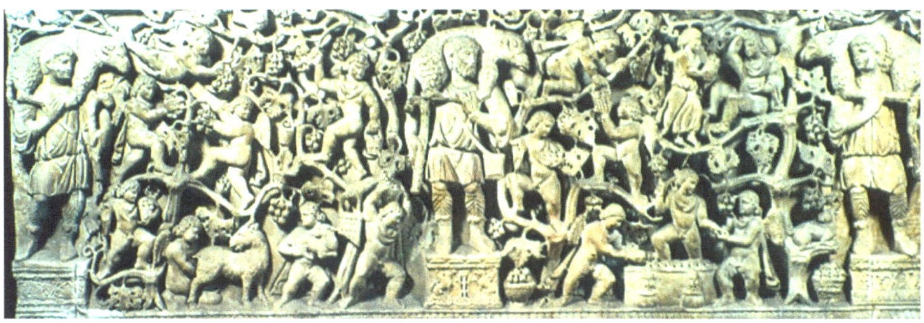

***The Three Shepherds Sarcophagus*, Pio Christian Museum, Vatican, early fourth century**

The figures of the shepherds may represent aspects of the Godhead, perhaps referring to the **Trinity**, God the Father, the Son and the Holy Ghost. Their differing maturity may alternatively refer to the ages of man.

Old Saint Peter's

Old Saint Peter's was commissioned by Constantine I (306-37) and built ca. 324. It used the basic basilical plan employed at the Lateran, which had been already built. But importantly here the plan focused at the west end on a ciborium over the supposed burial place of Peter. There was also a narrow transept (arms to either side of the apse), which would help the circulation of pilgrims. This plan was picked up in later basilical designs.

The basilica also contained other burials and so functioned as a funereal hall and, in the fourth century, funerary banquets following the Roman tradition would be held there. It could contain over a 1000 people at one time.

The atrium was accessed by an impressive flight of thirty-five steps through a *propylaeum*, a formal entryway. The courtyard had over forty columns and a central fountain. Five doors led into the church which had over eighty columns of various marbles, reused from earlier buildings. At the west end, the triumphal arch was decorated with a mosaic showing Constantine presenting the model of the church to Christ.

The focus was the shrine of Saint Peter. The *liber pontificalis* (see p. 82), explains that by request of Silvester, the bishop, Constantine enclosed Peter's coffin in bronze. The account continues:

> And above he set porphyry columns for adornment and other spiral columns which he brought from Greece. He also made a vaulted roof in the basilica, gleaming with polished gold, and over the body of the blessed Peter, above the bronze which enclosed it, he set a cross of purest gold, weighing 150 lbs.

Constantine also offered extremely valuable gifts to the church including 10-feet-high silver gilt brass candlesticks, depicting the acts of the apostles, each weighing 300 pounds, golden chalices decorated with gemstones, jars, pitchers, a golden paten with 215 gemstones and pearls, and a chandelier with 50 dolphins on it.

Subsequent emperors also gave lavish donations to the church. However, it was an enormous edifice to maintain and by the fifteenth century was in a state of disrepair.

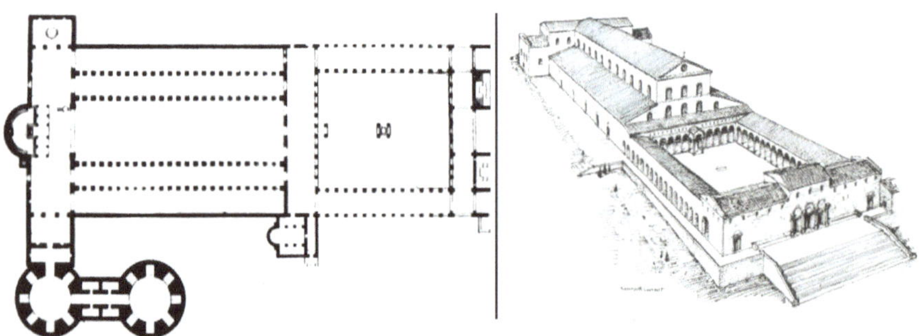

Old St. Peter's plan showing the five aisled basilica with the burial place of Peter at the west end; reconstruction

The round building at the end of the transept is an imperial **mausoleum** built by Honorius at the beginning of the fifth century. The round building next to it is a third-century rotunda dedicated as a church in the sixth century to **S. Andreas**.

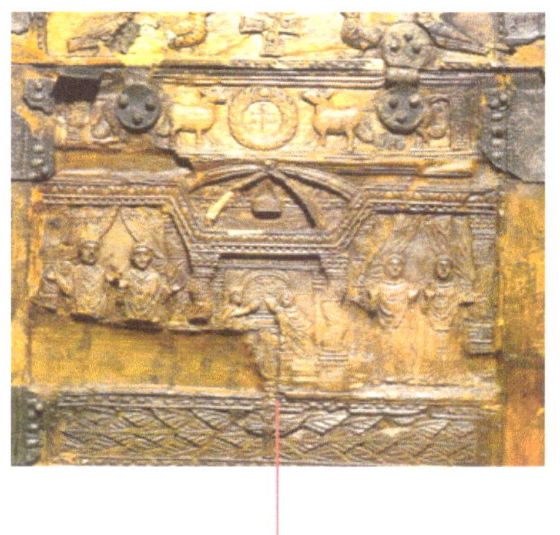

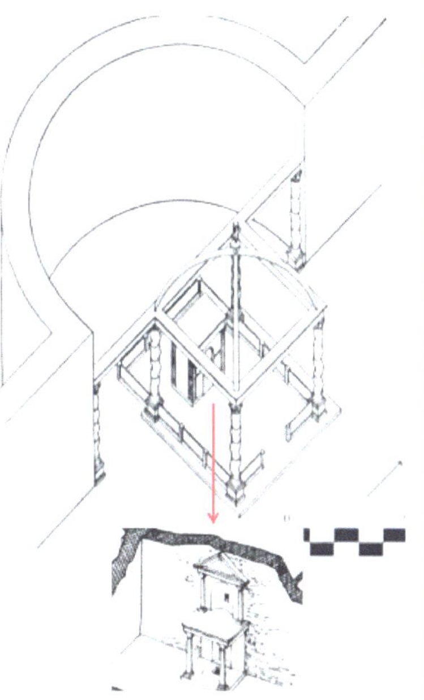

The Pola Casket, ivory, ca. 400, Archaeological Museum, Venice (left);

The *Pola Casket* ivory panel shows two men standing under the ciborium and dangling strings through open doors down to the shrine so that the string becomes sanctified by contact with St. Peter's relics.
The red arrow above and on the right indicates how the string, held under the ciborium would hang down to the shrine.

The fourth-century ciborium within the church (above the shrine) and, below, the shrine of St. Peter, late second century, below floor level.

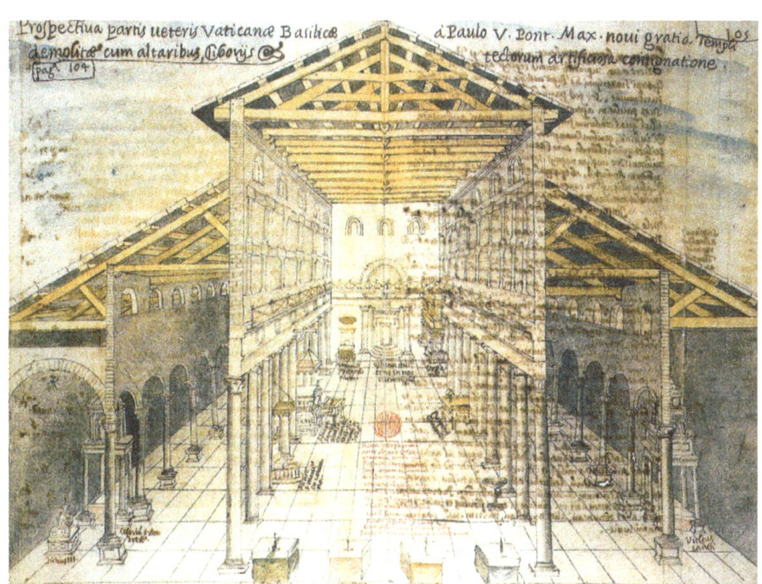

Jacopo Grimaldi, 1619, drawing of the interior of Old St. Peter's as it was in earlier times, Ms. Barbarini Lat. 2733, fols 104v-105r

Tituli and the early communities of Christians

Saints Peter and Paul are, by tradition, said to have been killed during a period of Christian persecution under the emperor Nero (54-68). There is no concrete evidence that Peter was in Rome but Paul's arrival is recorded in the Acts of the Apostles (28.14-15). The earliest Christian communities came from Jewish traditions and they may have kept up some of their Jewish practices in parallel with Christian ones, just as when pagans adopted Christianity, they maintained some pagan traditions, and we know that many (including Constantine I (306-37) were only baptised just before death. The two groups, those from Jewish and from pagan or gentile origins, are depicted in personifications in fourth and fifth century mosaics (see p. 57).

Christians met in houses, not purpose-built rooms, which later took on the name *domus ecclesiae*, where they gathered socially and ritually and took care of the poor. By the third century some were well established and by the fourth, 25 had become a *titulus*, known by the name of the owner, who was responsible for it. Churches were often built on these sites and were associated with early martyrs.

Constantine I (306-37) and the early development of Christian Rome

By the middle of the third century, there were some 100 bishops in central Italy, and it is thought that by then there were perhaps 15-20,00 Christians in Rome. Christianity was established in many key cities throughout the empire, particularly in the east at Jerusalem, Antioch and Ephesus. Constantine I used the administrative structure of the Church to extend and consolidate his rule and incorporated imperial-style dress and practice, such as processions, into Christian ceremony.

At this time he started to build covered cemeteries and major churches outside the city walls. These were areas of green belt, large villas and palaces, many of which were owned by the imperial family. The Lateran was built on the site of the barracks of the imperial horse guard and on land from his wife, Fausta's, family. A church, Santa Croce, the Holy Cross, was built by Constantine's mother on the site of her palace. St. Peter's likewise was built with imperial patronage.

Old and New Testaments and the Apocrypha

The Christian Bible consists of the Old and New Testaments. The former is writings derived from Jewish tradition and include books of law, history, prophesy and poetry. It was translated into Greek from Hebrew in the third century B.C.E. The New Testament contains the four Gospels, the Book of Acts, various letters to Christian communities and the Book of Revelation. These were written in the first two centuries and then compiled. Texts about Christian faith which were considered non-canonical were not included and are known as the Apocrypha. Some of these were very popular and gave rise to imagery illustrating them.

Second Coming

The Second Coming or *Parousia* (arrival in Greek) refers to Christ's reappearance at the end of the age. The theme is developed in Matthew 24 and 25: ' After a period of pestilence, the Son of Man comes in his glory, and all the angels with him, he will sit on his glorious throne' (Matthew 25.31). He then passes judgement, separating 'the sheep and the goats'. It is taken up in the Book of Revelation. Imagery in the early churches, particularly in the apses and triumphal arches, illustrates this subject, and it is evident that Christians were expecting Christ's imminent return.

CHAPTER SEVEN

BEYOND THE CITY

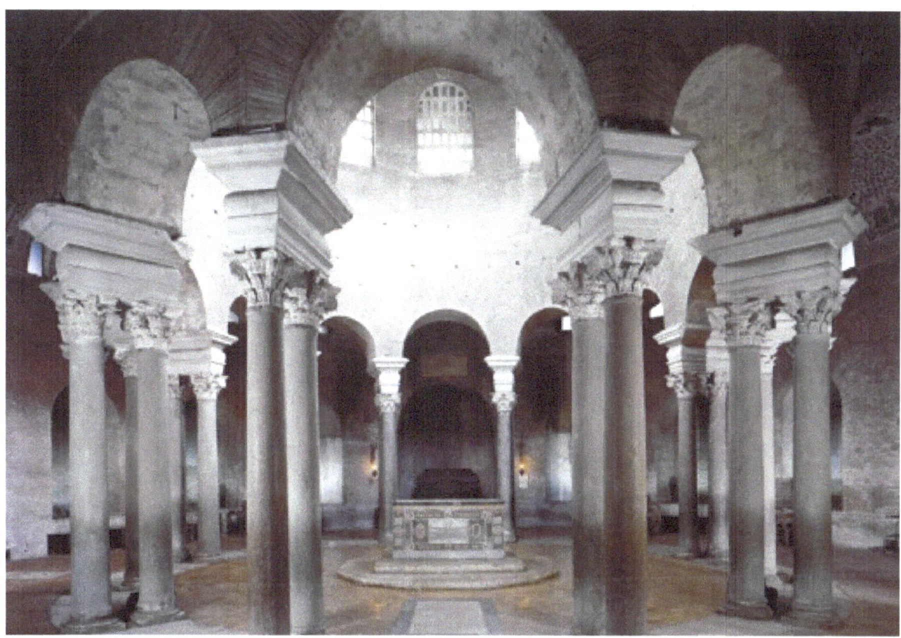

S. Costanza, interior, ca. 350

Sant'Agnese, Santa Costanza, the Catacombs, San Lorenzo fuori le Mura, Santa Croce in Gerusalemme, San Paolo fuori le Mura

Introduction

Roman and subsequently Early Christian burials were outside the city walls along the major thoroughfares, such as the Via Appia and Via Nomentana. Cremation was still practised, but from the time of Hadrian (117-138), it became more common to inhume bodies, particularly for Christians who believed in resurrection. Cult sites grew up at places where the second- and third-century martyrs were thought to have been buried, in catacombs or cemetery halls, and this drew other Christians to be buried in close proximity. Under Constantine I (306-37), large covered cemeteries were established, as at Sant'Agnese, and here his daughter, Constantia (also known as Constantina/Costanza), was probably buried, or in the adjacent specially-built mausoleum. The extensive catacombs, which were used by pagans, Jews and Christians, provided space for great numbers of burials.

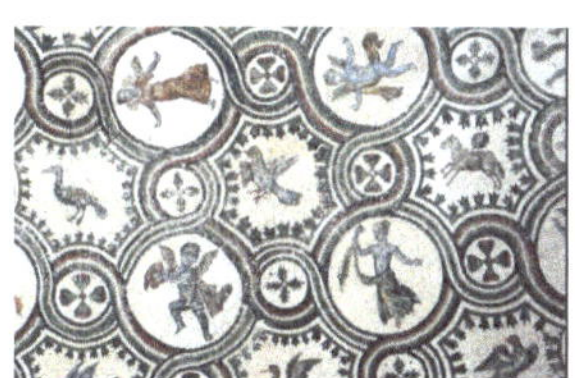

Ambulatory mosaics detail, S. Costanza, ca. 350

These mosaics in the vault of what is probably an imperial **mausoleum** are rich in pattern and not unlike many late antique floor mosaics in the Mediterranean world. They were presumably made by the same craftsmen who were working on secular buildings.

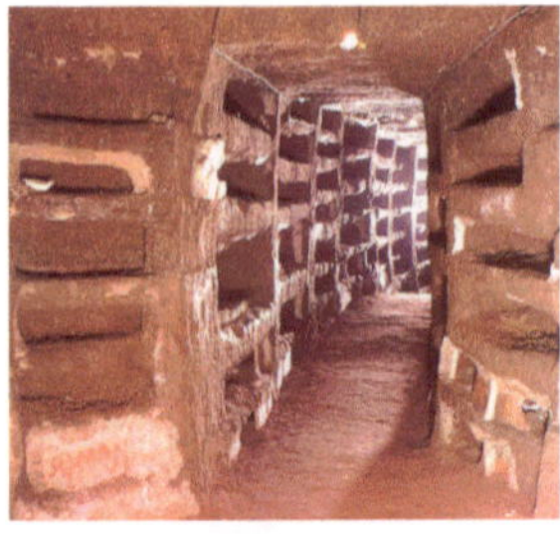

***Loculi* in the sides of a catacomb passage**

Bodies were wrapped in cloth and laid on these shelves, often with other bodies. The *loculus* (recess) was **sealed** with bricks or stone panels, sometimes with inscriptions or symbolic decorations.

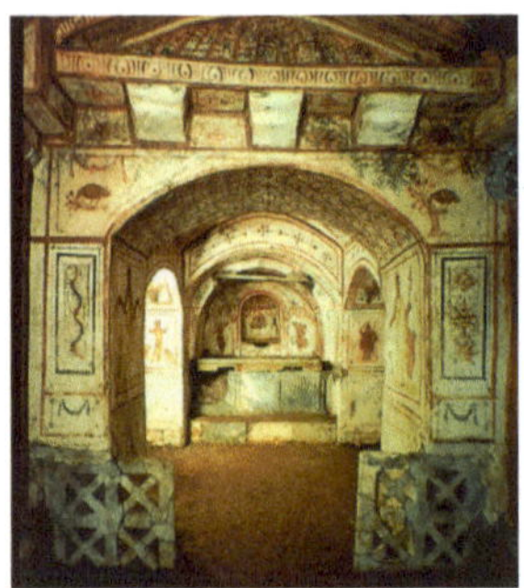

Cubiculum, Via Latina Catacomb, fourth century

Sarcophagi were used for the burials of people who could afford them and were placed in ***cubicula*** (excavated rooms with paintings). The space at the far end, like a large curved niche is called the ***arcosolium***. It contained the burial.

It seems as though pagan and Christian burials shared spaces in the catacombs as paintings from both beliefs occur together.

Following Roman tradition, feasts would be held near the burials to celebrate the dead. These would be conducted in light from lamps or candles and must have been very atmospheric.

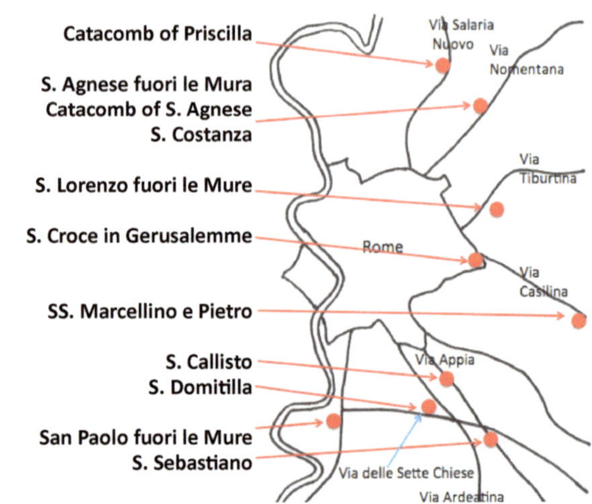

Map indicating the sites discussed in this chapter

Itineraries

The catacombs currently open to the public are San Callisto, San Sebastiano, Domitilla, Sant'Agnese, Priscilla, and Santi Marcellino e Pietro, although they may be closed for certain months/days, especially in winter, and the latter (with an imperial mausoleum) may not be accessible. It is possible to visit a few in one day. Sant'Agnese is beneath Sant'Agnese fuori le Mura basilica and adjacent to the remains of the Sant'Agnese funerary hall and the Mausoleum of Santa Costanza on the Via Nomentana, which in turn is not too far from the Catacomb of Priscilla on the Via Salaria Nuova, so they make a good group to visit together. The catacombs of San Callisto, San Sebastiano and Domitilla are similarly adjacent, situated in the Via Appia area. They can be very crowded. Santi Marcellino e Pietro is on the Via Casilina (the old Via Labicana) also to the southeast of the city. Two of the three large basilicas, San Lorenzo and Santa Croce are fairly near the Lateran, while San Paolo is closer to the southern catacombs. They will be approached in this order here in a brief survey intended to give a taste of what may be on view.

Sant'Agnese funerary hall

Arriving at the site, walk towards the Mausoleum of Santa Costanza. On your right is a vast area, walled, with a curved apse at the far end. This is the area built, probably, in the time of Constantine I (306-37) as a covered cemetery. It is typical of early funerary basilicas, where funerary banquets would be held and a mass held annually on the anniversary of the saint to whom it was dedicated. Saint Peter's originally had this function. It has been suggested that Constantia, Constantine's daughter, who died in 354, was buried, not in the Mausoleum of Santa Costanza, but in an apsed structure in the middle of the nave.

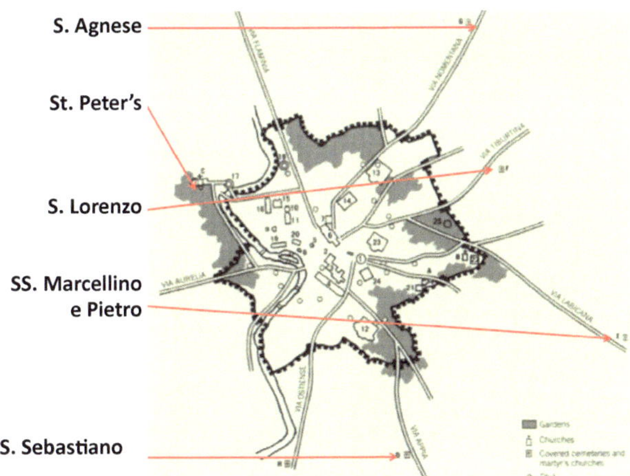

Rome of Constantine, ca. 330, Covered cemeteries and martyrs' churches, adapted from R. Krautheimer

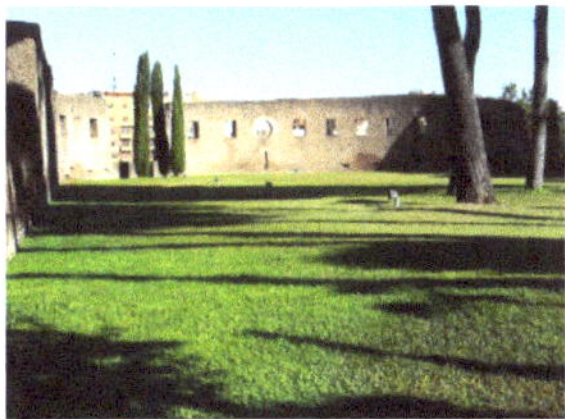

Remains of covered cemetery, Sant'Agnese, fourth century

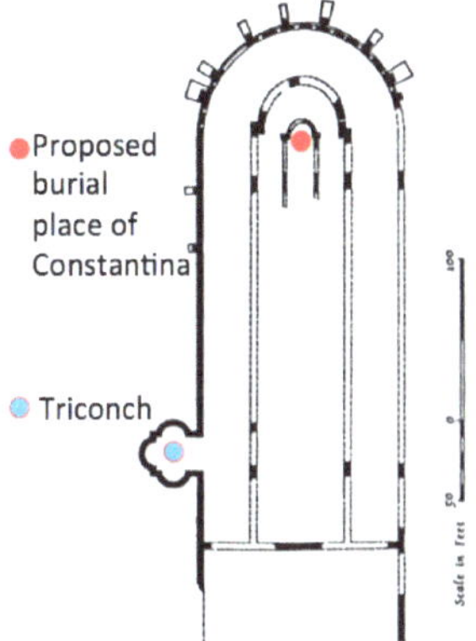

Plan of covered cemetery, Sant'Agnese, fourth century, after David J. Stanley

It has been suggested that Constantia was buried in this building.

The triconch (three-apsed building) shown on the plan (right), which has been excavated but is not visible and lies under the wall of Santa Costanza, may have been either a martyrium to honour Sant'Agnese or a baptistery. The *Liber Pontificalis* records that Constantia and her sister Helena were baptised at this location and the triconch appears to have been built at the same time as the funerary hall.

Santa Costanza

The large round building know as the Mausoleum of Santa Costanza is controversial in terms of its date and function and even if it was originally a pagan or a Christian building. It has, because of its circular form, been thought to be a baptistery, but the commonly-held view is that Constantine's daughter, Constantia, was buried here in 354. She was married to Gallus (351-4), the co-emperor in the East. Her sister, Helena, was married to Gallus' half brother, Julian (355-60), known as Julian the Apostate, since he held pagan beliefs. Helena died in 360 or 361. The remaining fourth-century decoration is not ostensibly Christian, so it has been suggested that Julian built it for his wife and, perhaps, also for his sister-in-law. However, mosaics in the dome (destroyed in 1620), which are known from seventeenth-century watercolours, have been interpreted as containing Old and New Testament themes. Of course, these could have been added later (and they have been dated by style to the 360-380s), after the short period of pagan resurgence.

The mosaics line the barrel vault of the circular ambulatory that surrounds the central dome supported by twelve antique reused columns. The building would originally have had marble sheets covering the walls and mosaics on the curved areas in the ambulatory and dome.

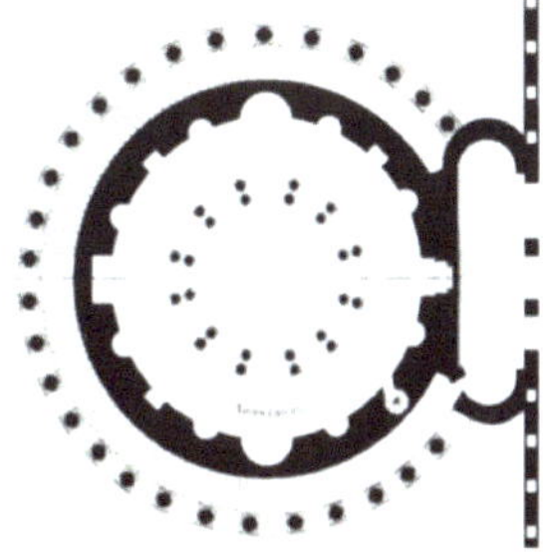

Plan of S. Costanza, mid-fourth century

The oval space to the right provides a narthex or entryway. The circular form has a wide vaulted **ambulatory** (walkway) with niches inset into the outer wall and is surmounted by a large dome.

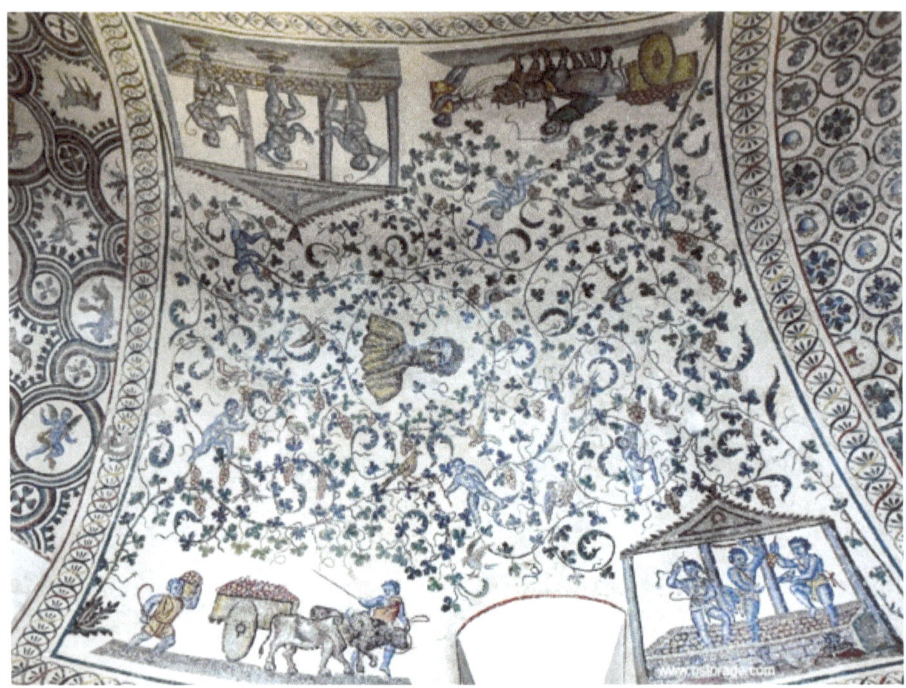

Ambulatory mosaics depicting the grape harvest, S. Costanza, ca. 350

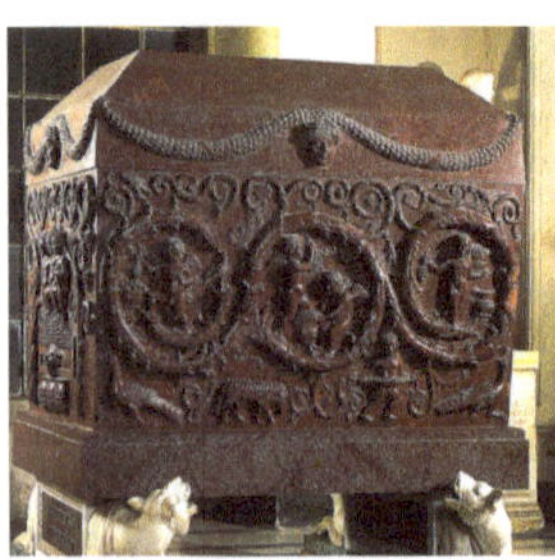

Porphyry sarcophagus with vine scroll and erotes, ca. 350

The sarcophagus, now in the Vatican (see p. 66), came from S. Costanza and, by tradition, was used by **Constantia**, Constantine I's daughter. It is decorated with acanthus scrolls and grape vines, garlands, lambs and *putti* busy at the grape harvest. **Porphyry** marble, dark red in colour and highly sought after, came from Egypt and was used for imperial sarcophagi and statuary.

The ambulatory vault mosaics survive, decorated in twelve sections with two sets of each design. Some are purely geometrical, others have roundels containing erotes and animals, full length and bust figures (not identifiable) as well as flora. Others have boys (looking like erotes or cupids) cultivating vines, goading oxen pulling carts full of grapes and pressing the grapes. The reference to wine may be associated with Christ as the true vine, or to the wine of the Eucharist, but there is no firm evidence that this association was made here. At this early period in Christian history, it seems that much of the imagery of the pagan past was comfortably adopted, even if the patrons were Christian.

There are also two later, probably seventh-century, and heavily restored mosaics in two niches, showing the *Traditio Legis* and *Traditio Clavium*, Christ giving the Law to Peter and Paul, and the Keys to Peter.

Catacomb of Sant'Agnese

This is accessed through the basilica of Sant'Agnese just to the left as you enter the church. It has three parts, one to the left of the basilica, one beyond the location of the apse, and one towards the mausoleum of Santa Costanza. They date respectively from the second to the fifth centuries. There are no paintings but many inscriptions.

Sant'Agnese fuori le Mura

The present church was built by Pope Honorius I (625-38) on the site of two earlier churches, the first dating from about 400. It marked the burial of Saint Agnes, who was killed by tradition at about the age of twelve, through a dagger in her throat. This took place ca. 304 during the Diocletian persecutions.

The great staircase (seventeenth-century) to the right as you enter is lined with various inscriptions from the catacombs. Much of the church has been altered, but the mosaic in the apse is a rare example of seventh-century work and shows Pope Honorius on the left presenting a model of the church to Agnes, in the centre, with a coronet and dressed in an elaborate jewelled garment, with Pope Symmachus (498-514), who restored the church prior to Honorius, on the right.

The extensive catacomb is below the church, entered from the north aisle. There are no paintings.

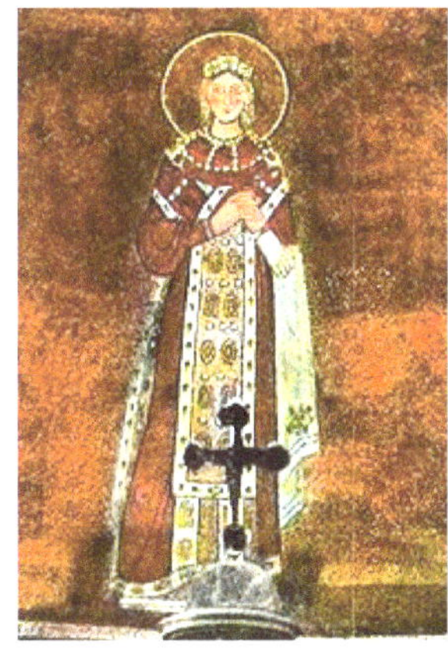

St. Agnes, apse, S. Agnese fuori le Mura, 625-38

Catacomb of Priscilla

This is a delightful place to visit, run by Benedictine nuns. A tour is provided of the upper of three levels, some of which is dated to the second century C.E. It was originally a private foundation, probably paid for by a woman named Priscilla Acilii, a member of a senatorial family.

In one of the vaults of the galleries it has a painting of a woman holding an infant, thought to be the Virgin and Child, with perhaps the Prophet Balaam or Isaiah to the left. The mother and child is a universal image and so the interpretation is hard to confirm.

The *Capella Greca* has exceptional paintings. There are various scenes from the Old and New Testaments. Look up to the first arch spanning the room for the Adoration of the Magi. An important image is of a group of seven eating together, including a woman (third from the right). Early Christians met to share meals in memory of Christ's last supper with his disciples, and the painting is interpreted as a group of Christians doing so.

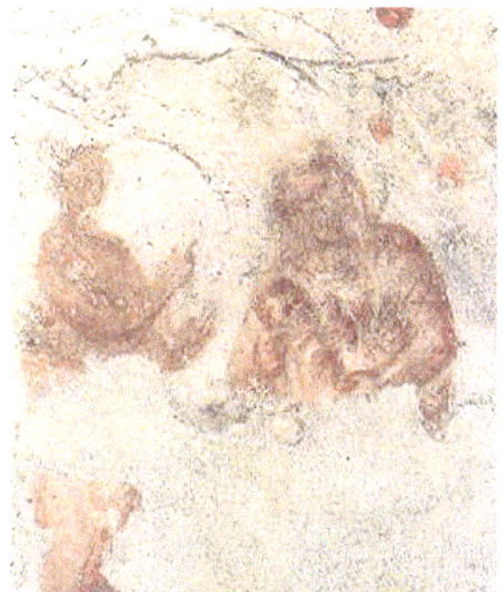

Possible representation of the Virgin and Child, Catacomb of Priscilla, third century

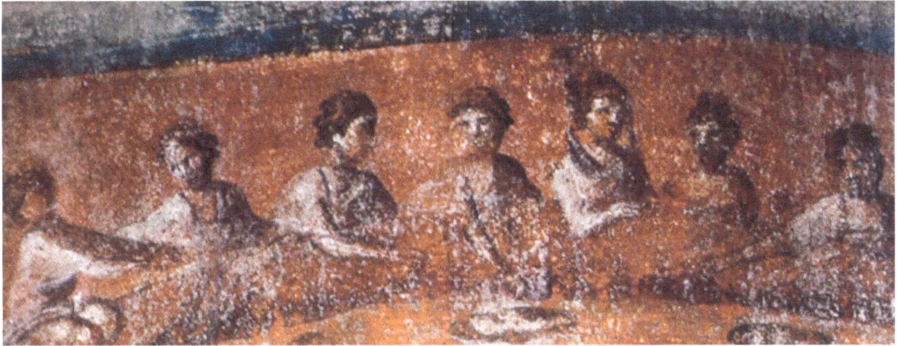

***Fractio Panis* (breaking bread), Catacomb of Priscilla, third century**

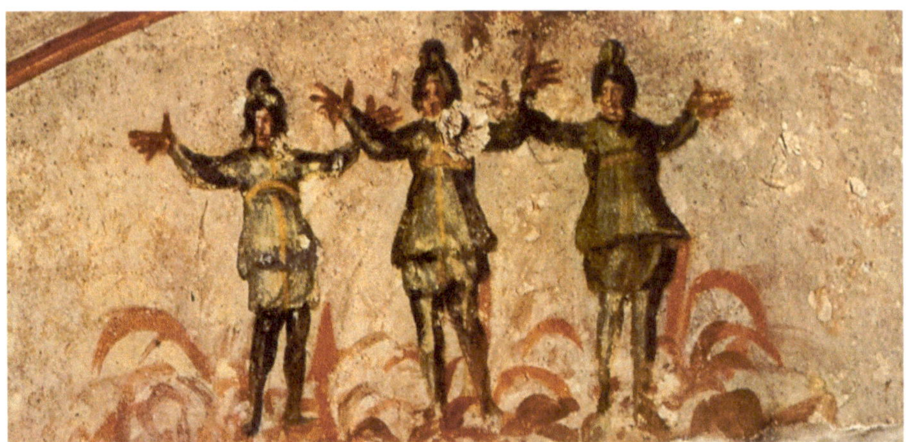

Three Hebrews in the Fiery Furnace, Catacomb of Priscilla, late third century

The rooms in the catacombs are mostly painted on plaster, often in **fresco** technique. They are necessarily made with speed and in little light, using oil **lamps** for illumination. The only daylight coming in was the occasional shaft to ground level but these are only in the upper areas, and many of the catacombs are several levels deep. The paintings reflect this rapid production, made with fast, fleeting brush strokes and a limited palette.

The choice of scenes is limited in scope, often with images from **biblical narratives**, traditional **Roman mythology**, or **portraits** of the deceased and their families as well as symbolic motifs.

The biblical iconography is also often repetitive with popular scenes associated with **resurrection**, such as the story of Jonah, Daniel in the Lions' Den, and the Hebrews in the Fiery Furnace appearing often. Other New Testament scenes associated with funerary banquets, such as the 'Fractio Panis' are also frequently found, as well as the reassuring image of **Christ as a shepherd** to lead and protect his flock.

In the Cubiculum of the Velata a woman is depicted in prayer as well as a Good Shepherd and the Three Hebrews in the Furnace.

Catacomb of San Callisto

When Callixtus I (217-22) became pope, he extended this, the earliest of the official cemeteries, and nine of his successors in the third century were buried here. Here also was buried Santa Cecilia, before her remains were moved by Paschal I (see p. 82). It was discovered in 1849 by Giovanni Battista de Rossi (1822-1894), who did extensive archaeological excavating and interpretation of Rome's catacombs. It is large, with over ten kilometres of corridors and rooms.

It has many paintings including, in the Cubiculum of the Sacraments, the Raising of Lazarus and the Miracle of the Loaves and Fishes and, in the Crypt of Lucina, Christ as the Good Shepherd.

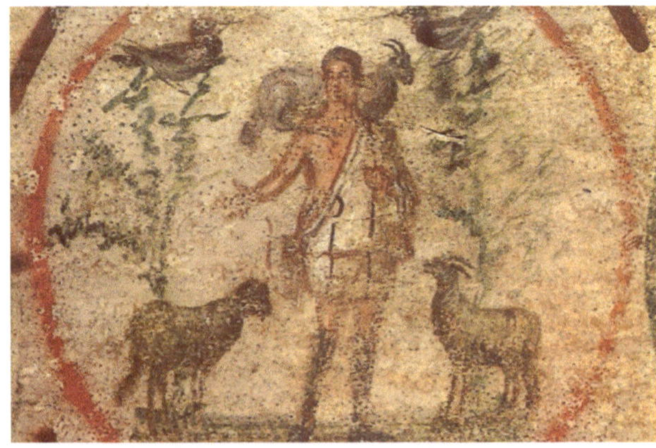

Good Shepherd, Catacomb of S. Callisto, third century

Catacomb of San Sebastiano

Originally the site of a stone quarry and later of villas and mausolea, this became a *memoria* to Saints Peter and Paul. It had a courtyard with stairs to a spring, and a small apsed building with columns at its entrance. In the fourth century a covered cemetery was built here, known as the *Basilica Apostolorum*. From the ninth century it has been dedicated to Saint Sebastian, a third-century martyr, and was it was rebuilt in 1612. There are remarkable pagan Roman tombs and the catacombs are extensive.

Catacomb of Domitilla

This is one of the oldest catacombs. It is named after a first-century Christian, Domitilla, who was the niece of Domitian's sister. It has very early paintings including ones of flowers and a Good Shepherd and a later one interpreted to be Christ surrounded by his apostles. The church is dedicated to Domitilla's two servants, Santi Nereo e Achilleo.

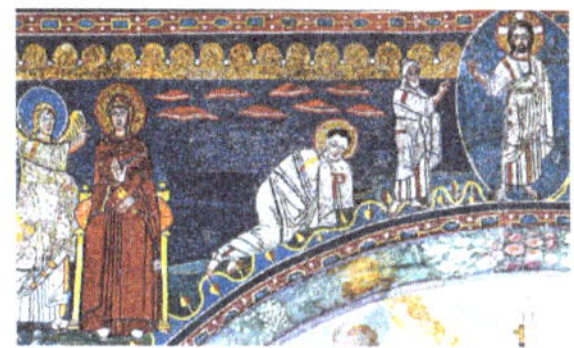

Annunciation and Transfiguration, arch, SS. Nereo e Achilleo, ca. 816

This church was rebuilt under Leo III (795-816). Above is the left half of the triumphal arch. To the right is the remaining part of the Transfiguration and the Virgin and Child presented by an angel.

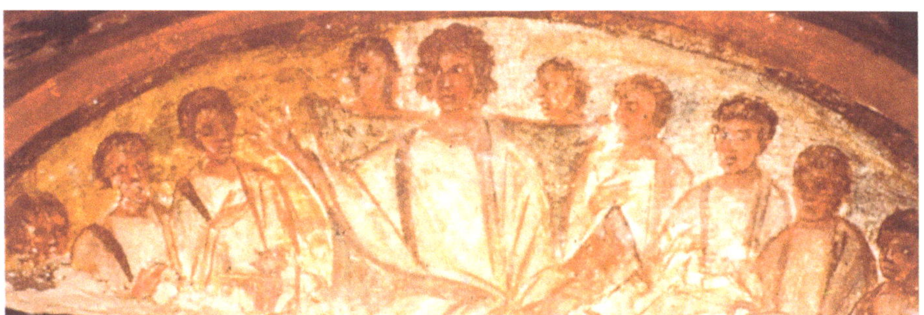

Christ and his disciples or a teacher with his students, Catacomb of Domitilla, fourth century

The traditional Roman toga is draped around the body and worn over a long loose tunic, with narrow sleeves and a black or purple bands, called *clavi* attached at the shoulders. It is known as the *tunica talaris.*

Interpretation and Dating of Catacomb Paintings

Much has been written about the function and interpretation of catacombs and their paintings. Burial in catacombs was the common practice among pagans, Jews and Christians. The style and some of the motifs in the paintings are similar and it is most likely that the same decorators were working in catacombs of various faiths.

It is often hard to determine precisely the iconography of early Christian paintings as so many of the traditional subjects and ways of depicting gods, leaders, followers, miracle workers and so on were adapted from those used in antiquity. Equally, scenes from the Old Testament, such as the story of Jonah, may have been used in Jewish settings (though none survive in Rome).

Equally, the dating is normally determined on stylistic grounds, or occasionally on what is known about the development of iconography, but as there is so little Christian imagery to survive from the third century, and perhaps none from the second, it is hard to make good comparisons. Most very early imagery comes from funerary settings, in part because it has survived being buried underground but it may also have been the most popular context for the creation of imagery.

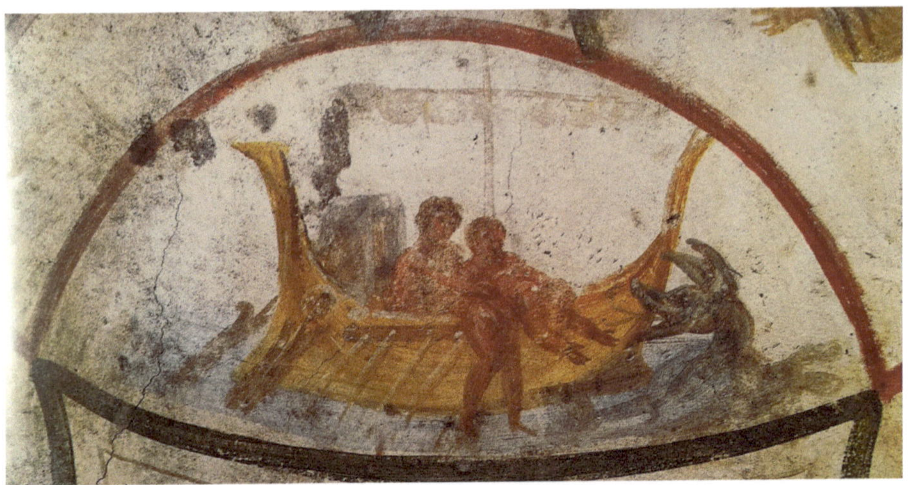

Jonah being thrown into the sea, Catacomb of Santi Marcellino e Pietro, mid third century

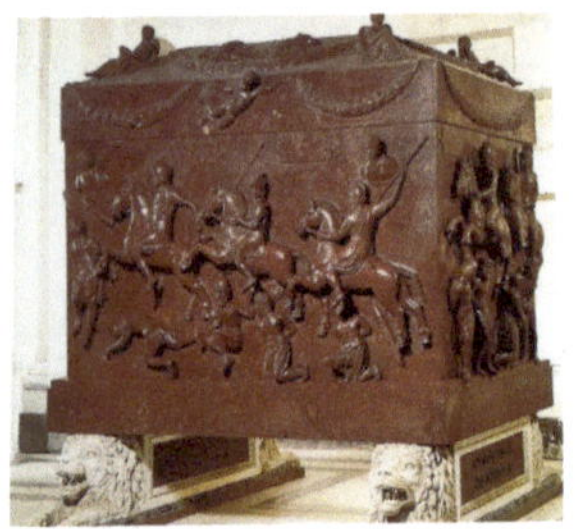

Sarcophagus of Helena, Vatican, early fourth century

This very fine sarcophagus is made from **porphyry** marble and has military scenes which have led scholars to suggest it was made for **Constantine**. He was buried instead in Constantinople in a mausoleum he built called the Holy Apostles in, probably, a relatively plain porphyry sarcophagus.

Catacomb of Santi Marcellino e Pietro

This is on the site of an imperial villa owned by Helena, Constantine's mother, and has the remains of her mausoleum. It has been suggested that the mausoleum was originally built for Constantine I (306-37), who also built a massive funerary hall. The sarcophagus, now in the Vatican, was perhaps also intended for Constantine (see left). There are many paintings, including a ceiling with scenes from the life of Jonah and a Good Shepherd.

Jewish Catacombs

Of the several Jewish catacombs in Rome, two may be open to the public. The fascinating paintings, mostly of Jewish symbols and religious implements, at the Villa Torlonia, set on the Via Nomentana, are from the third and fourth centuries. The catacombs at Vigna Randanini, on Via Appia Pignatelli, are beautifully decorated in a late antique style with birds, animals, and mythical beings. They were used from the second to fifth centuries.

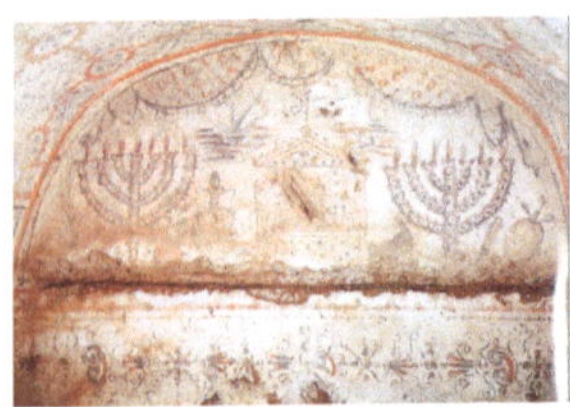

Menorahs and Ark of the Covenant, Villa Torlonia Catacomb, third century C.E.

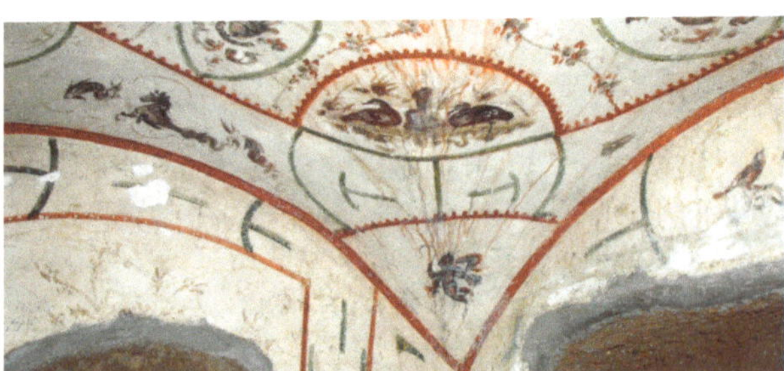

Birds, sea monster and *putti*, Vigna Randanini Catacomb, third century

San Lorenzo fuori le Mura

Located on the Via Tiburtina, this could be visited with the Priscilla catacomb and Sant'Agnese.

History

Saint Lawrence, one of Rome's seven deacons, and one of its most celebrated saints, was martyred in 258 by being roasted on a gridiron. He was buried in the catacomb on this site, owned by a Christian woman named Cyriaca. Constantine I (306-37) built an adjacent funerary hall (covered cemetery) with steps leading to the burial where he erected an apsed shrine. This was followed by several additions until in the sixth century a new church was built under Pope Pelagius II (579-90), constructed so that Lawrence's tomb was in the nave. Many alterations were made, principally in the thirteenth and nineteenth centuries. In the former, an enlarged nave and aisles were added by Pope Honorius III (1216-27) to the west of the early church, which then became the chancel.

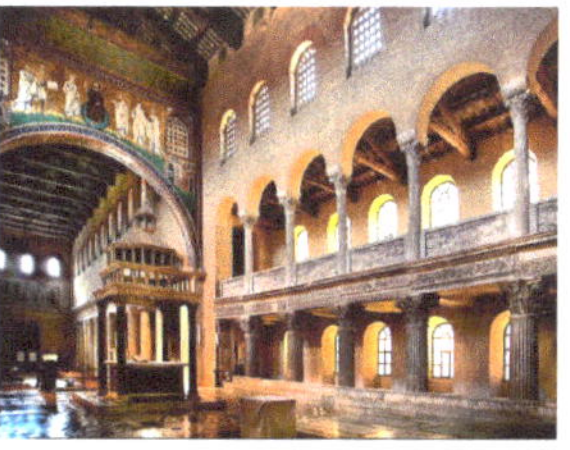

The sixth-century galleried nave, facing west with the thirteenth-century church beyond, San Lorenzo

The trabeated nave, with a horizontal entablature over columns, has an upper gallery and clerestory allowing light into the building, a feature of Byzantine churches of the time.

Interior

The relation of the various parts of the church are not immediately evident. On entering you are in the thirteenth-century nave. Note the paschal candlestick in the south aisle (on the right). Moving down the nave towards the east, steps lead down to the sixth century building, with the tomb of Saint Lawrence in the centre, and the sixth-century mosaic in the triumphal arch to the west. The narthex of the early church is at the east, adjacent to the twelfth-century cloister (which has early fragments). The Catacomb lies to the north with an entrance in the left aisle of the early church.

Before entering the sixth-century part (now the chancel), enter the Shrine of the Unknown Martyr, with frescoes from (probably) the time of John VII (705-7) showing *Maria Regina* (see p. 20), and from the ninth century, showing the Virgin and Child with angel, flanked by Saints Lawrence, Andrew, John the Evangelist and Catherine. The sixth-century building has twenty-four *pavonzetto* (fine variegated marble) columns (twelve on the ground floor, twelve in the gallery) erected with architectural *spolia*. Turn back the way you have come to see the sixth-century triumphal arch, very restored.

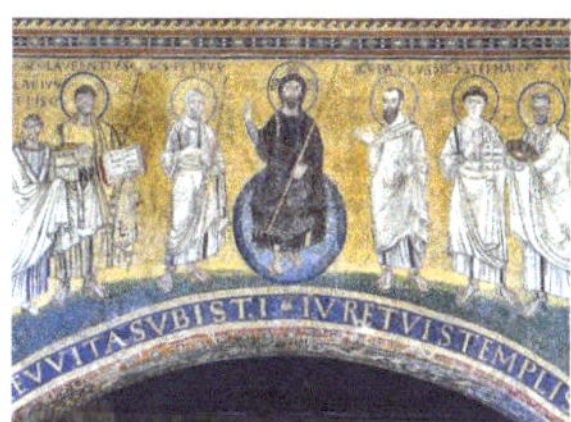

Christ and Saints, triumphal arch, S. Lorenzo, 579-90, heavily restored

Christ sits on a globe representing his realm. He is flanked on the left by Saint Peter, **Pope Pelagius** holding a model of the church and **Saint Lawrence** and on the right by Saints Paul, Hyppolitus and Stephen. The **inscription** reads, 'You once submitted, deacon, to martyrdom by flames; the sublime light duly returns to your sanctuary'.

The Patriarchal Basilicas

In Rome, five basilicas, all built in the fourth century, are ceremoniously assigned to the leaders of the Roman and the four eastern churches. They are San Giovanni in Laterano, assigned to the pope (the bishop of Rome), San Pietro (Saint Peter's), assigned to the patriarch of Constantinople, Santa Maria Maggiore, to the patriarch of Antioch, San Paolo fuori le Mura, to the patriarch of Alexandria, and San Lorenzo fuori le Mura, to the patriarch of Jerusalem.

Santa Croce in Gerusalemme

This rebuilt early church is a 20-minute walk from San Lorenzo. It can also be visited with the Lateran, which is a 12-minute or so walk away.

History

The church is sited on the Sessorian Palace, owned by Constantine I's (306-37) mother, Helena (c. 246/50-c. 330). By tradition, she built it after her pilgrimage to the Holy Land in 326-8 when she was about 80 years old. There is no evidence for the long-held tradition that she found there the cross on which Christ died, to which the church is dedicated. The church was built in one of the great halls of the palace and on the exterior, beyond the apse are remains of the palace.

It was rebuilt in the twelfth century under Pope Lucius II (1144-5) and again in the eighteenth, hence its high baroque appearance, but various parts of the early church can be seen.

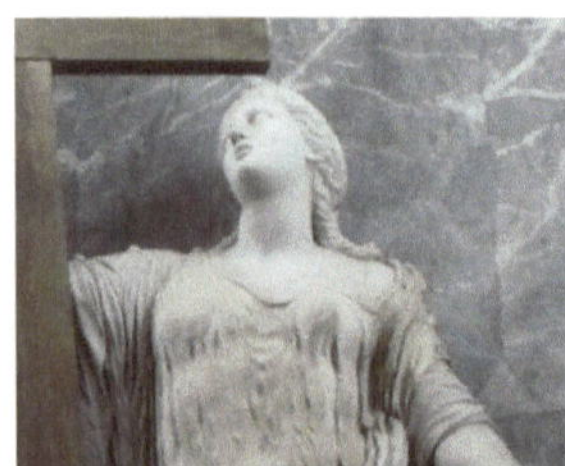

S. Helena, recut Roman statue, S. Croce

Chapel of Saint Helena

A key attraction here is the Chapel of Saint Helena, which is beyond the apse, reached via the left aisle. This is part of the original palace and church. By tradition the floor lay on soil brought from Jerusalem. Galla Placidia (regent 423-37)) was responsible for the mosaic in the vault, which is now represented by a fifteenth-century copy by Melozzo da Forlì (1480) (later restored). By the altar is a statue of Helena, adapted from one of Juno from Ostia.

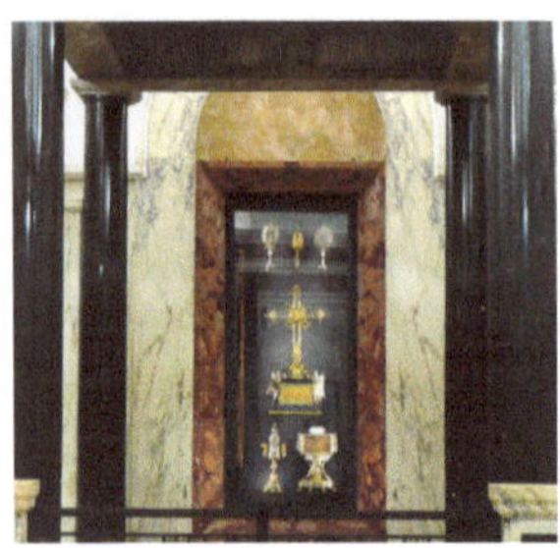

Relics in the Chapel of the Relics, S. Croce

The large collection of relics include the **True Cross**, a nail from the cross, two thorns from the crown of thorns and St. Thomas' index finger, a testament to the immense power held by relics in the early and medieval Church. The present austere setting perhaps minimises their cult value.

Chapel of the Relics

At the end of the north aisle is a long chamber (1930) that houses the extensive collection of relics.

San Paolo fuori le Mura

History

This church was burned down in 1823. Now rebuilt, it reflects the original design but with few original elements and appears rather sterile. A church was first built here by Constantine I (306-37) or by his sons, and a larger one was erected under Theodosius I (379-95) and Honorius (395-423), sited on the burial place of Saint Paul. It was altered considerably before its destruction. The supposed site of Saint Paul's burial and a first-century shrine with a second-century trophy (a niche or shrine commemorating a burial) were discovered in 1838.

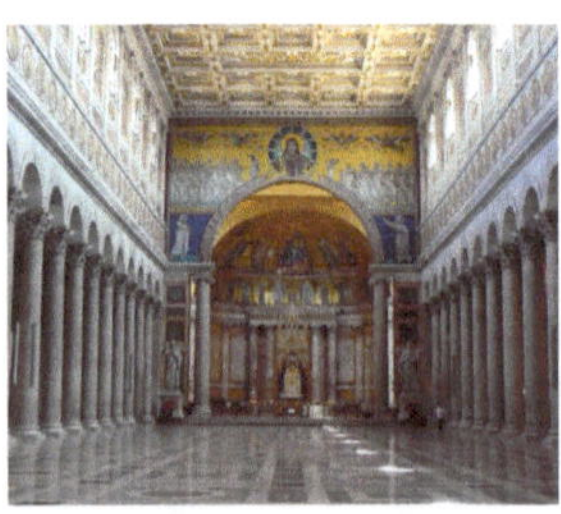

Nave, facing east, S. Paolo fuori le Mura, fifth century, rebuilt after 1823

Still evident is the vast size of this basilica, although the richness of its original decoration is partially lost.

Decoration

The present portico is nineteenth century but uses the original columns, of which the second column from the right on the inner row has a dedicatory inscription from Pope Siricius

(384-99). The second set of doors from the right came from Constantinople in 1070, given by a merchant named Pantaleone. They are made of bronze with images inlaid in silver and enamel (view from the inside).

The triumphal arch mosaic (heavily restored) was presented by Galla Placidia (regent 423-37) in 440, under Leo I (440-61). It shows Christ and the *tetramorph* (symbols of the evangelists), with the twenty-four elders of the Apocalypse. The dedicatory inscriptions refer to Galla and to Leo. This image was greatly influential on subsequent mosaic decorative plans in Rome which very often picture the End of Days and the Second Coming of Christ.

On the other side of this arch are damaged mosaics by Pietro Cavallini. The apse mosaic dates to the thirteenth century under Pope Honorius III (1216-1227) and, made by Venetian craftsmen, shows Christ (with Honorius at this feet) above the instruments of the Passion with Saints Peter, Paul, Andrew and Luke.

The high altar is above Saint Paul's shrine and, beneath a grill (ask to see) are two marble plaques from the fourth century naming Paul. The paschal candlestick to the right of the altar was made by Pietro Vassalletto (fl. 1154 – 1186), and the very fine baldachino over the altar is by Arnolfo di Cambio (1285).

The Lapidary Museum and the Library (which holds the celebrated Bible of San Paolo fuori le Mura presented to Charles the Bald in 870-75), are not open to the public but they may be possible to access: ask at the monastery.

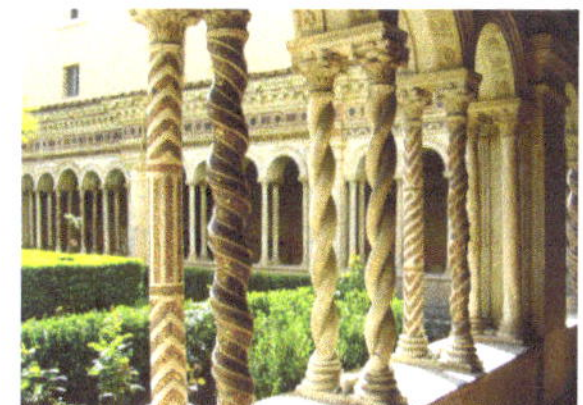

Cloister, S. Paolo fuori le Mura, 1208-35)

The cloister was sculpted by the Vassalletti family (who also worked on the Lateran cloister). It holds various Early Christian fragments.

The Chapel of the Reliquaries on its north side has various relics, including a set of chains said to be the prison chains of St. Paul and a fourteenth-century chalice.

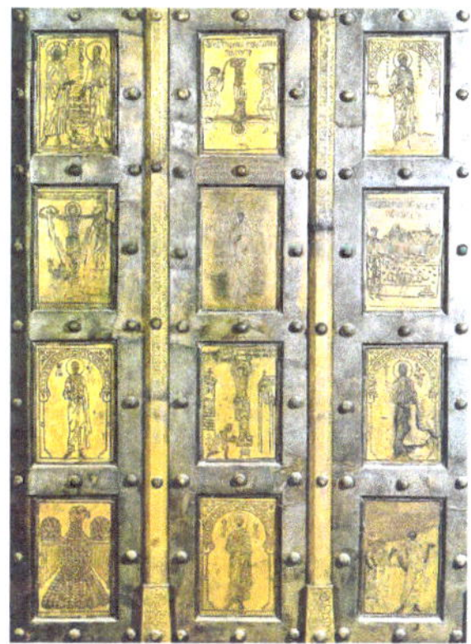

Bronze doors, lower left section, San Paolo fuori le Mura, 1070

The door from **Constantinople** has four groups of panels. One has twelve of the main feasts marking events in Christ's life; the others have twelve prophets, twelve apostles (including Paul who is shown with the donor **Pantaleone**), and twelve martyrdoms of the apostles. Additional panels make a total of 54. An inscription explains Pantaleone's intention in giving the doors: he hopes the door of life is opened to him so he can be close to God, as Paul is.

The Jubilee and the Pilgrimage of the Seven Churches

The pilgrim route of the seven churches was established by Pope Boniface VIII (1294-1303) for the Jubilee in 1300. In addition to the five papal basilicas (see box p. 79), it included San Sebastiano and Santa Croce in Gerusalemmme.

Byzantine Bronze Doors

We know of eight sets of bronze doors that were bought by Italian patrons to donate to churches in the eleventh and twelfth centuries. The doors were made in Constantinople or perhaps by workshops imitating work from the capital. It is surmised that the doors represent the Doors of Paradise. Two of the earliest, those at Amalfi (ca. 1060) and at San Paolo fuori le Mura (1070) were given by the same patron. The others were made for Monte Cassino (1087), Monte Sant'Angleo (1076), Atrani (1087), Venice (two: 1080, ca. 1112) and Salerno (first half twelfth century).

Byzantine artists, Iconoclasm and the influence of Byzantine Art

There were several Byzantine monasteries in Rome which housed Greek monks from the sixth to the twelfth centuries. Greek foundations were particularly important during periods of Iconoclasm, when the imperial authorities in the east banned the use of figural imagery, and they became a refuge for Greek monks. The Byzantine monasteries must have employed eastern artists, and they influenced various aspects of Roman life in terms of religious practice and art.

Examples of the monasteries that were in place from the early period, the sixth or seventh centuries, are Santa Maria in Schola Graeca (later Santa Maria in Cosmedin), San Giorgio in Velabro, and San Saba, which housed monks from near Jerusalem fleeing Islamic rule. They were decorated by Byzantine artists who we know travelled widely. For instance, they are recorded as going to Damascus to work on the Great Mosque built there by Umayyad caliph, al-Walid I (705–715), which was commissioned in 706.

The first period of Iconoclasm ran from 726 to 787. In 815 the Byzantine emperor, Leo V (813-25), reintroduced a period of Iconoclasm after just a short break and again banned the use of images in religious practice. As a result Byzantine monks and artists came to the west. The *Liber Pontificalis* (see below) records that a Greek congregation of monks sang the Greek psalmody at Santa Prassede, where Paschal I (817-24) had given them refuge. There is no evidence that the artists were Greek but it is likely. In the *Liber Pontificalis* are descriptions of the myriad of silks, including veils (to cover special objects), hangings (to hang between the columns), altar-fronts, and decorated ecclesiastical garments. The terms used to describe the techniques are Greek suggesting they either were made in the east or at the Greek monasteries in Rome.

In the second half of the eleventh century, there was a further spread of the influence of Byzantine painting connected with the Benedictine Abbey at Monte Cassino (about 80 miles from Rome). Abbot Desiderius sent to Constantinople for mosaicists to decorate the church he was rebuilding and had his monks trained in their skills. The style and techniques then spread to Rome, to elsewhere in Italy and beyond. The paintings in the lower church at San Clemente, dated to the end of the eleventh century, are probably by secular artists but also show the influence of Byzantine styles and, in some of the paintings, Byzantine style dress.

Liber pontificalis

This text, written in Latin and translated as the *Book of Pontifs*, records the biographies of the bishops of Rome. It is thought that the early part was first written in ca. 530 and reworked in the 540s. It was then left for some years and perhaps under Honorius I (625-38) taken up again. From that point the accounts are more or less contemporary with the popes. In the early lives much of the text addresses the various gifts of precious objects made to the churches.

Paschal I (817-24)

Paschal I was pope for a short period, but built three important churches in Rome, Santa Cecilia, Santa Maria in Domnica and Santa Prassede. They are all decorated with a similar style and iconography using mosaics. These may have been made by artists from Constantinople or at least from the Byzantine empire in the east. Paschal was a Roman and had worked caring for pilgrims. Iconoclasm (see above) had been revived in the east in 814, and shortly after, when Paschal became pope, he arranged for Greek monks fleeing from Byzantium to be housed at monasteries such as at Santa Prassede and Santa Cecilia. This period is often referred to as a 'renaissance', a flourishing of the arts, which began under Leo III (795-816).

CHAPTER EIGHT

FURTHER MUSEUMS

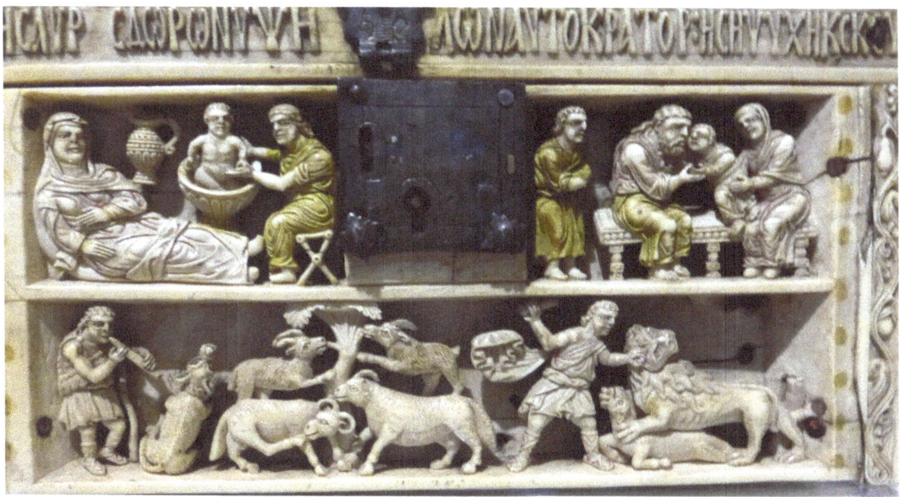

Byzantine ivory casket with scenes of the Life of David, 898/900, Museo nazionale del Palazzo di Venezia

Museo nazionale del Palazzo di Venezia, Crypta Balbi, Museo dell' Alto Medioevo

Introduction

The museums and galleries of Rome are extraordinarily rich in their antiquities and art from the Etruscan, Roman and post-medieval periods, particularly renaissance and baroque. These are world-famous and so flooded with visitors. On the other hand, the collections with Early Christian and medieval objects are rarely visited and poorly promoted. In the centre of the city, the Museo nazionale del Palazzo di Venezia, on Via del Plebiscito, and the Crypta Balbi, on Via delle Botteghe Oscure, are often quiet and create peaceful havens. Further afield, the Museo dell' alto Medioevo is in EUR, a Mussolini era enclave in the suburbs, itself interesting to see and not hard to get to, has an excellent display of late antique *opus sectile* work and other very interesting material.

Two other museums that have a little late antique material are the Museo nazionale Romano, Palazzo Massimo alle Terme and the Capitoline Museums (this also has a thirteenth-century sculpture of Charles I of Anjou).

The ivory box above shows scenes from the **life of King David**. The image in the top left of his birth is based on representations of the Nativity of Christ or of his mother, Mary, and the scene to the right, known as the *kolakeia*, is taken from the **apocryphal life of the Virgin** when the small child is fondled by her parents Joachim and Anna.

In the lower register David is playing a pipe for the animals and then slaying a lion.

The ivory shows signs of having been painted. There is controversy about how extensively ivory was **painted** in the medieval period, but it was probably often gilded and highlighted with brilliant colours. You can see the staining of the ivory on certain figures and in the patterns on the border.

Museo nazionale del Palazzo di Venezia

This museum, in an impressive fifteenth-century palace, mainly houses paintings and wooden sculpture as well as porcelain and bronzes from the renaissance on. It does however have a few important medieval objects, which are somewhat tucked away. Some material may not be on view or be rearranged.

A gallery on the regions of Lazio, Umbria and Marche has a thirteenth-century Head of Christ by a Roman artist who was influenced by Pietro Cavallini, a Roman crucifix originally at Santa Maria in Aracoeli and another crucifix from the early fourteenth century said to be by the Master of Saint Claire who worked in Assisi. There are three important early wooden sculptures. The oldest, colourfully painted and known as the Virgin of Acuto, could be as early as late twelfth century.

The gallery on Venetian material has several important paintings including the *Sterbini Diptych*, an altarpiece dated just after 1317, which shows the influence of the Sienese painter Duccio di Buoninsegna who adopted the iconography and style of painting from Byzantine works.

The most prized Byzantine object is a rare ivory casket, carved with stories from the life of King David and, on the top, Christ blessing an emperor and empress, signifying a wedding, probably that of Leo VI (886-912) and his third wife, Eudokia. There is also a fine tenth-century Byzantine triptych (the panels would originally have been hinged together), with Christ flanked by John the Baptist and the Virgin in the centre top register surrounded by various standing saints. The large probably Italian copper and enamel in Byzantine style of Christ is very distinctive, although somewhat damaged.

Virgin of Acuto, wood and polychromy, Museo di Palazzo di Venezia, late twelfth century,

This very fine example of medieval **woodwork** has been repainted.

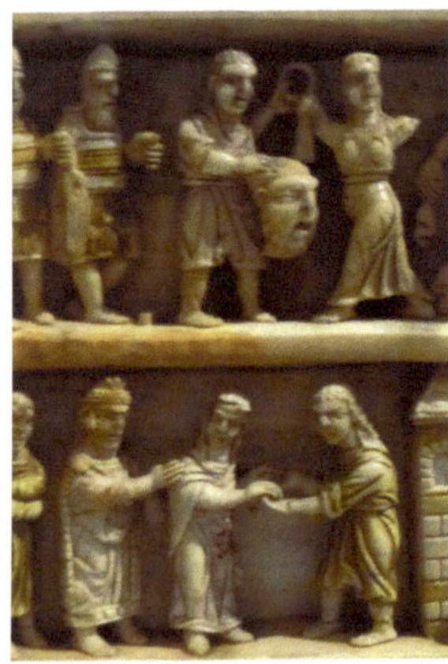

Byzantine ivory casket, David with the head of Goliath, Museo nazionale del Palazzo di Venezia,898/900

David was a popular biblical King emulated by **Byzantine emperors**. This box has unusual depictions of his life.

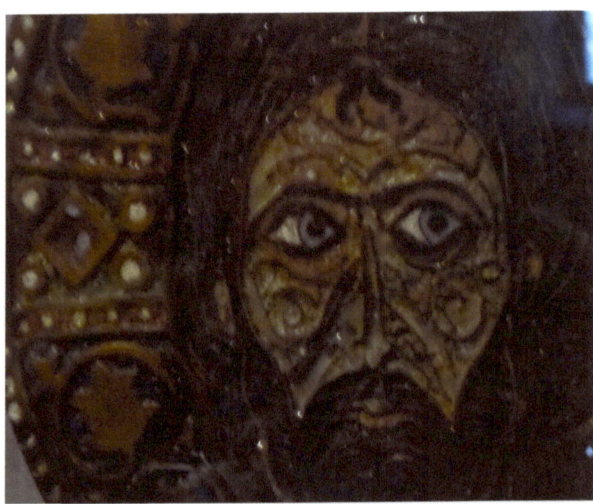

Italian (?) copper and cloisonné and champlevé enamel, Museo nazionale del Palazzo di Venezia, thirteenth century (?)

Crypta Balbi

This wonderfully displayed museum is only a five-minute walk from the Palazzo di Venezia. It is on the site of a Roman theatre (built by someone called Balbus) and a crypta (a large square building attached to the back of the stage) with later remains of a medieval church and monastery, which have all been excavated.

The ground floor rooms trace the history of the area from Roman times to the present using excellent maps and information. The medieval section shows objects from the monastery of San Lorenzo in Pallacinis, which was restored in the eighth century, and the church of Santa Maria domine Rose, as well as some ceramics.

The next floor has material from the fifth to tenth centuries, arranged thematically with engaging historical information. There are interesting everyday objects, seals, jewellery and lamps, coins and pilgrim *ampullae* (small bottles). There is good information on individual popes discussing their patronage and affiliations, using reproductions of mosaics and paintings in the city as illustrations, as well as various fragments from buildings and a very fine reconstructed eighth-century bishop's throne made in bone. An interesting section with excellent plans illustrates the eleven pilgrim routes across the city described in the Einsiedeln Itinerary, a ninth-century pilgrim guide.

Frescoes from the seventh to ninth centuries are rare, but displayed here are some from the church of Santa Maria in Via Lata on the Corso with scenes from the story of the Seven Sleepers of Ephesus and the Life of Saint Erasmus.

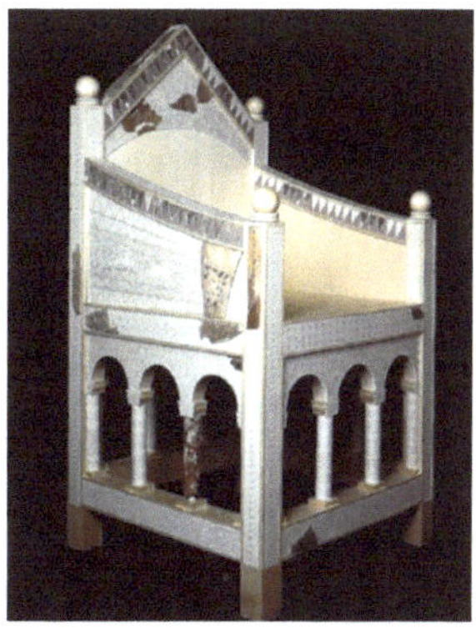

Bishop's throne, wood and bone, reconstructed, Crypta Balbi, eighth century

The area by the Crypta Balbi is thought to have been a centre for bone and ivory carving by the second half of the seventh century, and the workshop was perhaps in the monastery of **San Lorenzo in Pallacinis**. The throne may have been made locally. The bone is incised with delicate designs, including leaping antelope-like animals, and set onto a wooden core. The lower part between the legs is designed like a columned arcade.

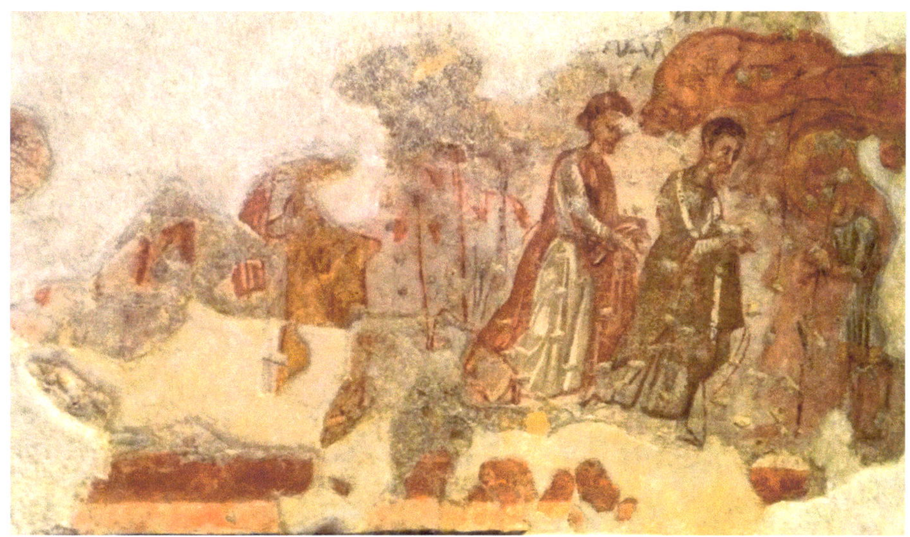

The first of the Seven Sleepers of Ephesus meeting the bishop of Ephesus and an imperial official, from Santa Maria in Via Lata, Crypta Balbi, seventh century

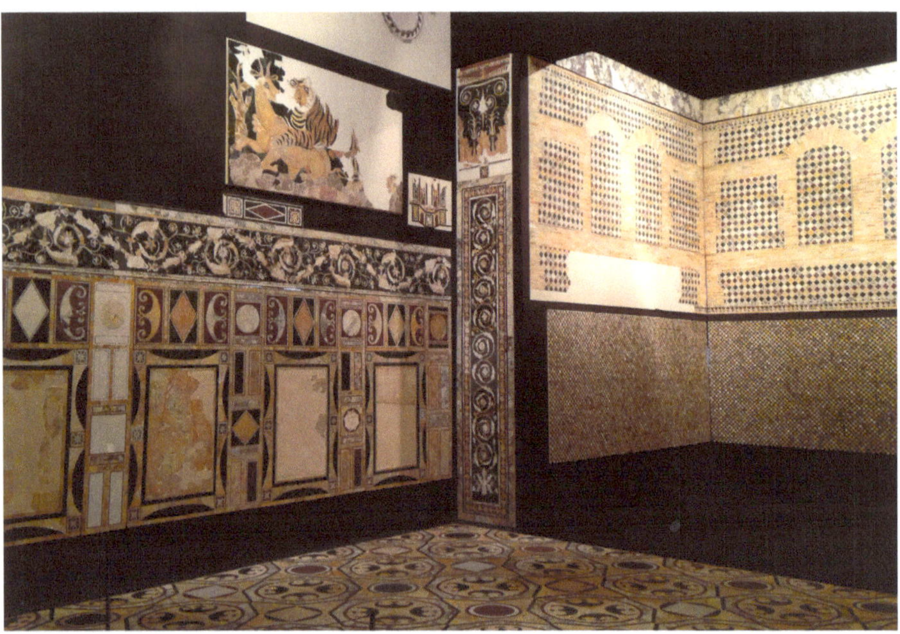

***Opus Sectile* hall from *domus* Porta Marina, Ostia, Museo Nazionale dell'Alto Medioevo, 383-8**

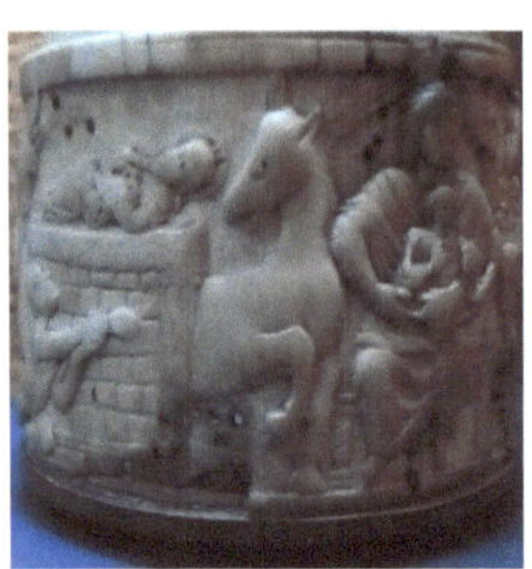

Ivory pyxis, Carolingian, Trier?, Museo nazionale dell'Alto Medioevo, after an early Christian model, eighth to ninth century

The scene shown here is the **Nativity** and includes an unusual feature which fell out of use about this time. The woman on the left holding her arm up is Salome, who, according to an apocryphal story, accompanied the midwife who was called to Christ's birth. She was healed from a withered hand as she touched Christ's crib.

Museo nazionale dell'Alto Medioevo

This is another under-recognised museum with some very fine material. It can be easily reached via EUR Fermi metro station. EUR was begun under Mussolini in the 1930s as a tribute to fascism. The museum dates to 1967 and holds fourth- to ninth-century ivories, metalwork, coins and jewellery, with some luxury Lombardic items, such as a gold sword hilt and a silver horse harness.

The highlight is the extraordinary *opus sectile* floor and wall

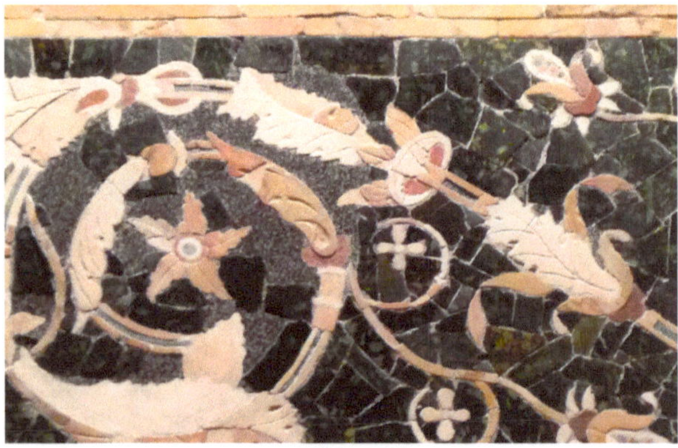

Acanthus scroll from *domus* Porta Marina, Ostia, *opus sectile*, Museo nazionale dell'Alto Medioevo, 383-8

decorations from a fourth-century house in Ostia, known as the *domus* Porta Marina. It was situated on the waterfront and began to be built in 384-5, known by a coin found in the mortar. It collapsed due to an earthquake in 392 just a few years later and at that time had not been completed. It was left buried until rediscovered in 1959.

The surviving room is an *aula* (a hallway) with a rectangular *exedra* (a recess). The floor has a geometric pattern in coloured stone, including *giallo antico*, serpentine, red porphyry and *pavonazzetto*. The walls have a panelled dado at ground level with an acanthus scroll frieze and above are fragments of scenes with wild animals, lions and a tiger, attacking a hart. There are thirteen types of stone used.

On the wall to your right (the west wall) is an image of a bearded man blessing, which has been interpreted as Christ, although there are no other distinctive references to Christianity. It is argued by Giovanni Becatti, who excavated the site, that it was the meeting-room of an Ostian group who had converted to Christianity. However, this is controversial, and it is often the case in this early period that pagan and Christian imagery could be used in various contexts.

Fragments of related stunning *opus sectile* work from the Basilica of Junius Bassus, located near Santa Maria Maggiore, are housed at the Museo nazionale Romano, Palazzo Massimo alle Terme and in the Capitoline Museums. Junius Annius Bassus was consul in 331 and the father of the owner of the famous sarcophagus (see p. 63). The fragments shows a charioteer, perhaps Junius himself, riding a biga (two horsed chariot), a scene from the myth of Hylas (Herakles' companion) abducted by the Nymphs (with very fine Egyptian figures in the border) and two scenes of tigers attacking their prey.

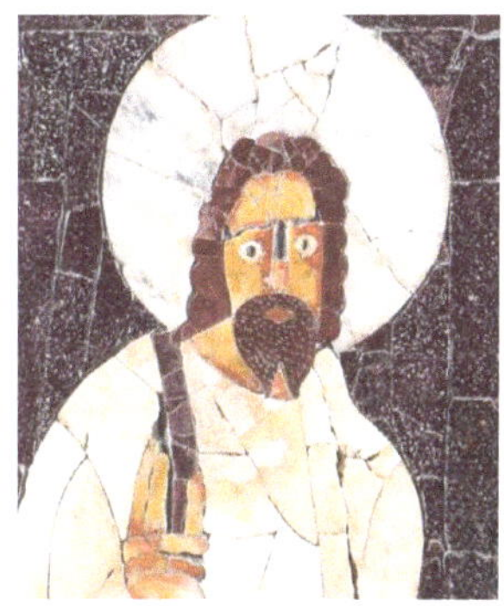

Male figure (Christ?) from *domus* Porta Marina, Ostia, *opus sectile*, Museo nazionale dell'Alto Medioevo, 383-8

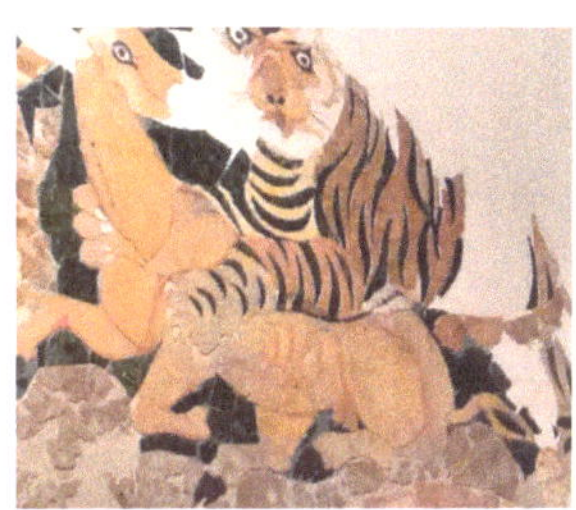

Attacking tiger from *domus* Porta Marina, Ostia, *opus sectile*, Museo nazionale dell'Alto Medioevo, 383-8

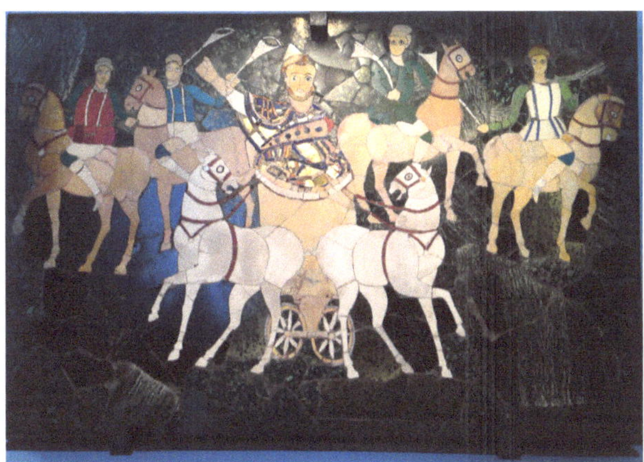

Charioteer, *opus sectile*, Museo nazionale Romano, Palazzo Massimo alle Terme, mid fourth century

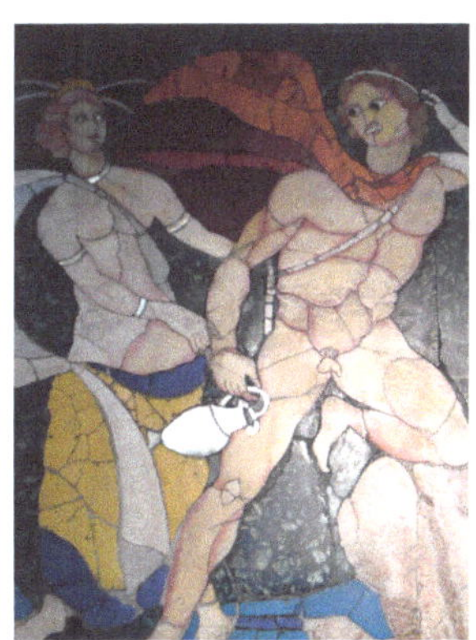

The Abduction of Hylas, detail, *opus sectile*, Museo nazionale Romano, Palazzo Massimo alle Terme, mid fourth century

SITES IN ROME IN ORDER OF DATE

These dates largely do not include the earliest foundations, but the date of the main part of the building now visible. Many of the dates are disputed. c.=century.		Papal Patrons if known
First c.	St Peter's Necropolis/*Scavi* (and later)	
Second c.	Various catacombs (and later)	
314-18	San Giovanni in Laterano (rebuilt 1646-90)	Sylvester (314-35)
324	Old St Peter's (rebuilt 1506-1626)	Sylvester (314-35)
ca. 330?	Santa Croce in Gerusalemme	
ca. 354	Santa Costanza	
Fourth c.	Casa Romane del Celio (fourth to twelfth c. paintings)	
379-423	San Paolo fuori le Mura, rebuilt after 1823	
390	Santa Pudenziana (apse mosaic from then survives)	Siricius (384-99)
425-32	Santa Sabina	
432-40	The Lateran Baptistery (original 314-18, mosaics fifth to seventy century)	Sixtus III (432-40)
432-7	Santa Maria Maggiore (triumphal arch and nave mosaic from then survives plus mosaic facade ca. 1288-97, mosaic apse ca. 1291-6)	Sixtus III (432-40)
432	Santa Sabina (doors and opus sectile survive)	Sixtus III (432-40)
468-83	Santo Stefano Rotondo (mosaics seventh c.)	Simplicius (468-83)
526	Santi Cosma e Damiano (apse mosaic survives)	Felix IV (526-30)
Sixth c.	Santa Maria Antiqua (paintings sixth to eighth c.)	Various but especially John VII (705-7)
Sixth c.	San Teodoro (apse mosaic survives)	
579-90	San Lorenzo fuori le Mura, rebuilt 1216-27	Pelagius II (579-90) Honorius III (1216-27)
609	Pantheon (consecrated as church)	Boniface IV (608-15)
625-38	Sant'Agnese fuori le Mura	Honorius I (625-38)
Seventh c.	San Saba (paintings eighth to fourteenth c.)	
Seventh c.	San Giorgio in Velabro (paintings ca. 1290)	
731-41	San Crisogono (site earlier, lower church paintings, twelfth c. rebuilding)	Gregory III (731-41)
757-67	Santa Maria Nova	Paul I (757-67)
772	San Giovanni a Porta Latina (rebuilt), (paintings 1191)	Hadrian I (772-95) Celestine III (1191-8)
772-95	Santa Maria in Cosmedin	Hadrian I (772-95)
796	Santa Susanna (some painting survives)	Leo III (795-816)
816	Santi Nereo e Achilleo	Leo III (795-816)
817-24	Santa Prassede and San Zeno chapel (mosaic)	Paschal I (817-24)
817-24	Santa Cecilia (original mosaic, paintings ca. 1290)	Paschal I (817-24)
817-24	Santa Maria in Domnica (original mosaic)	Paschal I (817-24)
827-44	San Marco (original apse mosaic)	Gregory IV (827-44)
1108	San Clemente (with paintings from seventh-eleventh	Paschal II (1099-1118)

	c. in lower church and Roman mithraeum)	
1110	Santi Quattro Coronati (paintings)	Paschal II (1099-1118)
1099-1118	Santi Giovanni e Paolo (paintings 1255)	Paschal II (1099-1118)
1138-43	Santa Maria in Trastevere (apse mosaics 1138 and ca. 1291)	Innocent II (1130-43)
1222-3	Lateran Cloister	Honorius III (1216-27)
1246	San Sylvester Chapel at Santi Quattro Coronati paintings)	Innocent IV (1243-54)
1278	Sancta Sanctorum at Lateran Palace (paintings)	Nicholas III (1277-80)
1300	Jubilee (various events/decorations)	Boniface VIII (1294-1303)

Building periods, church plans and decorative themes

By the early fifth century, the important large early basilicas were established and richly decorated in mosaic and wall paintings. Some building and decorating took place in the sixth and seventh centuries, mostly under Greek popes, and then there were two bursts of activity, at the beginning of the ninth and at the beginning of the twelfth century, the latter following damage to the city in 1084, when it was sacked by the Normans. And again, prior to the Jubilee in 1300 there was a great surge of activity in decorating the churches with mosaic, paint, and sculpture including the grand *ciboria* and candle sticks. While these elements are often still visible other features are either lost or hidden in treasuries: at each time of building or renewal, the churches would have been presented with many gold, silver and bejewelled objects used in their liturgy and precious fabrics, hanging over the altars and acting as curtains.

The influence of key church plans and decorative programmes is evident throughout the medieval period. Saint Peter's is referred to as 'the head and mirror of all churches' because of its great influence. Its plan, with atrium, aisled nave, transept and apse is used for other churches throughout the west but also in Rome, such as at San Paolo fuori le Mura and later at Santa Prassede, built in the ninth century. As this church was designed to hold the bones of dead martyrs it was appropriate to follow the plan of a martyrial church.

In terms of decoration, many themes were revived over time. Galla Placidia (regent 423-37), who ruled with her son Valentinian III (423-55) was a great patron of Christian buildings, and the triumphal arch mosaic at San Paolo fuori le Mura depicting Christ and the tetramorph (symbols of the evangelists), with the twenty-four elders of the Apocalypse introduced a theme that was often repeated in the churches. The surviving apse mosaic at Santi Cosma e Damiano of Christ's Second Coming (see box p. 70), accompanied by Saints Peter and Paul and saints associated with the church, with the tetramorph on the triumphal arch reiterates this theme and is picked up again in the sixth century at San Teodoro, in the ninth century in churches patronised by Paschal I, and again at San Marco a little later in the century. The apse mosaic at San Clemente's upper Church from the twelfth century (see pp. 36-7), while bringing in new elements draws on early Christian motifs, such as acanthus scrolls, the Rivers of Paradise, and the hand of God at the zenith of the apse surrounded by the light of heaven. Similarly the later iconography of the Coronation of the Virgin, also associated with the End of Days, is used at Santa Maria Maggiore in the thirteenth, but combined with traditional motifs. This reuse of familiar imagery emphasises the long traditions of the church.

GLOSSARY

This glossary covers some terms used in the text, especially those not explained when used.

Acheiropoieta, lit. not made by human hands, miraculously created icons

Alpha Omega, first and last letters of Greek Alphabet, used as a name for Christ (Revelations 1.8 etc.)

Ambo (pl. *ambones*), pulpit, usually two in an early church, on the left for reading the gospel, on right for epistle

Ambulatory, a place for walking, often covered, often used in a church or cloister

Anastasis, eastern iconography for Christ's resurrection, depicts him breaking down the doors of Hades

Apse, usually semi-circular end of a church or chapel

Architrave, a beam resting on columns; moulded framework around a door or window

Arcosolium, an arched recess used as a place of burial

Atrium, forecourt, used for churches

Baldacchino, canopy supported by columns, often used over an altar, sometimes referred to as ciborium

Basilica, used in Roman times as administrative centre, adapted for Christian use with nave, aisles, clerestory, apse

Biga, two-horse chariot

Byzantine, the culture of the eastern Roman empire, surviving until 1453 and ruled from Constantinople

Campanile, bell tower

Carolingian, Frankish dynasty ruling 751 to 987; from 800 holding the title of emperor under Charlemagne

Capital, decorative element on top of a column or pilaster

Catacomb, underground burial area outside city walls

Champlevé, enamelling technique

Chancel screen, separating the chancel at the east end of a church from the nave

Chi Rho, the first two letters of Christ;s name in Greek, used as a symbol

Ciborium, canopy supported by columns, often used over an altar, sometimes referred to as baldacchino

Clerestory, a high section of wall that contains windows

Clipeus (pl. *clipei*), from ancient word for shield, used for a decorative roundel

Cloisonné, enamelling technique

Confessio, area beneath the high altar containing relics

Cosmatesque, coloured marble, glass and gold leaf work, named after the Cosmati family

Cubiculum, pl. *cubicula*, lit. bedroom, used here for a room in a catacomb

Crypt, a space below a church or chapel, often used for burials or to house relics

Dado, lower part of a wall, decorated in some form

Diaconia, pl. *diaconiae*, early Christian charitable institution

Diptych, a two-part object, often painting or ivory panels

Domus, a Roman house

Ecclesia, personification of the Church

Enamel, powdered glass fused to metal

Eros, pl. *erotes*, associated with Aphrodite, child or youth-like figures, often with wings, cupids

Eucharist, Holy Communion, a sacrament partaking of bread and wine in memory of Christ's Last Supper

Exedra, a recess

Forum, public space in a Roman city, for commerce, judicial affairs and meeting

Fresco, painting done on wet plaster

Giornata, the amount painted in one session in fresco painting

Gold glass, typically Roman technique of placing gold leaf between two pieces of glass

Greek cross, cross with all four arms of equal length

Hetoimasia, an empty throne prepared for the Second Coming of Christ

Icon, generally used for a movable painted wooden panel

Iconoclasm, here to refer to periods in Byzantine history when figural images were banned (726-787, 814-843)

Iconography, the images and subject matter in a work of art and their interpretation
Liber Pontificalis, official biographies of the papacy
Liturgy, set forms of worship or ritual, used here to refer to Christian services
Loculus pl. *loculi*, rectangular hole created in catacomb walls for burials
Loggia, covered gallery or balcony
Mandorla, almond-shaped motif, often containing sacred figure
Martyr, person who voluntarily dies for beliefs
Martyrium pl. *marytria*, central-planned church or chapel, often used for the burial of a saint
Mausoleum, a building housing a tomb or tombs
Memoria, chapel in memory of deceased person/s
Mithraeum, temple to the god Mithras
Narthex, hallway at the entrance to a building
Nereid, sea nymph
Nimbus, ring of light around the head (halo)
Nymph, female nature deity/spirit
Normans, descendents of Vikings or Norsemen who settled in northern France
Opus anglicanum, fine English medieval needlework, often using gold and silver threads
Opus Reticulatum, masonry arranged in squares or diamonds
Opus Sectile, cut marble placed in decorative patterns
Orans, figure with arms outstretched, a traditional form of prayer or veneration
Ottonian, Saxon dynasty of German monarchs, 919-1024, ruled the Holy Roman empire from 962
Palimpsest, where later work is superimposed on earlier work
Parousia, in Christianity, Second Coming of Christ
Pallium, narrow band of white woollen vestment worn by the Pope and archbishops
Patriarch, used here as head of the church in the Christian east (Greek orthodox)
Pavonazzetto, white marble with red and blue veins
Pope, bishop of Rome
Porphyry, used here to refer to a purple-red stone from Egypt
Portico, roofed entryway to a building, often with columns
Putto pl. *putti*, childlike figures with wings, cupids, erotes
Relic, body part or possession of holy person and things he/she had contact with
Reliquary, container for a relic
Repoussé, relief work in metal, made by hammering from the back
Sacristy, room in a church where sacred vessels are kept and used for robing/disrobing
Sakkos, a wide vestment worn traditionally by the patriarch
Sarcophagus, pl. sarcophagi, a stone coffin, often decorated
Schola cantorum, enclosure in an early Christian church for the choristers
Solea, part of the bema (raised platform) that extends beyond the sanctuary into the nave
Spandrel, surface between two arches in an arcade
Spolia, reused building or decorative material
Square halo/nimbus, square shape behind head, used to show sanctity of a living person
Stucco, decoration made from fine ground gypsum modelled into delicate patterns
Tessera pl. *tesserae*, traditionally small stones but later cut glass or stone used in mosaic
Titulus, house or apartment used for Christian meetings, named after the owner
Transept, arms of a church at right angles to the nave
Triumphal arch, arch at the apse end of a church just in front of the apse
True Cross, by tradition, the cross on which Christ was crucified
Tufa, soft volcanic rock
Typology, the interpretation of figures and events in the Old Testament as foreshadowing the New Testament

MAPS

Chapter six: The Vatican

Chapter two: The Viminal Hill

Chapter three: The Forum and nearby

Chapter four: The Caelian Hill

Chapter five: Trastevere and the Aventine Hill

Chapter seven: Beyond the city

Chapter eight: Further museums

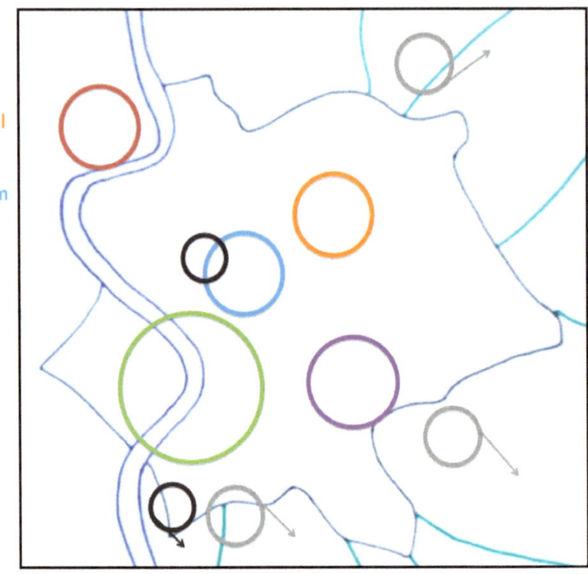

Overview map of areas covered by chapters

Key: Metro stations in red

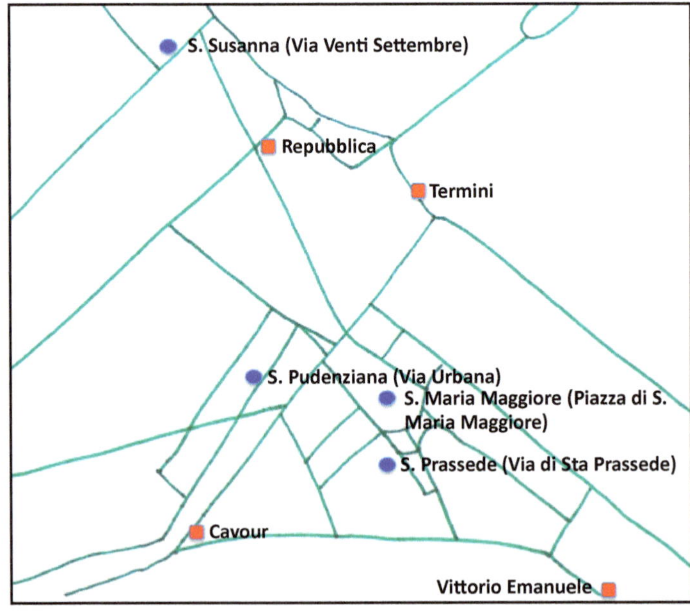

Chapter two: The Viminal Hill

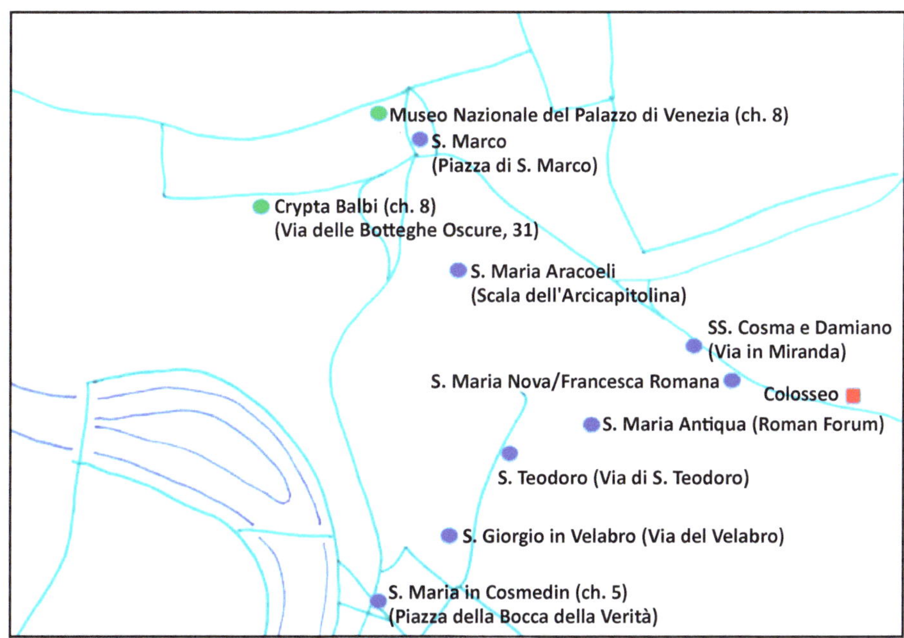

Chapter three: The Forum and nearby; Chapter eight: Further Museums

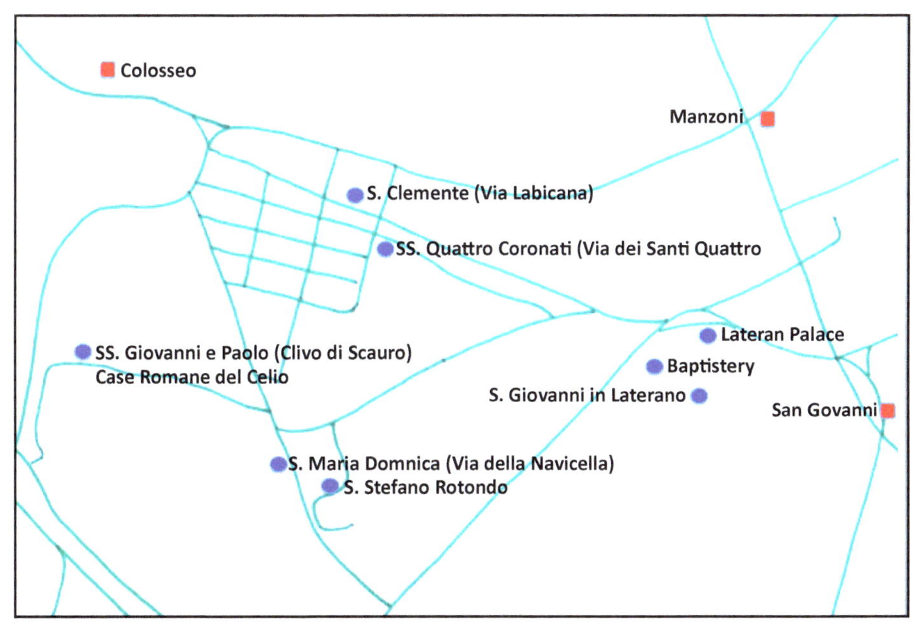

Chapter four: The Caelian Hill and nearby

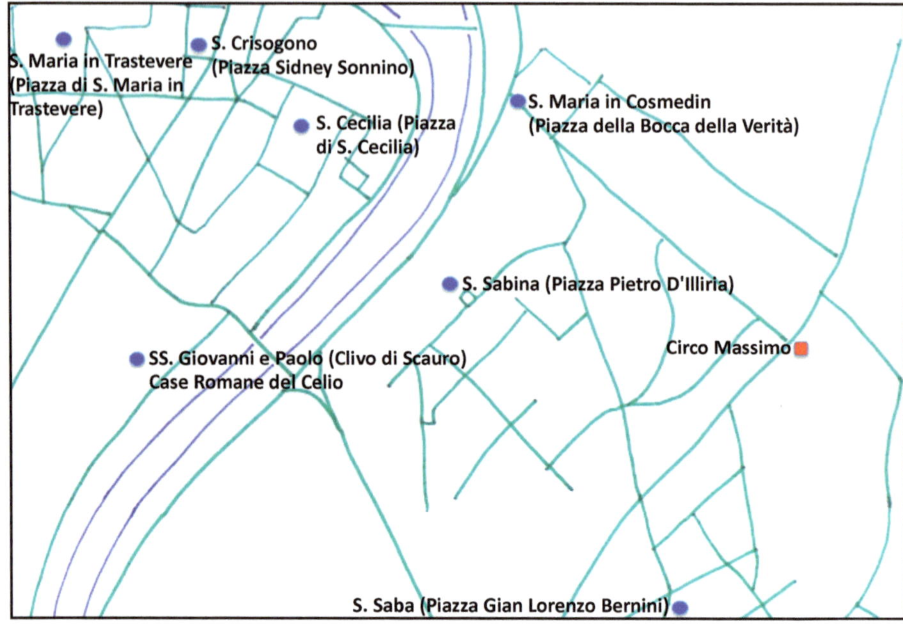

Chapter five: Trastevere, the Aventine Hill and nearby

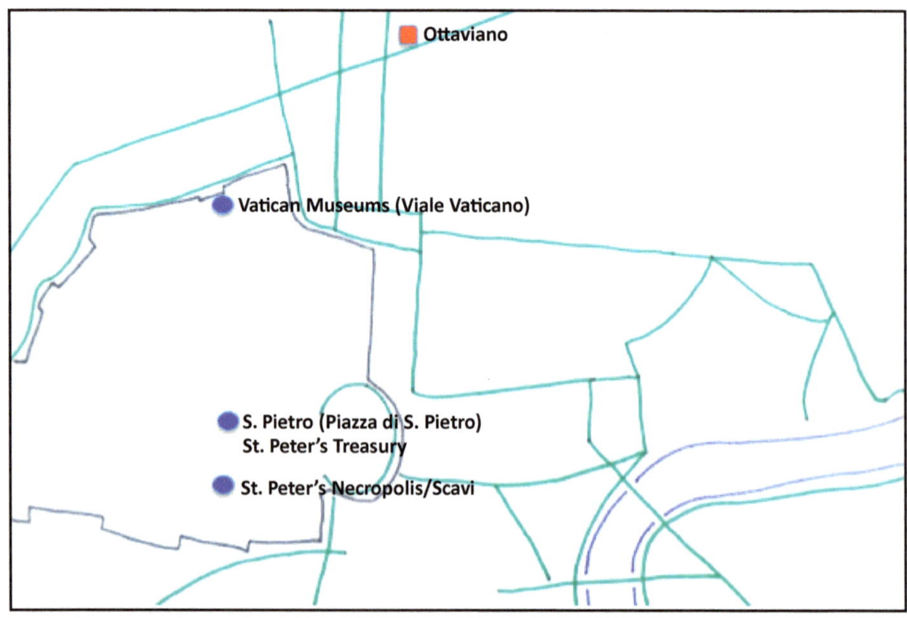

Chapter six: The Vatican area

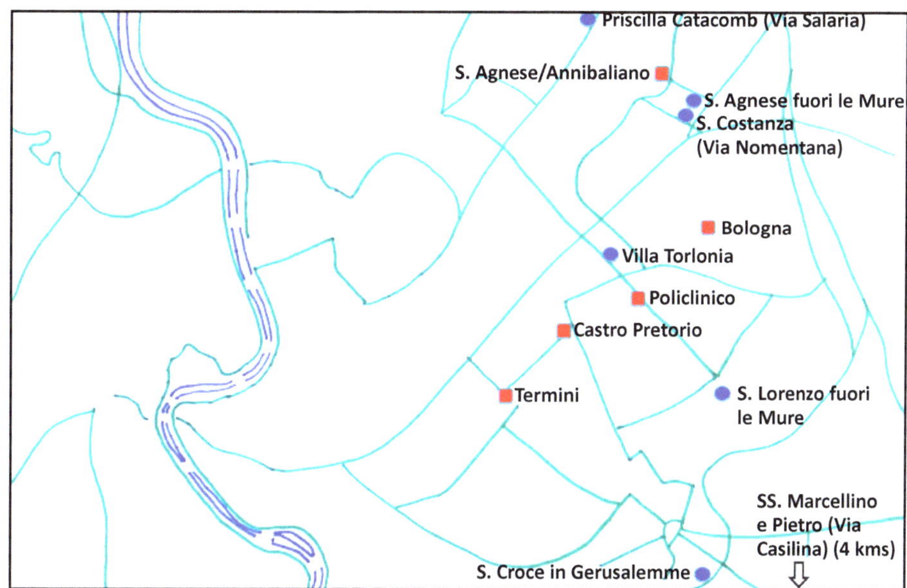

Chapter seven: Beyond the city (to the north)

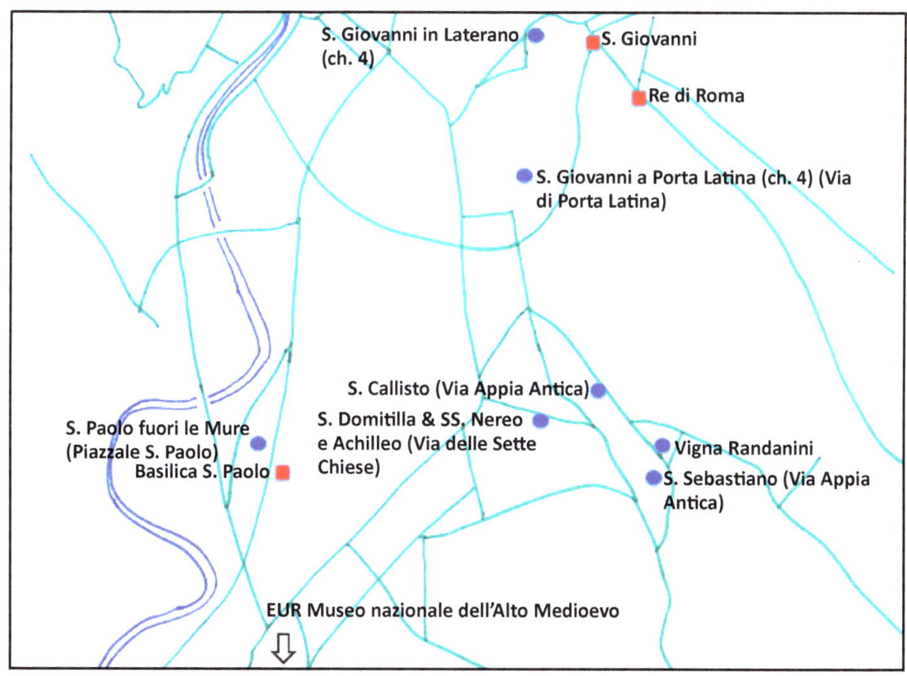

Chapter seven: Beyond the city (to the south); Chapter eight: Further Museums

SELECT BIBLIOGRAPHY

The bibliography on Rome is vast, and no attempt is made here to reference all the sources used.

Key books:
Kessler, Herbert L. 2000. *Rome 1300: on the path of the pilgrim.* New Haven; London.

Krautheimer, Richard. 1980. *Rome: profile of a city, 312-1308.* Princeton.

The key academic set of volumes on the early buildings is:
Krautheimer, Richard, et al. 1937. *Corpus basilicarum Christianarum Romae: the early Christian basilicas of Rome (IV-IX cent.),* Monumenti di antichità cristiana; 2 serie, 2. 5 vols. Città del Vaticano.

Very useful as a detailed and well presented guide up to the end of the ninth century with excellent floor plans but no illustrations:
Webb, Matilda. 2001. *The churches and catacombs of early Christian Rome: a comprehensive guide.* Brighton.

An excellent guide:
Claridge, Amanda. 2010. *Rome: An Oxford archaeological guide.* 2nd, rev. and expanded ed., Oxford archaeological guides. Oxford.

Also useful:
Macadam, Alta, 2006, *Blue Guide: Rome,* 9th ed., London.

Specific reference has been made to certain books and articles including:
Primary texts:
2000. *The book of pontiffs (Liber pontificalis): the ancient biographies of the first ninety Roman bishops to AD 715.* Rev. 2nd ed., Translated texts for historians; v. 6. Liverpool.

Eusebius. 1989. *The history of the Church from Christ to Constantine.* Rev. ed., London.

Eusebius. 1999. *Life of Constantine,* intro., trans., and commentary by Averil Cameron and Stuart G. Hall. Oxford.

For the Latin inscriptions (partially used for translations here):
Lansford, Tyler. 2009. *The Latin inscriptions of Rome: a walking guide.* Baltimore; London.

Secondary texts:
Belting, Hans. 1994, *Likeness and presence: a history of the image before the era of art.* Chicago.

Blaauw, Sible de. 1994. *Cultus et decor: liturgia e architettura nella Roma tardoantica e medievale: Basilica Salvatoris, Sanctae Mariae, Sancti Petri, Studi e testi.* Città del Vaticano.

Boyle, Leonard, 1989. *A Short Guide to St. Clement's.* Rome.

Cutler, Anthony, and Nicolas Oikonomides. 1988. An Imperial Byzantine Casket and Its Fate at a Humanist's Hands. *The Art Bulletin* 70 (1):77-87.

Draghi, Andreina. 2001. Il ciclo di affreschi rinvenuto nel Convento dei SS. Quattro Coronati a Roma: un capitolo inedito della pittura romana del Duecento. *Rivista dell'Istituto nazionale d'archeologia e storia dell'arte* 54:115-66.

Drijvers, W. J. 2011. Helena Augusta, the Cross and the Myth: Some New Reflections. *Millenium* 8:125-74.

Evans, Helen C., ed. 2004. *Byzantium: faith and power (1261-1557).*New York, New Haven.

Frazer, Margaret English. 1973. Church Doors and the Gates of Paradise: Byzantine Bronze Doors in Italy. *Dumbarton Oaks Papers*, 27:145-62.

Gardner, Julian. 2013. *The Roman crucible: the artistic patronage of the papacy, 1198-1304*, Römische Forschungen der Bibliotheca Hertziana; Bd. 33. München.

Hetherington, Paul. 1994. *Medieval Rome: a portrait of the city and its life.* New York.

Howells, Daniel Thomas, with a contribution by Andrew Meek; Chris Entwistle and Liz James, eds. 2015. *A catalogue of the late antique gold glass in the British Museum.* London.

Kartsonis, Anna. 1988. The Responding Icon. In *Heaven on Earth: Art and the Church in Byzantium* ed. L. Safran. University Park, PA, 58-81.

Krautheimer, Richard. 1983. *Three Christian capitals: topography and politics.* Berkeley; London.

Mackie, Gillian Vallance. 2003. *Early Christian chapels in the West: decoration, function, and patronage.* Toronto: University of Toronto Press.

Magnuson, Torgil. 2004. *The urban transformation of medieval Rome, 312-1420*, Suecoromana, 7. Stockholm.

Mancinelli, Fabrizio. 1981. *The catacombs of Rome and the origins of Christianity.* Florence.

Milner, Christine. 1996. 'Lignum Vitae' or 'Crux Gemmata'? The Cross of Golgotha in the Early Byzantine Period. *Byzantine and Modern Greek Studies* 20:77-99.

Osborne, John. 2008. The Cult of 'Maria Regina' in Early Medieval Rome. *Acta ad Archaeologiam et Artium Historiam Pertinentia* 21:95-106.

Spier, Jeffrey, ed. 2007. *Picturing the Bible: the earliest Christian art.* New Haven; London: Yale University Press in association with Kimbell Art Museum.

Stanley, David J. 1994. New Discoveries at Santa Costanza. *Dumbarton Oaks Papers* 48:257-61.

Stern, Henri. 1973. Review of *Scavi di Ostia, Edificio con 'opus sectile' fuori Porta Maxima, by G. Becatti. The Art Bulletin* 55:285-7.

INDEX

Numbers in **bold** refer to illustrations, numbers in *italics* to boxes
NT = New Testament, OT=Old Testament